Marching Toward Mad·

Marching Toward Madness

How to Save the Games You Always Loved

JOHN LEBAR & ALLEN PAUL

CAROLINA ACADEMIC PRESS
Durham, North Carolina

Library of Congress Cataloging-in-Publication Data

Names: LeBar, John, author. | Paul, Allen (M. Allen), 1939– author.
Title: Marching toward madness : how to save the games you always
    loved / by John LeBar, Allen Paul.
Description: Durham, North Carolina : Carolina Academic Press, LLC,
    2020. | Includes bibliographical references and index.
Identifiers: LCCN 2020002500 | ISBN 9781531018566 (paperback) |
    ISBN 9781531018573 (ebook)
Subjects: LCSH: College sports—Economic aspects—United States. |
    College athletes—United States—Economic conditions. | College
    sports—Moral and ethical aspects—United States. | National
    Collegiate Athletic Association.
Classification: LCC GV351 .L43 2020 | DDC 796.0430973—dc23
LC record available at https://lccn.loc.gov/2020002500

ISBN 978-1-5310-1856-6
e-ISBN 978-1-5310-1857-3

Carolina Academic Press
700 Kent Street
Durham, North Carolina 27701
Telephone (919) 489-7486
Fax (919) 493-5668
www.cap-press.com

Printed in the United States of America

Public faith in higher education cannot be sustained if college sports are permitted to become a circus, with the institution itself little more than a supporting sideshow.

— The late A. BARTLETT GIAMATTI,
former President of Yale and Commissioner of Baseball

Table of Contents

Acknowledgments and Approach

A major obstacle in writing *Marching Toward Madness* was the lack of published sources on the origins and evolution of the scholar-athlete, a uniquely American archetype that began to take shape in the late 19th century. In the century that followed, the scholar-athlete became a cherished ideal, only to be eclipsed altogether by the steady rise of a mega sports entertainment structure that came to dominate college sports after World War II. In nearly five years of research and writing about the scholar-athlete, we did not find one book on the subject but found many that addressed important facets of this long-neglected American ideal—among them Ronald A. Smith's *Sports and Freedom, The Rise of Big Time College Athletics;* Benjamin G. Radar's *American Sports, from the Age of Folk Games to the Age of Televised Sports;* Murray Sperber's *Onward to Victory: The Crises that Shaped College Sports;* and Charlie Clotfelter's *Big-Time Sports in American Universities.*

After much experimentation and several false starts in devising a structure for the book, we received indispensable advice on that matter from John Stauffer, a Harvard professor and prominent authority on the antislavery movement. He was coached at Duke by John LeBar and played No. 1 singles on the tennis team. He also gave us many valuable suggestions on draft chapters of the book. With John's help and that of several others, we finally settled on a four-part structure for *Marching Toward Madness* that spans from the historical elements of the scholar-athlete to the public focus today on fundamental reform of college sports.

The book is based on many primary and secondary sources. Most important among the former were recorded interviews in Columbus, GA, Dallas, TX, Durham, NC, Miami, FL, and Rehoboth Beach, DE, with John's former players. Our most important secondary sources came from Perkins Library at Duke whose staff provided unstinting support for our research.

We are indebted to many people who helped us at various stages of the project, none more importantly than Tom White, a mutual friend at North Carolina State University, who introduced us in June 2014. John's former players enriched the book enormously: through personal interviews, by reading and commenting on various chapters, by tracking down old photographs, by hosting us in various cities and through strong encouragement at every stage of the project. We are especially indebted to the following players, each of whom was a scholar-athlete at Duke: Chaim Arlosoroff, an orthopedic surgeon in Miami, FL; Paul Auerbach of Los Altos, CA, a professor of emergency medicine at Stanford University Medical School; Ted Daniel, a senior litigator at the Norton Rose Fulbright law firm in Dallas, TX; Chip Davis, an orthopedic surgeon in Orlando, FL; Ross Dubins, Tennis Superintendent for the City of North Miami, FL; Russell Gache, an intellectual property attorney in Birmingham, AL; Mike McMahon, who founded and ran a successful party boat business in Dallas, TX; Mark Meyers, a retired senior corporate attorney at Shell Oil and founder of a ministry to the depressed and suicidal in Houston, TX; Joe Meir, founding CEO of one of the largest real estate development firms in North Carolina's Research Triangle; David Robinson, an eye surgeon in Rehoboth Beach, DE, and founder of one of the largest eye care practices in the U.S.; John Stauffer of Cambridge, MA, who is mentioned above; Marc Flur, a financial adviser in Durham, NC; and Will White of Columbus, GA, whose firm has built several thousand apartments in six states. Although Nancy Hogshead-Makar, an all-time Duke swimming star and nationally recognized authority on gender equity and Title IX, did not play for John, she, too, made indispensable suggestions for this book.

We've been spared from many mistakes by our informal panel of expert readers. It included: Jean Bonner of Delaware City, DE; Pat Buckles of Phoenix, AZ; Gerry Chiaruttini of Alexandria, VA; Chris Pipkin of Mebane, NC; Linda Harrell Rudisill of Lincolnton, NC; and the late Gregg Heininger of Polermo, NJ.

Special words of thanks are due to those who advised us on various chapters: Mike Forbes, Director of Club Sports at Duke, who introduced us to several excellent sources; Stacy Flur (wife of Marc Flur, John's second All-American), a professional editor who volunteered to edit the first draft of our manuscript and made numerous invaluable suggestions; and Bartley O'Hara, an attorney in Washington, DC, and longtime friend of Allen's, who explained the current climate for reform in the U.S. Congress. In addition, Amy Perko, CEO of the Knight Commission, connected us to experts on several issues; Drew Daffron, who became our "go to" guy on the dos and don'ts of social media; and Rob Marks, an expert on information technology at Duke, who advised us on several computer-related issues.

These acknowledgements would not be complete without a warm word of appreciation to Keith and Linda Sipe, Publishers of Carolina Academic Press; Managing Editor, Ryland Bowman; and Marketing Director, Rachel Green. The manuscript was edited by Jessica Newman, who did a superb job. As a mid-sized publisher, CAP has a much-to-be-commended hands-on approach. Last, but by no means least, we wish to thank family members who read and commented on each draft of the manuscript. They include John's daughters, Leja LeBar and Rhonda Jenkins; Allen's daughter, Jennifer; his son, Mack; his brother, Jon; and sister, Mary. Our wives — Carole LeBar and Betsy Paul — read every version of the manuscript and made many excellent suggestions. Their patience, fortitude and encouragement were indispensable to the completion of this project.

Marching Toward Madness

Declining American Values

Impelled by runaway spending, rampant corruption and foolish panaceas, America's much-beloved games of college basketball and football are on the verge of being wrecked. The specter of mega-billions being showered on imperial coaches, insatiable athletic directors, hordes of support staff and lavish comforts for fat-cat fans at stadiums and arenas has led to a near-deafening roar to pay the players. The injustice of such sums being amassed, in the main, from the labor of young men of color—many of whom come from disadvantaged backgrounds—cannot be justified; yet, American society has allowed this intractable problem to fester for more than half a century. Lured by the glitter of untold riches, naive young players enroll year after year in colleges and universities expecting the ultimate reward of a highly paid career in the National Basketball Association (NBA) or the National Football League (NFL). Only a miniscule few will advance that far; even fewer will reap significant financial rewards. Overwhelmingly, our spectacular gladiators are faced with dim prospects once the dream dies. Instead of educating them, colleges and universities force them into full-time athletic "jobs" in which their labor is shamelessly exploited.

Small wonder that outraged critics claim an open-shut case

for paying the players with only sketchy answers to how such a radical change would work. The "pay them now!" bandwagon is filled with well-known sports analysts, academics, attorneys, advocacy groups, a prominent federal judge, members of Congress and even two presidential candidates. Most argue with the certitude of Jane Austen's opening line in *Pride and Prejudice*. To paraphrase: It is a truth universally acknowledged, that a college athlete in possession of superb talent, must be in want of pay. To paraphrase Austen's second line: This truth is so well fixed in the minds of patrons that many consider athletes their rightful property. Notwithstanding all the certitude, the case against pay for play is strong and the pro-pay bandwagon may be speeding toward a colossal wreck.

Marching Toward Madness will show that paying the players is a very bad idea. Chapter Twenty-One (The Folly of Pay for Play) cites 21 reasons why the pro-pay position is so wrong-headed—among them the near-certain prospect that the player talent pool will be concentrated to even fewer rich schools; recruiting wars that lead to greater and more frequent scandals; the potential for endless litigation under Title IX; and an exponential increase in the regulatory powers of the National Collegiate Athletic Association (NCAA), an organization sorely lacking in public trust and authority. Worst of all, pay for play will encourage colleges and universities to shirk even further the imperative to educate the young athletes who generate so much of their windfall revenues from basketball and football.

These young athletes' dreams are incubated by relentless indoctrination on the part of the professional leagues, their media allies and to a lesser extent by the colleges and universities that exploit them. The endless hype reaches hurricane force during the NFL draft of college players. The *Tennessean* reported that the NFL's three-day extravaganza in late April 2019 drew more than 600,000 fans to downtown Nashville and attracted a television audience of 47.5 million. Both were records. Each year, in the weeks leading up to the event, stories about who will be drafted in what order and what sort of contract they'll get dominate mainstream media. After the draft, the focus shifts to contracts signed by leading players. NBC Sports reported that on May 9, less than two weeks after the 2019 draft, the No. 1 pick—Oklahoma quarterback Kyler Murray—signed a fully guaranteed four-year contract with the Arizona Cardinals worth $35 million. It included a signing bonus of $23 million.

Such astronomical contracts cause countless players all over the country to dream, *Why not me?* But the odds against those dreams coming true are astronomical too. The NCAA reports that in 2018 there were 1,036,848 high school football players and 73,557 college players. High school seniors had a 0.08 percent chance of being draft by the NFL; seniors playing college football had an 8/10,000 chance of being drafted. In raw numbers, only 256 of 16,346 college players will hear their names called. Prospects for high school and college basketball players to be drafted by an NBA team are not much different.

Pay prospects also are grim. For every stratospheric pay package, many players make the $480,000 minimum specified in the NFL's standard first-year contract. Coupled with an average NFL career of less than three years, the typical player gets far from enough to retire on and risks crippling injury. To put these numbers in perspective, the Social Security Administration estimates that career earnings of males with a college degree are $900,000 more than that of high school graduates; for men with graduate degrees, the difference is $1.5 million. Even when the added cost of a college education is subtracted, a stark contrast remains. In general, college graduates have greater quality of life and life satisfaction than high school graduates.

Despite the hue and cry to pay the players, the real issue is educating them instead. Unfortunately, at most schools with big-time sports programs, athletics are given a much higher priority than academics. Most of the 347 colleges and universities in NCAA Division I—those competing at highest level where larger budgets, better facilities and more athletic scholarships prevail—have been operating sports entertainment businesses for decades. Their athletic departments are autonomous fiefdoms, but in any given year only 20 or so of the 347 Division I schools balance their books. Some with annual revenue of more than $100 million still lose money. In general, deficits are covered by university general funds, student fees or taxpayer funds at public institutions. Funding deficits from student fees is more and more difficult to justify because student attendance at so-called "must see" games keeps creeping lower and lower, while nearly 70 percent of students graduate with $30,000 in debt.

In recent years, the much-ballyhooed term "student-athlete" has become shallow and almost nonsensical. *Marching Toward Madness* advocates reviving an ancient and quintessential American ideal—the scholar-athlete, a once-popular archetype that millions looked up to. In Part I, the book traces how that ideal evolved beginning in the last quarter of the 19th century; Part II explains how sports mold character; Part III explores how players become champions and what they learn from that experience; and Part IV describes specific reforms that will put college sports back on a sustainable path. Most important, the book states the case for a return to basics—for putting college sports in proper perspective, for restoring academic integrity, for putting learning before athletics no matter how popular the sport may be.

The authors bring complementary capabilities to the writing of this book. After coaching two varsity sports at Duke University, John LeBar served as the school's director of undergraduate studies for 15 years. He coached 60 players in 12 years as head tennis coach at Duke. All 60 graduated, and at least 25 — or 40 percent — earned advanced degrees: nine in medicine, eight in law, six as MBAs and two as PhDs. Allen Paul has been a lifelong writer. His book *Katyn: Stalin's Massacre and the Triumph of Truth* was a bestseller in Poland and elsewhere in Eastern Europe.

How the scholar-athlete emerged and evolved has been largely forgotten today. In the last quarter of the 19th century, the closing of the frontier, rapid industrialization, mass migration to cities and the rise of office jobs requiring little or no physical effort brought about a rethinking of manhood. Fears arose that American men were becoming soft and effeminate. Long before he became President, Teddy Roosevelt advocated the strenuous life and a new form of manliness. "A man in the real world can't be efficient unless he is manly," he once wrote Walter Camp, the father of American football.[1]

The new masters of manliness excelled in the classroom *and* in athletics. These hybrid men were often called "gentlemen and scholars," a term borrowed from the British. While they were athletic, their scholarly side was unmistakable. By 1904, the pendulum had swung enough that the *Saturday Evening Post* declared that the ideal man was "primarily the scholar, the thinker and the gentleman."[2]

How that dimension of the ideal man declined to public invisibility over many decades is explored in detail in the pages that follow. Its decline does not mean the archetype no longer exists—just that too few Americans expect college athletes to be fleet of foot and brainy too. A Google search tool shows that since the 1930s books have barely men-

tioned the term scholar-athlete at all.[3] In contrast, the term student-athlete has been widely referenced. It was coined in the early fifties by the NCAA to help member institutions avoid workers' compensation claims filed by injured athletes. To many Americans, the term student-athlete is a far cry from the ideal. It has come to stand for something deeply flawed in our sports—a pendulum swing that has obscured the importance of education and learning. After nearly five years of research and writing on the subject, the authors have not found one book on scholar-athletes and very little in scholarly journals or the popular press either. And yet, our lives today would be impoverished without the cures they discover, the books they write and the enterprises, large and small, they found and lead.

As a mega, "win-at-all-cost" system mushroomed in size, scholar-athletes got squeezed out of the big revenue sports of football and basketball. Today, most scholar-athletes play non-revenue or club sports; they too have demanding coaches and require extensive travel and long practices that cut into study time. In parallel with the scholar-athlete's decline in visibility, the amateur ideal has been deeply eroded. It is often dismissed as an anachronism of "the British way" when gentlemen played games only for pleasure. But that slant was never embraced by Americans, who have always believed anyone so inclined should aspire to athletic excellence and play sports too.

After the Civil War, the ideals of manhood underwent a profound shift. For decades, the self-made man epitomized true manhood; being rugged *and* learned was not yet an ideal to most Americans. Popular magazines that heavily influenced middle class opinion—like *Munsey's, Collier's* and *Saturday Evening Post*—warned that education could "over-civilize" men and cautioned that cultured learning could get a man branded as a sissy.[4]

No one did more to change the ideal than Yale's Walter Camp, who established a football dynasty that has never been equaled. Between 1872 and 1909, Yale won 324 games while losing only 17; between 1890 and 1893, Yale did not give up a point. Harvard got so frustrated with Yale's success it considered giving up football. Camp, who both played and coached at the school, wrote that Yale's players would transfer "the experiences of the gridiron [to] those of the greater game of Life." He predicted that they would become senators, mayors and successful professionals, and he was right.

The ideal of the scholar-athlete enjoyed widespread popularity throughout the first half of the 20th century. Then, in the early fifties, major cheating scandals in basketball and football rocked public faith in the integrity of college games. As scandal after scandal occurred in the years that followed, public confidence never recovered. The fateful turn toward the mega sports entertainment businesses of today came in 1984 when the Supreme Court stripped away the NCAA's right to televise football games between its member at the time of 800 colleges and universities. The decision eliminated revenue sharing that helped level the playing field for smaller schools and other non-football powers. In a prescient dissent, Justice Byron "Whizzer" White, who'd been an All-American halfback at the University of Colorado, held that revenue sharing was critical to maintaining competitive balance among colleges and universities and to check the trend toward professionalization at dominant schools. "Even with shared television revenues," Justice White concluded, "unlimited appearances by a few schools would inevitably give them an insuperable advantage over all others and in the end, defeat any efforts to maintain a system of athletic competition among amateurs who measure up to college scholastic requirements."[5]

The latest figures on the revenues of schools with the largest football programs confirm that what Justice White predicted has come unmistakably true, but even he might be staggered by the extent of the imbalance engendered by the court's 1984 decision. In fiscal year 2014–15, half the teams in the NCAA's Division I Bowl Championship Subdivision—the so-called Power Five Conferences which have a total of 65 teams—earned a record $6 billion, or $4 billion more than all other schools combined.

"The gulf between college sports' haves and have nots has never been greater," Paula Lavigne of ESPN has observed. More specifically, she has noted, the richest schools now spend lavishly on private jets, perks for varsity athletes, such as barber shops and bowling alleys, and five-star hotel stays during travel.[6] Add to that the $28 million Ohio State paid its coaches and the $24 million Alabama, Michigan and Florida each paid theirs. Clearly, the richest few have gained the insuperable advantage Justice White warned against in his dissent.

Abuses have not changed all that much since 1929 when the Carnegie Foundation issued a scathing report on college athletic misconduct. Based on site visits to 130 schools, the report found that 112 were flouting rules with player inducements ranging from open payrolls and disguised booster funds to no-show jobs at movie studios.[7] Follow-up inquiries two years later by the *New York Times* found that not a single institution had reformed its practices.

Misdeeds in college sports have been amply documented in several excellent books—among them Murray Sperber's *Onward to Victory* and *Beer and Circus, The Game of Life* by James L. Shulman and William G. Bowen (a former president of Princeton University), and *Unwinding Madness* by Gerald Gurney, Donna A. Lopiano and Andrew Zimbalist. They advocate reforms like greater control over athletic departments for college presidents and an end to the "arms race" to build luxury boxes and lavish academic support centers where athletes are tutored, coddled and entertained. It's fair to say reform proposals have been languishing since the Carnegie Report was issued. Efforts to curb increased violence in football have had modest success at best.

In considering these bleak results, we'd do well to recall a famous tongue-in-cheek comment Dr. George L. Cross, a widely respected President of the University of Oklahoma, made to state legislators in the early fifties, shortly after Oklahoma won its first national football championship. A sleepy old senator aroused himself after Dr. Cross finished and said, "Yes, that's all well and good. But what kind of football team are we going to have this year?"

Dr. Cross replied, "We want to build a university that our football team can be proud of." His wry comment led to a mini-storm of media protest in which the respected educator was wrongly portrayed as pandering to the good old boys.[8] The moral for today is that ideals are not easy to explain and even harder to follow; each generation must define and embrace its own.

Our greatest scholar-athletes have set examples we can learn much from. The story of William Henry Lewis, the first African American to be named an All-American football player, has long been forgotten. A Harvard-trained lawyer, in 1911 he became the highest-ranking member of his race ever to serve in the U. S. government. In his long and active life, he broke many barriers. Byron "Whizzer" White, who wrote the Supreme Court dissent mentioned above, is seldom remembered for being one of the greatest scholar-athletes America ever produced. In 1937, he was a consensus All-American in football at the University of Colorado and a Rhodes Scholar too. (Lewis and White are profiled in Chapter Two.) Among the greatest of female scholar-athletes, there is no better example than Duke swimmer, Nancy Hogshead-Makar, who overcame posttraumatic stress disorder (PTSD) to capture three gold medals and one silver at the 1984 Olympics. A superb student at Duke and at Georgetown Law School, she is a nationally prominent expert on Title IX and gender equity. (Her profile appears in Chapter Nine.)

The lives of role models like these reflect the ancient Greek ideal of an integrated whole—a person with seven distinct traits: the *discipline* to find the right path and stick to it; the *empathy* to understand the needs of others and to see things from their perspective; the *passion* to produce great work and contribute to the public good; the *intellect* characterized by an inquisitive, analytical and creative mind; the *courage* to think and act independently, to weather adversity and solve problems without compromising principles; the *faith* to believe in a power greater than oneself; and the capacity to lead a high-impact life characterized by "giving back" to his or her community and beyond. In his role as head tennis coach at Duke, John LeBar helped many players develop these traits. All 60 of his players graduated and nearly half got professional or graduate degrees (see listing in the Appendix).

A word of explanation is needed on the alternating voice readers will encounter in *Marching Toward Madness*. Its "storytelling voice" shifts between first and third person to add authenticity to the narration. Parts I and IV are jointly narrated by the authors; Parts II and III are narrated by John LeBar, exploring his personal experience in molding scholar-athletes.

When all is said and done, we need to ask ourselves, "Are we prepared to discard the ancient amateur code?" To give up playing for the joy of the game, building character through fair competition, embracing sportsmanship in all aspects of play, learning to subordinate oneself for the good of the team and pursuing the integrated whole of becoming a scholar *and* an athlete? One may dismiss—even sneer at—these ideals as relics of a *rah-rah-sis-boom-bah* era, but doing so invites peril. Such ideals make us better humans beings, call on us to stand for something greater than ourselves and commit us to uniting every stratum of American society.

Part I
The Scholar-Athlete Ideal

How the ideal of the scholar-athlete emerged in the Victorian Era to become a uniquely American icon, before giving way to scandals and a win-at-all-cost mentality.

CHAPTER ONE

A Brief History of College Sports

The American sporting scene has always produced bona fide heroes who set standards we all can admire and aspire to. Separating the acceptable from the unacceptable in the full panoply of collegiate sports is an indispensable part of understanding how we lost our birthright and how it might be regained. The ideal of the scholar-athlete was enshrined early at Yale, where the best-known exemplar was Nathan Hale, an early hero of the Revolutionary War. Words he spoke moments before the British hanged him on September 26, 1776—"I only regret that I have but one life to lose for my country"—enshrined Hale in immortality.[1] At 21, he'd been caught spying for the Continental Army. A handsome, muscular young man with blue eyes and reddish brown hair, Hale had graduated from Yale with first class honors in 1773 and went on to teach in two Connecticut secondary schools. A diary he wrote in the early months of 1776 notes his avid interest in wrestling, checkers and football. He'd played football (then more a version of rugby) at Yale and is said to have performed the extraordinary feat of jumping from one waist-high hogshead cask into an adjacent one.[2] A statue of Hale stands today near City Hall in New York.

In his inaugural address on October 19, 1869, Harvard

President Charles W. Eliot gave an early definition of the scholar-athlete when he called the sons of Harvard an ". . . aristocracy which excels in manly sports, carries off the honors and prizes of the learned professions, and bears itself with distinction in all fields of intellectual labor and combat;. . ."[3]

Eliot's reference to manly sports reflected a Victorian obsession with muscular Christianity, which originated in mid-century England to keep public school boys from becoming too effeminate and to keep religion from being overly feminized. It soon became a rage in an America plagued by anxieties that closing of the frontier, the rise of Social Darwinism and the industrial revolution would expunge ruggedness and toughness from the male character. By the time Teddy Roosevelt embraced manly ideals in the 1890s, popular magazines—the main arbiters of taste and cultural mores—featured story after story on an authentic American hero: the manly ideal of the scholar-athlete.[4] A good example is the cover of the *Saturday Evening Post* for October 28, 1899, cited in Daniel A. Clark's *Creating the College Man*. It depicts two college men clasping each other's shoulder in a fraternal way, one in cap and gown with an arm full of books, the other in a football uniform cradling a pigskin.

The dual ideal of the scholar-athlete was firmly fixed in the public mind by illustrations such as this one from 1899.

"The cover graphically illustrates," Clark writes, "how the ideal college man now united two heretofore antagonistic ideals of American manhood—the cultured, genteel scholar and the resolute, courageous, and vigorous man."[5]

Ideals notwithstanding, by the time that cover appeared, college football was a gory mess but fast becoming the country's most popular sport. In 1878, a Yale player prepped for the Harvard game by dipping his canvas uniform jacket in slaughterhouse blood—to "make it look more business-like," explained Frederic Remington, whose future paintings, illustrations and sculptures of the American West would make him famous.[6] Five years later, at President Eliot's urging, the Harvard faculty voted to ban football because, by rule, a player could strike an opponent with a closed fist three times before being ejected.[7] Punching, scratching, clawing, gouging and other forms of mayhem were all part of the game. Over and over university athletic committees and college presidents, citing egregious abuses—even clever coaching tricks to injure opposing players—called

The COLLEGE MAN'S NUMBER

THE SATURDAY EVENING POST

An Illustrated Weekly Magazine
Founded A° D¹ 1728 by Benj.Franklin

Volume 172, No. 18   PHILADELPHIA, OCTOBER 28, 1899   5 Cents the Copy; $2.50 the Year

The Curtis Publishing Company, Philadelphia

1899 Cover of Saturday Evening Post. Illustration provided by Curtis Licensing

for bans; but each such plea failed as alumni, students and an adoring public adamantly insisted that the games go on.

That same streak of violence ran back through American sport to earliest times. In the Colonial Era, taverns on village greens were often the scene of rough and tumble sports with bloody outcomes—worsened, nearly always, by heavy drinking. Wrestling, cudgeling and various ball and bat games with violent twists were most popular among the common folk. In the South, horse racing was greatly favored by the gentry. Early on, the Church of England, the South's dominant denomination, took a *laissez faire* attitude toward sports. But by the 1730s and 1740s, evangelicals of the Great Awakening were urging suppression of sporting ways, though with scant success. In the North, generations before, Puritans and Quakers had tried the same to little effect. Americans were so imbued with love of sports that attempts at suppression only increased their ardor, which in time would grow exponentially.

By the early 19th century, the focal point of sporting attention had shifted from the village green to the college campus, where baseball and early forms of football based on rugby and soccer were being played. Intercollegiate competition of any kind had not yet occurred. The first took place in 1852: a rowing match between Harvard and Yale on Lake Winnipesaukee, New Hampshire.[8] At the time, rowing—driven by its practicality and a plethora of sporting clubs—was second only to horse racing as America's favorite sport. As a harbinger of the future influence of money on sports, the New Hampshire boat race was proposed by the superintendent of the Boston, Concord and Montreal Railroad, who offered to pay all expenses for a two-week vacation for both crews. On race day, a thousand spectators watched as the Harvard boat, Oneida, quickly took a one-length lead over Yale's Shawmut and won going away.[9] The winners were presented a prize of silver-tipped walnut oars by General Franklin Pierce, who would win the presidency that November. Lake officials offered a return match in 1853, but it failed to materialize due, most likely, to mediocre financial results for the railroad. Even so, a spate of rowing matches in the decade that followed pitted colleges and universities throughout New England and the Middle Atlantic states.

Long-simmering relations between Great Britain and the United States over British actions on behalf of the Confederacy during the Civil War prompted perhaps the greatest boat race ever held in 1869. By providing naval vessels to the Confederacy—in particular, the havoc-wreaking *Alabama*, a sail- and steam-powered commerce raider—it was said the British had lengthened the war by two years and caused incalculable damage. Some members of Congress were demanding $2 billion in reparations, which the British roundly rejected amid reckless talk of war on the American side.

Against this backdrop of friction and national pride, in April 1869, Harvard issued a challenge to Oxford for a four-oared race in August over a four-and-a-quarter-mile course on the Thames. On race day, the banks of the famous river were jammed with crowds estimated at upwards of one million, perhaps the largest ever to witness a sporting event. A coterie of British elite, including the Prince of Wales, Prime Minister William Gladstone, Charles Dickens and John Stuart Mill, watched while the usual gamblers and fast buck artists worked the crowd. It was a highly competitive race won by Oxford by a mere six seconds. Results were quickly flashed back to America via transatlantic cable laid only three years earlier. Both sides cited the results as evidence of their superiority in manliness and other virtues.[10]

Mother country norms and practices had always exerted strong influence in America, where the rich inheritance of British games was undeniable. But one source of conflict appeared in the late 19th century: It centered on who was eligible to play—a question that turned on the definition of an amateur at a time when professional sports were in their infancy. The British aristocracy and leisure class went to great lengths to shape an iron-clad answer that forbade participation by anyone who worked with their hands. The true amateur, the aristocrats held, played purely for the love of sport. To cement the concept in place, the British Amateur Athletic Club approved a so-called "Mechanic's Clause" in 1866–67, which barred from play all who were "born and bred below the salt"—i.e., anyone who earned wages by manual labor of any kind. In 1871, the club invoked the clause in a biking championship it was sponsoring by eliminating 17 of 20 entries. Much later, an American bricklayer was banned from the elite Henley Regatta under the Mechanic's Clause. In egalitarian America, such strictures seemed effete, unmanly and decidedly undemocratic. On the frontier, each man stood on his own merits and aristocrats did not dictate the rules.

The first intercollegiate baseball games were played in the 1850s, but the game's rise to America's favorite pastime took place mainly on professional diamonds. Intercollegiate football got its start on November 6, 1869, when Rutgers and Princeton, using rugby rules, fought to a 6–4 Rutgers win. Harvard beat Tufts 1–0 on June 4, 1875, to become the first game to follow modern football rules (though modern scoring came even later). Over the last quarter of the 19th century, the game gained enormous popularity, spreading quickly from its New England and Middle Atlantic origins to colleges and universities throughout the land. All through this period, Walter Camp, who captained Yale's 1879 team, and others tinkered with rules, mainly adapting rugby to systematize the game and give it a rational order.[11] Camp's innovations as head coach and later master strategist at Yale included the line of scrimmage, the system of downs, the center snap, the seven-man line and four-man backfield, including the new position of quarterback and the yardage markers on the gridiron itself.[12] Small wonder that by age 33, Camp was widely acknowledged as the father of American football.

By the 1890s, Thanksgiving Day games in New York were receiving saturation news coverage and drawing crowds in the 40,000 range.[13] Gradually, the sport became a national ritual. The historian Ronald A. Smith writes, "The Thanksgiving Day game had combined the educationally elite colleges on the athletic field with the social elite in the stands. The 'Gilded Age' in American history was seen no more clearly than at the football stadium. . . . Many of the prominent attended the games, from multimillionaires, such as Cornelius Vanderbilt, and state governors, to playwrights and social celebrities such as Mrs. William Whitney."

By this time, the United States was well on its way toward joining its educational system and popular sports at the hip, a trend that would accelerate dramatically in the century to follow. In contrast, other countries made sports the province of amateur and professional clubs that often played before huge throngs. A major influence in shaping the American system was a new craze for fitness and athleticism advocated as the true path to manliness by such popular figures as Theodore Roosevelt and Walter Camp. The trend took root toward the end of the 19th century, as training in physical education and sports found their way into the curricula of colleges and universities and even secondary schools.[14]

In 1903, Harvard built the first large stadium using reinforced concrete, and a nationwide boom in stadium construction followed. But now, the game found itself in the grip of its first great scandal over violent extremes on the playing field. In 1905 alone, there were 18 football-related deaths and 159 serious injuries, including concussions, punctured lungs, snapped spinal cords and broken necks.[15] In all, 45 players had died since 1900. In 1893, President Grover Cleveland had abolished the annual Army-Navy game after learning that 24 Navy players had been admitted that year to the hospital and that the team had experienced 82 sick days.[16] By then, several colleges and universities were threatening to abolish the game. The level of violence in 1905 turned out to be the breaking point; the game's existence hung by a thread.

At that point, one of football's greatest enthusiasts intervened to help save the game. That October, President Teddy Roosevelt called representatives of Harvard, Yale and Princeton—the so-called "Big Three"—to a White House luncheon to discuss how to make play safer, "especially by reducing the element of brutality in play," the *Washington Post* reported on October 10, 1905.

"Nearly every death may be traced to 'unnecessary roughness,'" the *Post* reported. "Most victims had been found unconscious beneath a mass of other players, often kicked in the head or stomach, so as to cause internal injuries or concussion of the brain. . . ." Even so, per the *Post* account, "Roosevelt liked football and apparently thought being roughed up wasn't necessarily a bad thing. 'I believe in outdoor games, and I do not mind in the least that they are rough games, or that those who take part in them are occasionally injured.'" Roosevelt's view that the football field was a proving ground for the battlefield was validated by the performance of his Rough Riders, many of whom were former football standouts.[17] "In life, as in a football game," he wrote, "the principle to follow is: Hit the line hard; don't foul and don't shirk, but hit the line hard!"

As the historian Benjamin G. Radar writes, "Through much of the nineteenth century, the popular media took delight in depicting the typical undergraduate male in effeminate terms—as a dyspeptic, shriveled up, and cowering scholar. . . . Football, on the other hand, projected the typical college man as rugged and fearless, as one who could hold his own in the world outside the walls of academe."[18]

After the White House luncheon, on the train ride back north, the Big Three representatives discussed the President's request and agreed to send him a joint telegram pledging their willingness to cooperate on reforms.

Theodore Roosevelt speaking from the balcony of the Hotel Allen, Allentown, Pennsylvania, 1914.

Fundamental reforms were soon adopted that legalized the forward pass, abolished dangerous mass formations, created a neutral zone between offense and defense and doubled the first down distance to 10 yards.[19] Thereafter, fatalities began waning—to 11 in 1906 and 11 in 1907. A resurgence in 1909 led to more reforms that spread formations and encouraged the high-octane passing game of the modern era. One footnote: among changes brought about at Roosevelt's request was a recommendation to form a purely advisory intercollegiate organization that later became the National Collegiate Athletic Association (NCAA).

It's worth remembering that no team would ever dominate football as had Yale in the lead-up to the modern era. From 1872 to 1909, Yale football teams won 324, lost 17 and tied 18. From the last game of the 1890 season to the ninth game of the 1893 season, Yale scored 1,265 points to none for its opponents.[20] Yale so dominated archrival Harvard that the Crimson "felt a certain loss of manhood in not winning a single game in the 1880s and only two in the 1890s," wrote Harvard historian S. E. Morrison. Harvard philosopher George Santayana even went so far as to identify Harvard with ancient Athens and Yale with ancient Sparta. All this could mean only one thing: Schools everywhere emulated Yale and its legendary son, Walter Camp.

By the turn of the century, administrations everywhere had discovered that football was far more effective in attracting public attention than an institution's reputation for scholarship or outstanding teaching.[21] In the postbellum era, most colleges and universities were attended by men from society's upper crust; and a degree from an Ivy League institution was seen as a ticket to the privileged class.

The dramatic rule changes adopted between 1905 and 1912 opened football up, led to many more spectacular plays and led to a sharp uptick in fan excitement. These changes, coupled with another lesser known factor—the inclusion of athletics in military training—helped set the stage for the Golden Age of Sport in the 1920s.

On the eve of World War I, as James Mennell explains in the *Journal of Sports History*, recommendations were made to President Woodrow Wilson that the military provide organized recreation in training camps. In a remarkably short time, camp teams were organized, equipped and playing games. Fortunately, many men in the camps had played or coached football, thus filling capable teams was not that difficult. Enthusiasm for football among soldiers and sailors was so high that games soon followed between camps and colleges in major stadiums.[22] Sportswriters soon saw and lauded the superiority of service teams. The biggest attendance draw of the 1917 season matched a service team against Harvard. Relations between service teams and colleges soured the next year. Mennell notes that fewer and fewer colleges would schedule service teams to avoid a loss of standing. Thus, the six leading service teams could schedule only six of their 27 games with college teams in 1918.

Mennell also writes that ". . . the most dramatic game of the 1918 season occurred when national champion Pitt agreed to play a powerful service team, the Cleveland Naval Reserve, in a postseason showdown between service and college teams. In 1917, Pitt had been regarded by many observers as the national champion, but had refused to play a postseason game with a strong service team. . . ." Cleveland won the [1918] game 10 to 9.

While game attendance fell during the war years, it rebounded sharply in the 1920s. During the Golden Age, attendance doubled and gate receipts tripled. Americans couldn't get enough of the game; their appetites were whetted by amped-up accounts written by legendary sportswriters like Grantland Rice of the *New York Herald Tribune*.[23] Rice's lead paragraph on the Army–Notre Dame game on October 18, 1924, described an immortal Irish backfield and became the most famous ever written:

> Outlined against a blue-gray October sky, the Four Horsemen rode again. In dramatic lore, their names are Death, Destruction, Pestilence, and Famine. But those are aliases. Their real names are: Stuhldreher, Crowley, Miller and Layden.

Rice also lionized home run king Babe Ruth, heavyweight boxing champion Jack Dempsey, tennis star Bill Tilden, and golfing great Bobby Jones. But he reserved his most memorable monikers for Red Grange, the University of Illinois halfback whose exploits on the gridiron electrified the nation. In naming Grange "the Galloping Ghost," Rice coined one of the most memorable sobriquets ever. It fit because Grange's phantom-like moves made him seem illusory as he dodged and weaved through masses of players on long runs. Rice also called him "the Wheaton Iceman," the "Will o' the Wisp" and a "Human Tornado."

His breathless prose earned Rice a six-figure income and a host of imitators. With radio and newsreels still in their infancy, newspapers were the public's main source of news. Americans wanted their sporting heroes to be larger than life and full of derring-do. Sports fans weren't nearly as interested in the rising chorus of complaints about college football's cut-throat recruiting, sham courses and runaway commercialization. These and other symptoms of deep-seated corruption were documented in a

Carnegie Foundation report issued in 1929 after three years of investigations and site visits to 112 campuses. Investigators found that three-quarters of the schools visited had violated the NCAA's code and principles of amateurism. The authors of *Unwinding Madness,* an excellent study released in 2017, note that, "A follow up study in the *New York Times* in 1931 found that not a single college had changed its practices in response to the Carnegie Foundation report."[24]

Charles Clotfelter, professor of public policy, economics, and law at Duke says, "What is most striking about the (1929) Carnegie Foundation report is how contemporary its findings sound today."[25] Charlie's book *Big-Time Sports in American Universities* is one of the very best on the subject.

In the decade that followed, Hollywood produced several films that poked at the hypocrisy of college sports, among them *Horse Feathers* starring the Marx Brothers, *Saturday Heroes* and *Hero for a Day.* These films helped establish near-universal public recognition that college football was rife with abuses that required correction.[26]

By this time, a new sport—an American original—had emerged and was being played worldwide. Dr. James Naismith, a Canadian-born physical education teacher,[27] had asked the janitor at his Springfield, Massachusetts, school to nail a peach basket on a balcony 10 feet above the floor. Using a soccer ball at first, he challenged his students to throw the ball into the basket any way they could. When one succeeded, the janitor brought out a ladder, climbed up and retrieved the ball. Naismith's previously bored students eagerly embraced the challenge. From these humble origins, the game quickly spread nationally through the YMCA network and soon was being played at a host of colleges. Improvements made along the way quickened the pace of play, and by 1936 basketball had become an Olympic sport.

It became a national sport centered in New York in the 1930s. In 1934, a former sportswriter named Ned Irish rented Madison Square Garden, which had seating for 16,000, and pitted outstanding local teams against the strongest rivals he could attract from other parts of the country. Two years later, Irish matched Long Island University (LIU), a perennial powerhouse, against Stanford University and its star, Hank Luisetti, whose one-handed shot created a rage. LIU boasted a 43-game winning streak, but Stanford won 42–31. Irish-promoted games had become a legend, and college basketball was established as a national spectator sport. During World War II, service teams composed of recognized stars did much to increase the game's popularity through a quicker pace and standardized play. After the war, the game became a source of pride in communities of all sizes with good teams. It also attracted stars from ethnic neighborhoods and a growing number of African Americans. Unlike football, the recruitment of one or two star players could transform a team in a single season, and players in general were improving their skills.

But disaster struck in 1951 when New York District Attorney Frank Hogan announced that 32 players from seven colleges, among them several of the nation's best teams, were guilty of point shaving. Three players from the University of Kentucky, which had won the NCAA title three times since 1948, pleaded guilty in the scandal. When it broke, their famous coach, Adolph Rupp, told the media the gamblers ". . . couldn't touch my boys with a ten-foot pole." As the sports historian Murray Sperber writes in *Onward to Victory,* "The point spread changed everything. Suddenly games between mismatched squads became interesting. If the bookie made the superior team a ten-point favorite, the bettor could wager that the underdog would do well enough to come close, at least not to lose by ten points or more." Interest in the point spread soared as millions of dollars got wagered, and incentives for fixing the spread became much too tempting for gamblers to ignore.

Revelations of widespread point shaving in basketball and widespread honor code violations at West Point threw cold water on cherished American beliefs and deeply shocked the public. Even the sporting press began to back away from defending what the public saw as inexcusable behavior. Suddenly deemphasis of college athletics became a cry heard throughout the land. The *New York Times* demanded a "total collegiate sports cleanup." For months, the college coaches and presidents battled each other over reforms.

"Most Americans wanted college football players to be superb athletes *and* authentic students, thus fulfilling the classic norm," writes Sperber. He goes on to say, "Some exceptional scholar-athletes could handle these conflicting demands (between athletics and the classroom) . . . but tens of thousands of participants in big-time college sports fell short, particularly academically."[28] The system could not support the traditional scholar-athlete ideal.

To their credit, college presidents, acting through the American Council of Education (ACE), proposed an impressive list of reforms: a ban on bowl games, abolition of spring football practice, an end to athletic scholarships. At the behest of coaches and athletic directors, the NCAA mounted an aggressive counterattack. In the end, NCAA prevailed, and the *New York Times's* influential columnist Arthur Daly would characterize the results as "a step in the right direction." It was Daly's view that "the NCAA took the lofty, utopian proposals of the college presidents and watered them down slightly."[29] *Slightly* was a poor choice of words; in effect, the NCAA had gutted ACE reforms. But with the *Times* imprimatur on the NCAA's side, other media fell in line and public outrage abated. With that, one of the last moments when the game might have been fundamentally reformed slipped away.

In the early 1950s, the flood gates opened, and money from television began pouring into college football coffers for the first time. NCAA television contracts authorized a "Game of the Week," plus regional broadcasts that shifted national viewers to the most interesting regional games.[30] Commercialization in the form of sponsored TV broadcasts began its inexorable rise to dominance over collegiate sports. Televised games were so popular fans quickly forgot the basketball point shaving scandals or shady practices dating back to the 19th century that most schools playing big-time football still used.[31]

From the Harvard-Yale boat race on Lake Winnipesauke in 1852 to the point shaving scandals of the late 1940s and early 1950s, a century of big-time college sports had fed voraciously on commercialization and a trend toward professionalization. "Ringers and tramps," who rarely, if ever, went to class, were getting paid just as in yesteryear; athletes were being coddled with kid gloves to a greater extent than ever before; coaches and athletic directors still steamrolled with impunity faculty and media demands for reform; college presidents still turned a blind eye to egregious abuses, hoping for "jackpot" championships that would lure more students to their campuses; and the "win-at-all-cost" sentiment among boosters and fans remained completely out of control. Everything had come full circle except for one new and catastrophic threat: Vast sums pouring in from television over the next half century and beyond would push commercialism to stratospheric heights and lead to levels of hypocrisy never experienced before.

CHAPTER TWO

Towering Achievers

Between the 1890s and World War II, the United States became a global power and forged a distinctive national culture defined in no small part by its scholar-athletes. As the Gilded Age came to an end and a new century dawned, Americans were still shell-shocked by a rapidly evolving form of capitalism marked by the Financial Panic of 1893, frequent and bitter labor strikes, small but heady wars of expansion and massive waves of immigration. For the first time, as the scholar Steven W. Pope writes,

> The Thanksgiving sporting tradition had truly become a national passion. In 1893, a four-hour Thanksgiving parade went up New York City's Fifth Avenue and wove through Harlem to the Polo Grounds where 40,000 spectators watched Princeton beat Yale.[1]

A week later, Richard Harding Davis, a journalist who would become the first American war correspondent, hailed the tradition of the Thanksgiving Day football game—at the time barely a decade old—as "the greatest sporting event and spectacle combined this country has to show."[2] More and more, sports served as the flame beneath the melting pot—a realm of pursuits that helped to unify newly arrived Polish steelworkers in Cleveland with Scotch-Irish millwrights in Birmingham and Serbian bricklayers in St. Louis. Regional, racial and ethnic differences all were bridged by an irresistible imperative to "Americanize." Walter Camp, the father of American football, proclaimed sport as "the folk highway" of the nation, contending that, "More people march together and contentedly and in democratic spirit along the [folk] highway than along any other of the roads trod by human kind."[3]

The careers of two scholar-athletes—both consensus All-American football players—were bookends to the half century of ferment and change between 1890 and the eve of World War II: William Henry Lewis, the first African American so recognized for his play at Harvard in 1892–93, and Byron "Whizzer" White, the nation's most popular collegiate sports hero in 1937–38. He played at the University of Colorado and went to Oxford in 1939 on a Rhodes Scholarship. Both men had exceptionally high-impact professional lives.

Lewis's parents were former slaves. He was born three years after the Civil War when it seemed that America's promise of full equality and citizenship for his race was all but assured. With two-third majorities in the U.S. House and Senate, Republicans had enacted bold plans for a "Radical Reconstruction" to be administered by the U.S. Army. Black Americans would be enfranchised, hold public office, get land and have public and private schools. In Special Field Order No. 15, issued on January 16, 1865, General William T. Sherman had mandated that black Americans along the so-called rice coast of South Carolina and Georgia be granted 40 acres of land (he later added a limited number of mules).[4] Southerner planters responded with implacable fury, and Radical Reconstruction quickly unraveled late that same year when President Andrew Johnson ordered that lands set for redistribution be left in the hands of the planters. Northern concern for the plight of newly freed southern black Americans soon began to wane as white Americans gradually regained control of the courthouses and state houses of the old Confederacy.

In the words of the leading black historian of the day, W.E.B. DuBois, who was born the same year as Lewis: "The slave went free; stood for a moment in the sun; then moved back again toward slavery." While the tragedy of black regression continued apace, an ideological debate over the so-called "Negro question" gave rise to what DuBois described as "one of the most stupendous [propaganda] efforts the world ever saw to discredit human beings, an effort involving universities, history, science, social life and religion."[5] In essence, the African American in the postbellum era was portrayed *and seen*—in the North and the South—as lazy and shiftless—a subhuman species with little prospect for improvement. One widely advocated solution was to establish African colonies to which the African American population would be exported.

The career and accomplishments of Lewis can only be appreciated in this context for they gave rout to the lie of racial inferiority and served as a beacon of possibilities that any fair-minded person could not ignore.

The first of the Horatio Alger rags to riches stories was published the year before Lewis and DuBois were born. It is doubtful that any offering in that series of 120 installments could outshine Lewis's story for sheer pluck and hallmark accomplishments. Lewis was born in the village of Berkley, Virginia, which is tucked between Portsmouth and Norfolk. His parents were the offspring of white, slave-owning fathers and African American slave mothers.[6] His father, Ashley Henry Lewis, had been freed in North Carolina by the Union Army and was mustered out of the military in Norfolk. He was working on the docks in Norfolk when William Henry was born, then moved his family to Portsmouth, where he became a Baptist minister.

At a mere 15, William went off to Virginia Normal and Collegiate Institute (now Virginia State University) where he came under the watchful eye of its President, John Mercer Langston, an African American abolitionist and lawyer. It is likely that Langston guided young William to Amherst College, where he enrolled in the fall of 1888. Up to that point, William had not played an organized sport and had engaged in little meaningful exercise. At Amherst, where development of the mind and body was strongly emphasized, his routine would quickly change. Choosing to play football, William would later say, "I didn't have a uniform, and wore my street clothes. That first day I got my clothes all torn off and my feet stepped on. The next day they gave me a uniform."[7]

Lewis was among several talented young black Americans who were warmly accepted and educated at elite liberal New England schools—prodigies who would be among the most prominent African American leaders in the new century. Apparently, he and an older classmate, William Tecumseh Sherman Jackson, were introduced to Massachusetts Senator

George Hoar by Virginia Normal President Langston. Hoar, in turn, seems to have introduced them at Amherst.[8] Lewis and Jackson traveled there together and were joined by a third young black American, George Washington Forbes of Wilberforce University in Ohio.[9]

Lewis and Jackson both went out for football as sophomores and quickly made the starting lineup with Lewis at center and Jackson in the backfield. Lewis drew rave reviews and would continue as a star for the rest of his career at Amherst. In his last season, he was elected captain, the first of his race to hold that position on a mixed-race team. The accolade was more than a perfunctory tribute because at that time the captain called plays and largely dictated on-field strategy.

In the final game of the 1891 season, Amherst and Williams played to a scoreless tie. Football historian William Edwards called Lewis's performance "one of the greatest exhibitions of grit ever seen in a football game.... [He] was all over the field on defense. When the game was over, his teammates tried to carry him off the field, but he refused to leave until the final whistle."[10]

At Amherst, race was a thin barrier to Lewis. He got elected to the Student Senate his junior year and was selected to compete for the prestigious Hardy Debate and oratory prize. He also gained membership in the Hitchcock Society of Inquiry, a prominent literary organization. Even more telling, in his final year, his classmates elected Lewis to give the class oration. In it, he observed: "Here is no snobbery, no caste, no invidious social distinctions. Every man is a fellow, a member of the true college fraternity."[11]

The Amherst Record noted that the world at large should know "... that the color of a man's skin has no bearing whatsoever on the part he may take in the student or social life at Amherst college."

It is noteworthy that several African Americans from Boston, including DuBois, attended Lewis's graduation. A young woman named Elizabeth Baker was among them. She came from Cambridge and Wellesley. After that visit, she and Lewis began a courtship that would lead to marriage. She may well have influenced Lewis to go to Harvard Law School because it was only a stone's throw from her home. They married the year he earned his law degree.[12]

Lax eligibility rules permitted Lewis to play football for Harvard in 1892 and 1893, his first two years of law school. His reputation for prowess on the gridiron preceded him, and he quickly cracked the Crimson's starting lineup. At five feet ten inches tall and 175 pounds, Lewis was small for a center but made up for that with incredible quickness. As one national writer put it: "Lewis is a man thoroughly versed in all the fine points of the position . . . and being very quick . . . he can not only play his position but get out and into almost every play, and to do a surprising amount of tackling."[13]

In 1892, Lewis made the prestigious All-American team chosen by Casper Whitney, editor of *Harper's Weekly*. He earned even more plaudits the following year and closed out his college career by leading Harvard to a rousing 26–4 victory over Penn on Thanksgiving Day. An injury had sidelined the Crimson captain, so Lewis was chosen to replace him. Once again, Whitney named him to his All-American team, extolling Lewis as ". . . not only the best centre of the year, but the best all-around centre that has ever put on a football jacket." The legendary Walter Camp also named Lewis to his All-American teams for 1892 and 1893. He later named Lewis to his mythical team of the eleven greatest football players of all time and credited him with revolutionizing his position by emphasizing mobility over fixed stability.[14]

Lewis might have played during his last year of law school but stricter eligibility rules adopted by Harvard and other schools ruled him out. With that, he moved to the sidelines where he became a much-admired assistant coach for 13 years. Once again he broke new ground as the first of his race to hold such a position. During that period, Cornell and several other schools offered Lewis their head coaching jobs. Part of his allure was his authorship in 1896 of *A Primer of College Football*, which was serialized by *Harper's Weekly*. By then, Lewis had developed a national reputation as one of football's greatest strategic wizards.

While Lewis coached, he also practiced law—first as a partner in the Boston firm of Lewis, Fox and Andrew and then on his own. By 1899, he had ventured into politics by getting elected to the Cambridge City Council. He followed that with a term in the Massachusetts state legislature but lost his bid for reelection in 1903. In 1907, President Teddy Roosevelt appointed him as Assistant U.S. Attorney for Massachusetts. As a fellow Harvard alum, Roosevelt admired Lewis's gridiron success and had entertained him in 1900 at his Oyster Bay estate on Long Island.

In 1911, President William Howard Taft appointed Lewis as an Assistant

Attorney General of the United States, a position that required confirmation by the U.S. Senate. Southern senators blocked his confirmation for eight months, but he was finally confirmed and served in the position for two years. It made him the highest-ranking African American ever to serve in the federal government. When he was fired by President Woodrow Wilson in 1913, he returned to Boston and private law practice.[15]

Over the course of his long career, Lewis was involved in several high-profile cases. No other African American had ever argued a case before the U.S. Supreme Court alone and won, but Lewis did that in 1930.[16] He was confident and strong in the courtroom, and the press often described his arguments as brilliant.

As the rise of the Ku Klux Klan became more and more ominous and as race relations sharply deteriorated, Lewis's strategy for improving the lot of black Americans evolved from confrontational to conciliatory. After law school, he became one of the "Boston Radicals," a small but vocal group of well-educated black Americans who opposed the accomodationist philosophy of Booker T. Washington, the powerful architect of the so-called "Tuskegee Machine" based at Tuskegee University in Alabama. The Radicals vehemently objected to the centerpiece of Washington's program to improve the lot of black Americans by providing them with industrial education in lieu of the traditional liberal arts education. Washington and the Radicals clashed at a meeting at a Boston hotel in 1898. The last speaker was Lewis, who advised Washington to go "back to the South and leave to us the matters political affecting the race."[17]

But Lewis changed sides just two years later. His turn toward Washington's philosophy was marked first by an exchange of letters with President Roosevelt. Lewis wrote first to push for a much stronger defense of civil rights. In his reply, Roosevelt urged Lewis to meet with Washington, writing that he "is a man for whom I have the highest regards." Apparently, Lewis's wife, Elizabeth, was urging him about the same time to give up on confrontation. All this led, ultimately, to an exchange of letters between Lewis and Washington in which Washington made it clear that he could help Lewis further his career. It was on Washington's recommendation that Roosevelt named Lewis as Assistant U.S. Attorney for Massachusetts.

The rupture between Lewis and the Radicals came to a head in 1903 during a visit Washington made to Boston. At a meeting chaired by Lewis, several Radicals interrupted Washington's talk. When Lewis's warnings to settle down were ignored, he called in the police and a melee ensued, which became known as the "Boston riot." One of Lewis's former Harvard classmates, William Monroe Trotter, was tried for his part in the disruption and got 30 days in jail. Lewis was the key witness at his trial. Trotter later called Lewis "the dirtiest cur" and accused him of capitulating to the accomodationist side to further his own career.[18]

In retrospect, the charge seems overly harsh. Lewis fought valiantly his entire life for black equality. When a white Cambridge barber refused to shave him, he sued and ultimately secured passage of a statewide law prohibiting racial discrimination in places of public accommodation. After he joined the American Bar Association, the organization's hierarchy learned that he was an African American and tried to boot him out in 1912. No less a personage than George Wickersham, the U.S. Attorney General, came to his defense by threatening to resign his own ABA membership if Lewis got kicked out. The ABA then backed down. Three years later, Lewis tried and failed to get the film *Birth of a Nation*, which glorified the Ku Klux Klan, banned in Boston. In all, he tried 12 cases before the Supreme Court, winning some and losing some. At age 80, he suffered a heart attack in his Boston apartment and died on New Year's Day 1949.

William Henry Lewis, who was imbued at Amherst and Harvard with the scholar-athlete ideal, became the quintessential public man. His long list of "firsts" served as a beacon of hope to fellow African Americans who desperately needed ideals to hold dear. He was closely followed and much admired by the black press. The *Cleveland Gazette* proudly called him "the most talked of Afro-American in New England." An elitist philosophy—the belief that educated and culturally advanced white and black Americans shared similar values—prompted liberal colleges and universities of that region to educate a significant number of black Americans who became leaders early in the new century. Because they eagerly seized that opportunity, these talented young black Americans played an instrumental role in defining the scholar-athlete ideal, which became a powerful beacon to all Americans in the new century.

¤ ¤ ¤

No scholar-athlete ever tested more fully the absolute limits of what could be achieved in either sphere than the curt and unassuming Byron Raymond White. In January 1961, he was having lunch at a restaurant near the Justice Department in Washington, where he had just become the Deputy Attorney General to Robert F. Kennedy, the President's brother, when a curious waitress asked, "Say, aren't you Whizzer White?" Eyeing her warily, White took another sip of coffee and replied, "I was."[19]

It was White's way of saying that his Whizzer years were over and he fully intended to keep them that way. He had never liked—and at times even loathed—that sobriquet. He'd been saddled with it his sophomore year just before suffering a season-ending football knee injury. It appeared in a one-column *Denver Post* headline and was repeated in a two-paragraph story below with no byline. It gradually snowballed from there, but who coined the "Whizzer" label was never clear. White called that sophomore season a double loss because "I couldn't play and I got rechristened."[20] By the time he was a senior—and well on his way to becoming a consensus football All-American—Grantland Rice, the dean of American sportswriters, would tell radio listeners that "Whizzer White is the ideal moniker for a triple threat tailback." Rice went on to say he believed White would live up to that name.

His reply to the waitress was told and retold so often it became folklore. One of his former law clerks, Dennis J. Hutchinson, a law professor at the University of Chicago, even gave his fine biography the somewhat cryptic name *The Man Who Once Was Whizzer White*.

In fact, White's spectacular athletic and academic exploits did elevate him, quite early in life, to near-mythic status. As his reputation grew, Whizzermania obsessed the public, which all too often meant the press camped out on his doorstep. He began with the generous assumption that the press had a job to do and knew how to do it, but he soon turned brusque and unavailable with many of the writers who pursued him. His modesty made him dislike attention; he also put a high value on his privacy. When photographers tracked him down on a San Francisco-bound train en route to an interview for a Rhodes Scholarship, he sullenly told them, "Members of the committee [conducting the Rhodes interview] might think I'm getting the big head or something, getting pictures taken of me every time I turn around."

The question *Who was he?* is not easy to answer. His former law clerk, Andrew G. Schultz, and Tenth Circuit Court judge, David M. Ebel, answered it as well as anyone could in a special tribute:

He accorded dignity and respect equally to presidents and cafeteria workers, and did not consider that his accomplishments and titles placed him above any other person. He was a fierce competitor, who truly loved to win in competition, and yet he valued fair play more. He held awesome power in his hands for thirty-one years as a Supreme Court Justice, but was an apostle of judicial restraint. He lived in the rarified intellectual world of constitutional theory, yet he grounded his most significant decisions on common sense learned in Wellington, Colorado. He was a man of the world, but also a man of deep faith. He was at the same time one of our country's most public and well-respected people, and yet one of its most private citizens.[21]

White was born in Wellington, Colorado, a tiny sugar beet town on the high plains about 70 miles due north of Denver and 13 miles north of Fort Collins. Neither of his parents had gone to high school, but both strongly emphasized education to their offspring. Young Byron's brother, Sam, was four years older and a near-perfect role model. Growing up, both worked hard in the beet fields and doing odd jobs around town. Sam was outgoing and gregarious, a star quarterback and valedictorian of his class. Byron was introspective and taciturn, but a superb student and valedictorian of his class, though it had only six students. Sam and Byron both won Rhodes Scholarships as seniors at the University of Colorado. Evelyn Schmidt came to Wellington High School in 1928 to teach English and drama. She was fresh out of teacher's college but proved to be a great influence on both boys. She would later recall that "Sam knew how brilliant he was, right from the start." Of Byron, she observed, he "had no idea how good he was. He was always challenging himself, always trying to find his limits. He pushed and dug and went further than anybody in school, including his teachers."[22]

By state law, the valedictorian of any Colorado high school could attend the state university in Boulder tuition-free. Room and board were not included, so Byron waited tables at sorority and fraternity houses all four years to support himself. He supplemented that income by doing odd jobs in the summer, mainly on the CU campus. He had a lot to juggle because he carried a full academic load and played three demanding sports: football, basketball and baseball, excelling at all three. Remarkably, he may have been even better on the academic side, earning a Phi Beta Kappa key and becoming valedictorian of his senior class. He also was junior class president and student body president his senior year. He'd gone to CU planning to follow in Sam's footsteps and pursue a medical career. But at the end of his sophomore year, he switched studies from chemistry, mathematics and science to the humanities and economics. Later, he entered the honors program for sociology and economics.[23]

His greatest year on the gridiron came as a senior in 1937. By then, he had developed a taut, lean body and weighed 187 pounds. He cut an imposing figure at six feet one inches tall with a powerful leg drive and oaken arms near-perfect for stiff-arming would-be tacklers. Early on, Grantland Rice and other national sportswriters mentioned him as a possible All-American. On November 3, 1937, White scored all CU's points in a 17–7 win over Utah. The local press billed the result: White 17, Utah 7. Their hero had become the number one scorer in the country, but back east no one knew. Then, the following Monday, it all changed. In an eyewitness report, a national columnist, UPI's Henry M'Lemore, crowed that White deserved "the gold watch, the parchment scroll, the double-breasted sweater and all the other items a man named on the All-America comes in for" for his performance. The column ran in 412 newspapers, and overnight White became a national sensation.[24] In time, he would become the most talked about college football player of the year in 1937 and 1938.

After the M'Lemore column, the sporting public could not get enough of him; Whizzermania ruled the day. For Coloradans, the only questions for the rest of the season were: Would Colorado get a New Year's Day bowl bid, and would Whizzer be named an All-American? In the attention-starved West, such questions could lead to fighting words.

Colorado closed out an 8–0 undefeated season on Thanksgiving Day with a 34–7 rout of Denver University to win the Rocky Mountain Conference Championship. White figured in all the scoring and ended up leading the nation in that category. He finished second in balloting for the Heisman Trophy, due mainly to doubts back east about the competition he had played.[25]

Shortly after the Denver game, CU got the New Year's Day bowl bid its fans had been clamoring for—to play Rice University in the Cotton

Bowl. Their second wish came true when White was made one of three unanimous choices to the prestigious Collier's All-American team. The selections were made by an advisory board headed by Grantland Rice. On December 11, one day after the Collier's announcement, the National Football League drafted players for the '38 season. White was picked fourth by the Pittsburg Pirates (later the Steelers). Nine days later, he was interviewed by the Rhodes selection committee, which deliberated late into the night. Finally, at 11 p.m., it announced that White had won; he was the seventh CU student so honored.[26]

CU lost the Cotton Bowl by a decisive 28–14 score, but White lived up to his billing. He threw a 7-yard touchdown pass in the first quarter and kicked the extra point to make the score 7–0. Later, he intercepted a pass, ran it back 47 yards for a touchdown and again kicked the extra point to put CU up 14–0. But it was all Rice after that. White had a tough day running, averaging only 2.3 yards per carry for a total of 54 yards. Even so, one of Rice's best players called White "the best back we have met this season."

Byron "Whizzer" White

After the bowl game, White turn his attention to basketball. But all through the season and the spring and early summer, the press obsessed about "Will he? or "Won't he?"—the questions being whether he'd accept the Rhodes Scholarship or play pro football. Pittsburg owner Art Rooney had made him a very public offer of $15,000 for the '38 season, double what most players made, but White steadfastly maintained he'd go to Oxford.

While his choice was always couched in either/or terms, his brother Sam, who was just wrapping up his last year at Oxford, found a third way. A classmate told him the Rhodes trustees rarely, if ever, granted one-year deferments but might agree to a one-semester delay. Sam immediately began exploring that option, and a formal request was made. But there was still no answer by the time Sam got home. As it turned out, the trustees were worried about a publicity backlash in the United States if they denied White's request. Their answer granting the deferral was cabled to Wellington on July 28. The next day, White cabled Rooney to ask if Pittsburg's offer still stood; on August 1, they agreed by phone on a contract that would fetch White $15,800 for one year.[27]

Although the money mattered a good deal to a poor boy from Wellington who was still bussing tables at a sorority house, his decision was swayed much more by his great passion for competition. Many in the sports cognoscenti had derided Rooney as foolish for "wasting" such a high draft choice on a player who, by consensus, had fed on weak competition; naturally, White was eager to prove them wrong and did so with a huge exclamation point: In the '38 season, he led the league in rushing on a subpar team and made all pro. Playing in '40 and '41 for Detroit Lion teams with losing records, he was just as good.

Even so, there was never a chance he'd not go to Oxford. He arrived there in January, 1939 and stayed in Europe until the war all but broke out. Earlier, in the spring, he met John F. Kennedy, who was touring the continent ostensibly to gather material for his senior thesis at Harvard. They met again in Munich in early July and narrowly escaped a rock-throwing incident when several young Germans spied the English plates on their car. Kennedy went touring elsewhere while White stayed on unobtrusively studying Roman law. On August 29, he cabled his parents that he'd left Munich—and none too soon: Three days later Germany invaded Poland, and the continent, ultimately, would go up in flames.

White's ship, the *Manhattan,* docked in New York on October 1, and he avoided the press in debarking. The next day, he paid $450 in cash for tuition at Yale Law School in New Haven.[28] He finished first in his first-year class and went back to Boulder to attend summer law school classes there. His decision to wait tables at his old fraternity class made national news; it astounded readers that, after being the highest-paid player in professional football, he'd take such a menial job. The ever-modest White explained, "It's a good way to earn your food and you don't make money to go to school."

A more lucrative job soon beckoned. On August 17, White signed a contract with the Detroit Lions for $7,500 for the season with an option to renew for a second year. Unbeknownst to him, Art Rooney had sold his contract for $5,000 to Lions owner Freddie Mandell, Jr., a Chicago department store magnate. White reported to the Lions' training camp the day after signing with Mandell.

"The reason I returned to football is because I love to play it," White explained.[29]

Thus, his law studies became truncated and compressed. Arrangements were made for him to take his exams for the summer law school session at CU at the Detroit law offices of a Yale law alumnus. Because of the war, his work at Yale would consist of the full year in 1939–40, the spring semester of 1941 and a semester and a summer in 1946 after mustering out of the Navy. Despite the lack of continuity, he still finished first in his Yale class.[30]

In contrast, his new team was not nearly so successful: Detroit finished 5-5-1 in '40 and 4-6-1 in '41. White led the league in rushing again in 1940 and compiled an enviable record the following year. In the last football game White would ever play, the Lions dispatched the Chicago Cardinals 21–3. In it, White ran an intercepted pass back 81 yards for a touchdown; ran back a punt from Detroit's two-yard line 63 yards to the Cardinal 35-yard line; threw a 23-yard pass for a touchdown; and quick-kicked a 62-yard punt. It was a memorable farewell—one of the greatest games in NFL history. Like most men his age, he'd soon be wearing a uniform.

He was driving back to Colorado when he first heard news of the Japanese attack on Pearl Harbor. On May 6, 1942, he was appointed an ensign in the naval reserve and sent to Dartmouth College for advanced intelligence training. He was subsequently sent to Tulagi, a remote Pacific island in the Solomon Chain to help protect Guadalcanal, which U.S. Marines had captured early in 1943. By coincidence, Lt. John F. Kennedy was stationed in the Solomon Islands too, where he commanded the patrol boat PT 109 and was tasked to disrupt Japanese convoys attempting to reinforce their troops on North Georgia Island through treacherous waters locally known as "the slot."

On the night of August 1, three patrol boats, including PT 109, were patrolling the slot when a Japanese convoy made up of four destroyers led by the Amagiri came through at top speed (30 to 35 knots) under blackout conditions. Suddenly, the convoy spotted a patrol boat closing fast. About 10 seconds later, it struck the starboard side of the vessel and severed its front quarter. The vessel was PT 109, which seemed to disappear. The destroyers following the Amagiri all strafed the waters where it had been sighted with machine gun fire. Two crewmen were killed in the crash, but Kennedy led the survivors on a four-hour swim through shark- and crocodile-infested waters clinging to debris. They finally made it safely to an island, but Kennedy moved them to avoid detection by the enemy. After they were rescued by Australian coast-watchers, Kennedy's actions were deemed both heroic and slipshod. PT boats were the Navy's fastest vessels and not one had been run down by a destroyer until PT 109 got sunk. The main reason was that Kennedy had only one of three powerful engines running when the Amagiri struck—and that engine was idling, rendering the vessel helpless. This was against squadron policy, and Kennedy was heavily criticized in the fleet for his actions. Some even said he should be court-martialed, but postmortems raised many other pertinent questions, some of which had extenuating answers.

Fortunately for Kennedy, and entirely by coincidence, it seems, Lt. Byron R. White was assigned to write the after-action report for the controversial mishap. The so-called White Report emphasized that barely 10 seconds elapsed between the time the vessels sighted each other and the collision. The report was written in a professional way and focused narrowly—as White had been tasked—on what caused PT 109's sinking. After the war, the incident was portrayed in a way to make JFK heroic.[31] The White Report was not declassified until 1959.

On May 14, 1945, White was on the bridge of the aircraft carrier Enterprise when a kamikaze struck the flight deck and sent a 500-pound bomb down the elevator well, exploding with an ear-splitting roar.[32] He escaped unscathed and overall casualties were light. The Navy released him in time to attend the January 1946 semester at Yale. That summer—despite all the disruptions—he once again finished first in his class. He got married too—to Marion Lloyd Stearns, the daughter of the president of the University of Colorado. Soon after that, he began a prestigious one-year clerkship under newly appointed Supreme Court Justice Fred Vinson.

In August 1947, at the age of 31, White joined the four-man firm of Newton, Davis & Henry. He helped build the practice with his name, by recruiting promising young lawyers from Yale and through transactional work that included prodigious research. He worked mostly for large clients such as the Denver National Bank and IBM but studiously avoided capitalizing on his fame in sports. He was successful in carving out a pleasant and productive life with Marion in the Mile High City. They had two children: a son, Charles Byron (Barney), and a daughter, Nancy Pirkin.

His somewhat quiet life changed after Robert F. Kennedy asked him to serve as Colorado Chairman for his brother's presidential campaign. Even though he was a newcomer to high-stakes politics, White organized an energetic and effective campaign: Kennedy won 13.5 of the state's 21 votes at the Los Angeles convention. Kennedy emerged there as the victor but lost Colorado and its four electoral votes that fall. Notwithstanding the loss, White gained much in stature with the new President and his brother. On December 16, JFK announced that his brother Robert would be the new Attorney General and that Byron White would be Deputy Attorney General.

Once again, he proved himself adept in vetting and recruiting top-notch staff and judges. But the new team had little time to settle in: On May 4, 1961, black and white "Freedom Riders" left Washington, DC, bound for New Orleans bent on testing segregated terminals and buses throughout the South. A Mother's Day riot occurred in Birmingham where a mob of 1,000 met and beat them on arrival. They were jailed in so-called "protective custody" by Bull Connor, the city's infamous police commissioner. The dangerous confrontation caught the Justice Department by surprise, but the department swiftly arranged for a highway patrol escort with Alabama Governor John Patterson to get the Freedom Riders to Montgomery. Meanwhile, White devised a plan to quickly deploy a contingency force of 550 marshals and other federal agents to get the Freedom Riders to New Orleans safely. Unfortunately, the safe conduct pass did not prevent a second, even bloodier clash when the bus arrived in Montgomery. By then, White had flown to Maxwell Air Force Base near Montgomery to take on-the-ground command of his ad hoc force.

Despite an injunction issued by a federal judge barring the Klan from committing further violence, a mob formed outside a church in Montgomery where the Rev. Martin Luther King was scheduled to preach. White's makeshift force of federal agents had to use tear gas and night sticks twice to turn back the mob. A call to mobilize troops at Fort Benning, Georgia, was about to be made when the state police finally stepped in and restored order at 10 p.m. Tense moments also occurred as the Freedom Riders passed through Mississippi, but violence was avoided. While the Justice Department's performance was criticized as lacking in coordination, a potential bloodbath was avoided, and the Freedom Riders did reach their destination in safety. White was calm, organized and decisive throughout the conflict. If anything, his stature rose even higher with the Kennedy brothers.

On April 3, 1962, President Kennedy appointed White, then only 44, to the Supreme Court, and he was unanimously confirmed by the Senate eight days later. "He has excelled at everything," the President said. "And I know that he will excel on the highest court in the land."[33]

White served as an associate justice for 31 years. Frequent attempts by the press and legal scholars to typecast him as either liberal or conservative were futile. He never subscribed to a judicial philosophy or any formulaic approach to the law; instead, he rigorously pursued fact-based findings. For him, facts were paramount; he had a painstaking eye for detail and was herculean about research. In general, he sided with New Deal-type expansion of government. He was dead set against rulings that smacked of or veered toward legislating from the bench. His frequent dissents were succinct, often caustic and could be somewhat dismissive of the majority. He joined the court under Chief Justice Earl Warren but, more than once, made clear that his was not a vote Warren could count on. He may have been closest in philosophy to Justice William Rehnquist, who joined the court in 1971 and became Chief Justice in 1986.

Rehnquist joined White in what was, perhaps, his most prescient dissent ever: *NCAA v. University of Oklahoma Board of Regents*, a landmark 1984 decision that held that the NCAA had violated the Sherman

Antitrust Act by limiting football teams at its 1,000 member schools to no more than six appearances on national television during a two-year period.

As *Washington Post* sports columnist Sally Jenkins would write years later, "The Hofstras got a cut of Oklahoma's TV checks. But, White asked, so what? It was a small price to pay, he suggested, for holding off rampant commercialization at the door"[34]—what White would call "an essential aspect of maintaining some balance of strength among competing colleges and of minimizing the tendency to professionalism in the dominant schools." To that, many today would add an emphatic "Amen!"

A major factor in the high court decision to clip the NCAA's wings may well have been its reputation for highhanded and coercive rule. Having been a high-profile college athlete himself, White was bound to have known this. Even so, he stressed that "unlimited appearances by a few schools would inevitably give them an insuperable advantage over all others and, in the end, defeat any efforts to maintain a system of athletic competition among amateurs who measure up to college scholastic requirements."

His last point is especially powerful because it anticipates the demise of the scholar-athlete, which he knew, from his own experience, to be one of America's highest values.

Liberals were deeply disappointed with his strongly worded dissents in two landmark cases: *Roe v. Wade* and *Miranda v. Arizona*. In the first—which granted women the right of abortion—White mainly chastised the majority for preventing states from protecting unborn life. In the second, the court imposed restraints on heavy-handed policing tactics. White held that the ruling would make law-abiding citizens less safe. Liberals were pleased when White joined the majority to invalidate laws that discriminated based on sex. White joined four other justices in *Furman v. Georgia* to strike down several state statutes on capital punishment. He consistently voted for civil rights in busing cases and affirmative action to boost minority admissions at universities. He was considered tough but fair throughout his tenure, but never stopped grilling attorneys in open court. His distrust for the press never changed. Requests for interviews often went unacknowledged. On occasions when he did encounter a member of the national media, any answers he gave were likely to be clipped and not particularly helpful. He always made exceptions for small news outlets in Colorado—especially *The Black and Gold*, his alma mater's student newspaper.

He retired on June 28, 1993, and returned to Colorado, where he died on April 15, 2002, at age 84. He was awarded the Medal of Freedom posthumously by President George W. Bush.

No one epitomized the ideals of the scholar-athlete more completely than Byron Raymond White. He was America's best-known and most popular collegiate athlete in 1937 and 1938—a distinction he would not have earned had it not been for his stellar academic accomplishments. Americans were proud that a dazzling halfback could also finish first in his class and be a Rhodes Scholar. Throughout his inspiring and eventful life, he remained humble, fair, courageous and diligent in applying his exceptional intellectual gifts. From the sugar beet fields he worked as a boy to the inner chambers of the highest court in the land, he brought integrity to every task he undertook. He thought nothing of busing tables after his highly paid years in the NFL; it was not beneath him: for him, it was the practical thing to do, and that was the kind of thinking that always grounded and guided him. He set standards few could meet or surpass, but many were benchmarks everyone could admire and aspire to.

When he retired from the court, Justice Lewis F. Powell called him "a national treasure, one of the greatest sons our nation has produced . . . seldom, if ever, will the court or this nation see his likes again. The national issues and mood have changed constantly, but he has been a constant, steadily crewing our Ship of State. Truly, he was, remains, and always will be, the best and the brightest."

To that the ever-modest White would never have replied—as he once did to a Washington waitress—"I was."

CHAPTER THREE

The Rise of Iconic Women

Long suppressed by the myth of female fragility and other barriers to their participation in sports, women finally smashed the gates and overran sanctuaries of male exclusivity in two epic battles in the early 1970s. The first ended on June 23, 1972, when the Civil Rights Act of 1964 was amended to include Title IX: *No person in the United States shall, on the basis of sex, be excluded from participation in, be denied the benefits of, or be subjected to discrimination under any education program or activity receiving Federal financial assistance.* Before Title IX, one in 27 girls played sports. Today that number is two in five.[1] In 2016, Donna de Varona, President of the Women's Sports Foundation, noted that the percentage of girls playing high school sports had increased by nearly 1,000 percent.[2]

The second clash, on September 20, 1973, was a true battle of the sexes—what the *London Sunday Times* called "the drop shot and volley heard 'round the world"—pitting Billy Jean King, who'd won her second straight singles crown at Wimbledon three months earlier, against a brash but aging Bobby Riggs, who'd won at Wimbledon in 1939. The heavily hyped, made-for-TV extravaganza in the Houston Astrodome attracted a worldwide television audience estimated at 90 million. In the run-up, Riggs, who had the look of a waif in outsized spectacles, played the role of cheeky male chauvinist to the hilt with inflaming comments like, "Women belong in the bedroom and the kitchen."

The match was not a contest between two scholar-athletes: after going to college for a year, Billie Jean decided to pursue tennis fulltime. But the contest opened the eyes of millions of young women and girls to their own athletic potential.

When the lights went bright, Riggs was carted into the Astrodome before a crowd of 30,000 on a rickshaw pulled by six models he called his "bosom buddies." Not to be outdone, King rode in on a sedan chair borne by four bare-chested, toga-clad Rice University track stars. She'd felt forced into playing after a so-called "Mother's Day Massacre" four months earlier when Riggs had routed Margaret Court, then the world's number one ranked woman, by a score of 6–2, 6–1. That lopsided victory had landed Riggs on the cover of *Time* and *Sports Illustrated* and made his taunts to defeat all female comers impossible for King to ignore—especially after a winner-take-all prize of $100,000 was posted.

King even agreed to the longer, more grueling men's format: best three of five sets instead of best two of three favored by the women's tour. Once the match began, it was evident that any problems with stamina would be on Riggs's side: He was slower getting to anything hit wide and deep and relied heavily on "junk" shots—soaring lobs in particular that he hoped King would lose in the lights of the cavernous Astrodome. His trickery fell flat against a superbly conditioned King who won in straight sets 6–4, 6–3, 6–3. When it was over, Billie Jean laughingly called Riggs "Roberta."

Years later, she would recall: "It's pretty scary to remember how people thought back then. Like women always choke. They belong at home. People really believed that. I did it to prove that women could walk and chew gum at the same time. To keep pushing that philosophy that women need equal opportunity."[3]

As a measure of how far they'd come, in 1896, the founder of the modern Olympics, Baron Pierre de Coubertin, had held, "It is indecent that the spectators should be exposed to the risk of seeing the body of a woman being smashed before their very eyes. Besides, no matter how toughened a sportswoman may be, her organizm [sic] is not cut out to sustain certain shocks." And yet, a woman barred from the marathon at the '96 games, Melpomene, ran the same course, finishing in four hours

Billie Jean King and Bobby Riggs in 1973

and 30 minutes.[4] Even so, women were not allowed to compete in the Olympics until 1920.

An impressive succession of trailblazers came after that. In the 1930s, Alice Marble, the first woman to serve and volley like a man, won three U.S. Open Championships and won at Wimbledon in 1939. Babe Didrikson Zaharias was as iconoclastic as Billie Jean. In 1945, she became the first woman to qualify for and play in a men's pro golf tour event, the Los Angeles Open. Before that, she won three Olympic medals in track and field and three Women's U.S. Open Golf Championships. In 1957, Althea Gibson, the Jackie Robinson of tennis, became the first African American to win at Wimbledon and at the U.S. Open. In 1960, at the Rome Olympics, Wilma Rudolph became the first American woman to win three gold medals. She'd had polio as a child and wore a foot brace until age eight, but overcame that to become the world's fastest female.

Like Billie Jean King, these women were not scholar-athletes, though King did attend Los Angeles State College (now California State University, Los Angeles) for two years before quitting to concentrate full-time on tennis. It took that to reach the pinnacle of athletic success. But the influence she and other icons had on girls and young women rippled throughout the land and inspired many brainy females to take sports seriously.

Pat Summitt was one of them. She began studying for her master's degree and coaching and teaching at the University of Tennessee in 1973, the same year Billie Jean beat Riggs. To her, that contest was,

> the grandest example of competitive ferocity and performance under pressure I'd ever seen from a woman. Under the most intense spotlight, in a chaotic setting with blaring trumpets and marching bands and fanfare, King didn't wilt. Instead she handled the carnival chaos coolly. . . .[5]

Summit, a star of the '72 Olympic basketball team, would become iconic as the most successful women's basketball coach of all time, accruing 1,098 wins and eight national championships before she retired. Over the course of her 38-season coaching career, she mentored 78 people, many of them scholar-athletes, who became basketball coaches or worked in administrative positions associated with the game. Hall of Fame coach Sylvia Hatchell at the University of North Carolina was one of them. A graduate assistant at Tennessee under Summitt, Hatchell has gone on to win over 1,000 games and one national title.[6]

When he finally broke Summitt's win record on March 17, 2018, Duke Coach Mike Krzyzewski said she'd have won "hundreds more" had her career not been cut short by an untimely death in 2010. "Pat could have coached men," he said. "She was as good a coach as there was in the country. She really was a pioneer and set up the glory that the women's game has right now."[7]

Slowly but surely women are closing the gap with men on a leveler playing field where they can develop their athletic talent to the fullest. The concentric circles of influence radiated outward by the early trailblazers have never stopped. Once a man's world, sport has become much more egalitarian; and playing field success has opened many more doors for women who now manage leagues, franchises, networks, brands and athletic conferences.

When she hit a last-second shot for Wake Forest to beat Duke in the

Amy Perko as a star at Wake Forest

Atlantic Coast Conference (ACC) tournament in 1985, Amy Perko never dreamed that one day she'd be the chief executive officer of the Knight Commission, the most influential U.S. organization on intercollegiate athletic reform. The NCAA has adopted several major reforms developed at the Knight Commission under Perko—which puts her in the vanguard of the leadership on collegiate athletic reform.

Perko was an academic and athletic star at Wake Forest; a Phi Beta Kappa and summa cum laude graduate, she also won the university's award for excellence in history. She was All-ACC in basketball twice and a three-time Academic All-American. She was named an ACC Legend in 2005 and was inducted into the Academic All-America Hall of Fame in 2008. After earning a master's degree in sports management from the University of Richmond, she became an investigator at the NCAA and an associate athletic director at the University of Kansas. She and her husband Rick have two daughters: Anna, a student at Wofford College, and Kate, who is still in high school. Amy says being a mother "is the most rewarding gift in my life."

During Perko's 20-year tenure in leading the Knight Commission, the organization's commitment to raising educational standards has been unwavering. In 2011, the NCAA adopted a recommendation Knight had long pushed for—that teams must graduate 50 percent of their players to compete in postseason championships. The new rule was quickly put to a stern test: The University of Connecticut won the 2011 Men's NCAA National Basketball Championship but failed the 50 percent graduation test that same year. That meant the defending champions were banned from the 2012 NCAA and Big East tournaments. By 2018, graduation rates for big-time football programs were markedly improved but remained significantly lower than the rate for all male students; rates for black players lagged even more so.

Since 2011, Perko says, "schools like Connecticut have changed their priorities. Overall, [the 50 percent rule] has established a benchmark that coaches know they must meet. . . . It goes back to making sure the entire system, the incentives in the system, the regulations are all driven by the mission of developing human potential—not the mission of 'we've got to generate as much revenue from TV as we can.' That's where college sports have gone off the rails."[8]

Another major Knight recommendation adopted by the NCAA will base the distribution of TV revenues from March Madness on academic performance. Between 2019 and 2032, more than $1.1 billion will be awarded to member schools based on the academic success and graduation rates of their teams.

Perko says Knight's highest priority now is to improve the health and safety of college football players. On May 2, 2017, its leadership challenged the governing board of the College Football Playoff (CFP) to allocate a substantial portion of its revenues to player health and safety. The CFP, which generated $1.6 billion in revenues in its first four years, rejected Knight's recommendation early in 2018, claiming that the NCAA and Football Bowl Subdivision conferences and institutions should pick up the tab. Perko says the Knight Commission will keep pushing the CFP to change its position and predicts that it will.

Knight Co-Chairman Arnie Duncan, a former U.S. Secretary of Education, points out that ". . . budgets aren't just numbers on a piece of paper—budgets always reflect our values. The distribution of revenue reflects what we choose to value in college sports. And we're always going to push to make sure we get those values right."

Next to the military, Duncan says, college sports do the best job of developing leaders. Perko, herself, is a good example of how athletic success can prepare one for a demanding leadership position. She emphasizes that success in sports and the workplace both require unwavering attention to detail and a relentless focus on teamwork to accomplish big goals.

For more and more women, athletic success is the stepping stone to a lucrative, high profile professional career. The *Harvard Business Review* reports that 52 percent of C-Suite women (those serving as a CEO, CFO, COO or as a board member) played a collegiate sport. Only 3 percent did not play a sport at any level.[9]

Success in sports certainly gave Laura Holden, 33, a big edge in her rapid rise as an investment banker on Wall Street. She had no shortage of grit as a high school senior at Maryvale Prep, an all-girls school in Brooklandville, Maryland, where she was valedictorian and scored three goals despite a torn ACL to beat Bryn Mawr 9–6 and win the conference lacrosse championship. She wore a brace and took Ibuprofen to minimize her pain. Holden went on to star in lacrosse at the College of William and Mary, where she co-captained a team that narrowly lost to Hofstra in the conference championship her senior year. Her performance in the Colonial Athletic Association title game earned her a place on the All-Conference team.[10]

In 2006, with a newly minted degree in business finance, she was hired by the investment banking arm of HSBC (Hong Kong and Shanghai Banking Corporation), a British multinational holding company, and was sent for training in London. After breaking in as an analyst in New York, she went back to London in 2010–11 for six months to work fulltime with the consumer mergers and acquisitions team. Once she settled permanently in New York, she spent the grueling hours of a young analyst on mergers and acquisitions, working many nights until 2 a.m. At the time, she told herself: "This isn't that bad, because I'm dry and warm and not getting hit (as she had been in lacrosse) . . . just the mental toughness that you need, a lot of that came from lacrosse." She says she is "a huge proponent" of hiring scholar-athletes because they are smart, disciplined and team oriented.

In 2012, Holden left HSBC to join the investment banking arm of Stephens, where she works with middle market companies—many of them family businesses—by helping them team with institutional investors who could provide growth capital as well as open doors to new growth strategies. Most recently, Holden helped a yoga company go public and advised Utz Quality Foods on an acquisition. Along the way, she rapidly progressed from Analyst to Associate to Vice President and Senior Vice President. She was about to be named a Managing Director at Stephens in 2018 when she joined Financo, a much smaller firm, where she will help develop a niche in the healthy living segment.

In 2017, 15 years after graduating from Maryvale Prep, Holden gave the commencement address there. In it, she encouraged her audience to keep good friends, read good books, take risks, don't be reckless with anybody's heart, don't tolerate anybody who'd be reckless with yours and to pray. Her last words of advice were a clarion call to women for professional advancement: "Be an advocate for yourself." It was not a strident or militaristic exhortation. She'd found the system benign enough; more than one male mentor had given her a boost up the corporate ladder. Her point dealt with psychic make-up: how most women tend to shy away from self-promotion, while most men don't.

"I'm not a limelight player," she notes. "In lacrosse, I preferred assists to goals." She says that can be a risky position to take; even when a woman's substantive contribution is superb, "Plenty of men are willing to take credit whenever they can." Holden is acutely aware that Wall Street is still male-dominated—"but many don't recognize the world is becoming more inclusive every day, that the client may be married to someone from another race, ethnic group or the same gender. Those who fail to recognize this are building bridges to nowhere."

As the quintessential modern woman, Holden understands her strengths, has the confidence to compete with anyone and is savvy enough to self-advocate when the need arises.

CHAPTER FOUR

The Mirror of Public Ideals

At the turn of the 20th century, the mirror of public ideals reflected the unblemished image of the heroic athlete—also said to be gentlemanly, which implied civilized and scholarly. That ideal was one of the miniscule few who went to college and were expected to climb the ladders of economic and social success. As noted in Chapter One, Harvard President Charles W. Eliot had offered, on October 19, 1869, one of the first visions of scholar-athletes when he called them an aristocracy that excelled in the manly sports and the learned professions, too. But that lofty promise belied deep postbellum anxieties over the closing of the frontier, rapid industrialization and a still-new survival of the fittest credo. As Michael Oriard writes in *Reading Football*, ". . . the American male was cut off from the physical demands of everyday outdoor life, through which his manhood had once been routinely confirmed."[1]

Eliot's reference to "manly sports" was pregnant with meaning. Five months earlier, on May 10, 1869, a golden spike had been driven at Promontory Summit in Utah Territory to mark the completion of the Transcontinental Railroad. Despite fierce attacks by Native Americans all through Nebraska, Wyoming and Colorado in the years before the line was laid from sea to shining sea, it seemed that the frontier had vanished. To many, a place of great expectations was gone, one where self-made men had gone to make their mark.

Fears that men would soon go "soft" worsened considerably after Charles Darwin's *Origin of Species* was published in 1859. His theory of evolution based on natural selection among plants and animals had been extended, without scientific basis, to individuals, groups and peoples in half-baked notions of Social Darwinism. In its worst form, it was used to defend imperialism and racism well into the 20th century. By the 1890s, the idea that males were being overcivilized had made its way into the cultural mainstream, where it joined a strong current of muscular Christianity.[2] As Daniel A. Clark writes in *Creating the College Man:* "Originating in England in the 1850s and then picked up with enthusiasm in the U.S. later in the century, the movement embraced physical activity, bodily strength, and competitive sports to nurture a new Christian manliness in the hope of energizing Protestant churches worried about the feminization of religion and the enervating effects of urban life. Eventually linked with broader anxieties over racial fitness and culminating with Theodore Roosevelt's cult of the strenuous life, muscular Christianity preserved much of the traditional Victorian 'character,' while introducing more modern elements exalting the masculine passions needed for the increasing fires of competition."[3]

Athletes played many games on American village greens in the antebellum era but were rarely in the public eye. By the end of the century, the pages of mass circulation magazines such as *Muncie's, Collier's, Cosmopolitan* and the *Saturday Evening Post*—the country's first true national media—were filled with college athletes portrayed as public heroes and cultured gentlemen—true exemplars of the masculine achiever.[4] In New York and other large cities, daily newspapers chimed in with massive coverage as well. The meteoric rise of Joseph Pulitzer's *New York World*, from a lowly circulation of 15,000 in 1883 to two million less than a decade later, was driven by an unwavering focus on entertainment often featuring saturation coverage of football.[5] The principal proving ground for America's new paragons of manliness soon became the gridiron, as football spread from elite eastern universities like Harvard, Yale and Princeton to high schools in nearly every hamlet.

While large newspapers ballyhooed baseball as America's pastime, and the masses never wavered in their love of the game, its popularity on college campuses began to wane in the 1880s. Lacking the ferocity of football, baseball never became a convincing test of manliness. By 1900, football was widely seen as "the college game" with a fandom spreading from social elites into the middle class, including many who had not been to college but were anxious to emulate the upper crust.[6]

Throughout, manliness remained the watchword for criers of change, and no one called for it more forcefully or with greater conviction than soon-to-be-President, Teddy Roosevelt. His clarion call for "the Strenuous Life" came in a famous speech on April 10, 1899, at the Hamilton Club in Chicago: "Let us therefore boldly face the life of strife, resolute to do our duty well and manfully . . . for it is only through strife, through hard work and endeavor, that we shall ultimately win the true goal of national greatness."

No American would become more closely identified with the manly ideal than Roosevelt. He had transformed himself through vigorous exercise and athletic pursuits from a sickly, asthmatic youth into a muscular, barrel-chested 200-pound man. Arresting photographs of TR—many of them staged—exuded manliness, including one in 1885 at age 27 in a buckskin outfit holding a rifle. Later, a profusion of heroic images depicted TR leading his Rough Riders—a regiment of college athletes, cowboys and outdoorsmen—in their famous charge up San Juan Hill. Two years after he returned from Cuba, those images helped elect him president.

TR is often said to have saved football at a moment when its "lawless underside" threatened to destroy the game, though that overstates his impact during the crisis considerably.[7] Serious injuries, and even deaths, had long plagued football, but in 1905, fears were aroused that control of a sport the public still cherished might soon be lost. As mentioned in Chapter One, TR had long seen the game as the manliest of sports and readily agreed to host a White House meeting on October 9 to discuss the situation. Two representatives each from Harvard, Yale and Princeton attended, including Walter Camp of Yale, who was widely considered the father of the American game. TR opened the meeting by citing specific examples of what was wrong, but the Yale and Princeton representatives pleaded ignorance to what he said. Later, TR asked the group to draft an agreement for reform on their train trip home, and the group complied.[8]

But their recommendations were too little too late; by the end of the season their notions were a dead letter. It was clear that it would take much more than a presidential nudge to the Big Three to reform football.

The 1905 season proved to be the bloodiest on record, resulting in 18 deaths and 159 serious injuries.[9] TR's own son, Ted, suffered a broken nose in the Harvard-Yale freshman game and required surgery. By the end of the year, an old guard—mainly Ivy League schools—under the influence of Camp was at war with smaller and less influential schools over reforms to establish a seven-man line of scrimmage, ten-yard yardage markers to earn a first down and the forward pass, which Camp adamantly opposed. One new development was the formation of an Inter Collegiate Athletic Association (ICAA) pledged to root out professionalism in the sport. Five years later the ICAA would become the NCAA, though it remained relatively toothless.[10]

Bitter battles would continue throughout that period with Harvard and Yale at each other's throats constantly. Harvard bitterly resented Yale's near-complete dominance under Camp's leadership. Between 1876 and 1909, incredibly, Yale lost only 14 times.[11] Never the school's coach, Camp operated more as a master strategist and athletic director, but Yale's success gave him more than enough cache to dominate football rulemaking for decades. And his innovative mind spawned all sorts of practical improvements, among them the snap-back from center, the system of downs and the points system. Surprisingly, at a time when women were expected to be demure and retiring, Camp's wife Alice became an innovative strategist in her own right. Yale All-American Alonzo Stagg, who became an iconic coach at the University of Chicago, called her "More coach than he (Camp) was."[12]

Harvard, in turn, sneered at Yale's football success. At the height of the 1905 crisis, an anonymous author in *Harvard Graduates' Magazine* wrote that Yale had contributed nothing to the science of educational method, only to the science of football.[13]

Another rash of injuries in 1909 made the need for thorough-going reform mandatory. In April and May of 1910, the logjam was broken and warring factions finally agreed to a comprehensive set of reforms, which eliminated mass plays like the flying wedge, a "V" formation in which players locked arms and crashed into a weak point on the opposing line. Two other major reforms provided for a seven-man line of scrimmage and made the forward pass a dynamic and much more exciting part of the game.[14] TR had brought reform to the fore with his 1905 White House meeting, but the principals of the sport—college presidents, coaches, administrators and influential alumni—had provided expert solutions that saved the game and made it much more exciting and popular than ever.

In the Roosevelt Era, the manly ideal of the scholar-athlete got a glossy update in the form of "gee-whiz" heroes of pulp fiction and dime novels written for boys. Best known of the genre was Frank Merriwell: "Frank for frankness, merry for a happy disposition, and well for health and abounding vitality" is how Gilbert Patten, creator and author of the series, explained his protagonist's name. Beginning in 1896 and continuing for 17 years, the Merriwell series ran in *Tip Top Weekly*. It continued after that until 1930 in the form of dime novels, though toward the end of that run other authors using the same pseudonym, Bert L. Standish, wrote them.[15]

For most of those years, Patten's series outsold any other for boys. His fictional Merriwell went to Yale and excelled at every sport he tried, especially football. But the narratives were about more than sports; they drew back the curtain on the traditions and rituals of an exclusive school—the rough-housing, social life, dances and, especially, the secret societies. Asked if he loved his Merriwell character, the author replied: "Yes, I loved him. And I loved him most because no boy, if he followed in his tracks, ever did anything that he need be ashamed of."[16]

More serious fare than the Merriwell series could be found in *Stover at Yale*, published in 1912 by Owen Johnson. It recounts what Yale undergraduate life was like in 1900. The protagonist, John Humperdink Stover, a football captain in prep school, pursues a varsity letter on the gridiron and hopes to join one of the secret societies, like Skull and Bones. Later, an existential crisis forces him to reassess his values and to see, as the author later explained, ". . . the rapidly growing tendency of our colleges to become not great institutions of learning, but mere social clearing houses."[17] F. Scott Fitzgerald would later describe the book as "the textbook" of his generation.

The last of the highly influential gee-whiz genres appeared in the late 1940s. Chip Hilton was a modern Frank Merriwell, written by Clair Bee, who would be named to the National Collegiate Basketball Hall of Fame in 1968. (See Chapter Five for an account of Bee's role in the postwar point shaving scandals.) In all, Bee wrote 24 installments of the Chip Hilton series, the first of which appeared in 1948; the series remained popular until the mid-1960s, selling more than 2.2 million copies.[18] An article in the 1996 Raleigh *News and Observer* described Chip as a "clean-cut, All-American scholar-athlete" who excelled in basketball, football and baseball—"a perfect son, great friend and A-plus student."

As popular as Bee's Chip Hilton character was, a Frank Merriwell patina flickered over college football for the first half of the 20th century. It was the image of a clean-cut, modest scholar-athlete whose benchmark qualities the public remembered and expected real-life stars to live up to.

Not all icons of manliness were derivatives of Harvard President Charles W. Eliot's 1869 inaugural address. From the turn of the century to the mid-1920s, a new type of male identity emerged in American popular culture as a vast audience became enamored with heroes like Tarzan and Eugen Sandow, the father of modern bodybuilding. To many, they embodied the perfect man without the braininess. These cultural fantasies of manliness held sway with millions but were always, unapologetically, white.

The 1920s were the Golden Age of sports—a time when increases in income and leisure time caused college football to explode in popularity. Practices that flagrantly professionalized the sport—the use of non-students known as "ringers and tramps," under-the-table payments and academic abuses such as sham courses and rigged grades—had long plagued the game and brought near-constant demands for reform. But a new type of crisis occurred in 1925 when the game's most famous player, Red Grange, turned pro after his last game at the University of Illinois and before he graduated. At the time, as Michael Oriard observes in *King Football,* his fine history of the game's Golden Age, "professional football was about as respectable as professional wrestling and considerably less popular." The Galloping Ghost (Grange's nickname) was guided by pro football's first sports agent, Charlie "Cash and Carry" Pyle—a name that hardly engendered trust.[19]

Grange drew astonishing crowds on a nationwide barnstorming tour—65,000 alone at New York's Polo Grounds—far more than ever for the pro game. It forced sportswriters and fans to face up to a troubling question: Had Grange betrayed his alma mater and his obligations as a scholar-athlete? The press was especially enraged by how much Grange was making and often wildly inflated his take with headlines like: "Red

Grange gets $82,000 in Eleven Days." Even more troubling from a long-term perspective was the public's growing concern that college football was becoming a semiprofessional sport. But, as Oriard writes, "In 1925, the critics were not yet ready to concede the intercollegiate sport's commercial nature as a permanent condition."[20]

The year after the Grange controversy broke, the NCAA commissioned the Carnegie Foundation to investigate professionalism in college athletics. Its representatives made site visits to 112 institutions and found that only 28 were not violating the NCAA's code and principles of amateurism. Unethical practices included slush fund payments to athletes.[21] The report concluded that "A change in values is needed in a field that is sodden with the commercial and the material. . . ."[22] But when the report was released in 1929, it caused barely a ripple of public concern. The irascible columnist, Westbrook Pegler, called it a waste of time.[23]

The *New York Times* published a follow-up study in 1931 that found that none of the schools investigated by Carnegie had put an end to their abuses. Later, the NCAA would conclude that abuses "have grown to such a universal extent that they constitute the major problem in American athletics today."[24]

Burdened as they were by a Great Depression, most Americans wanted to believe in the innocent, simple days of yore. They reveled in stories of the "little guys" beating the "big guys," none more widely acclaimed than a 1921 upset of mighty Harvard by tiny Centre College, a school in Danville, Kentucky, with a mere 300 students. When the two teams played the year before, Harvard was coming off an undefeated national championship season. But Centre had taken a shocking 14–7 halftime lead before losing 31–14. Both games were played in Harvard Stadium. When the rematch took place on October 29, 1921, the Crimson were undefeated and unscored on. The first half had ended in a scoreless tie, but after the break, Centre's star quarterback, Bo McMillan, made a 32-yard sideline dash with two Crimson defenders in hot pursuit to score the game's only touchdown. The Praying Colonels won 6–0.[25]

Afterward, Harvard's coach, Bob Fisher, said of McMillan: "Centre has a man who is probably the hardest in the country to stop." The next day's headline in the *New York Times* declared, "David Skunks Goliath at Harvard." The article called the game "arguably the upset of the century in college football." The win was no fluke: Centre finished the 1921 season

10–1, also defeating such powerhouses as Virginia Polytechnic Institute, Auburn, Arizona and Clemson.

In 1935, the Downtown Athletic Club in New York gave its first DAC award (changed to the Heisman Trophy in 1936) to the nation's most outstanding college football player. It went to Jay Berwanger, a halfback at the University of Chicago, who epitomized the understated, do-it-all type of hero so admired in that era. He was a versatile All-American who played nearly every position on offense and defense. In a 1934 game against Michigan, he gave fellow all-star and future President Gerald R. Ford a memorable keepsake: a gash beneath the left eye. In 1936, Berwanger became the first player picked in the inaugural National Football League draft but turned down the chance to play professionally to go into business; he later became a successful manufacturer of plastic car parts. Berwanger was so modest about his Heisman Trophy that he left the heavy cast bronze statue with his Aunt Gussie, who used it for years as a doorstop.[26]

In the 1930s, "talkies" came into their own, and the dime novel lost much of its popularity to the 25-cent flick, as movies rapidly became America's favorite pastime. Most American families often went to the movies once a week, which meant they could share favorite heroes and storylines with relatives who lived in faraway places. Popular sports talkies in the early thirties included: *The Champ*, a boxing film that won the Academy Award in 1931; *The Crowd Roars*, an auto racing film with Jimmy Cagney in 1932; and *Horse Feathers* starring the Marx brothers in 1932. It featured many jokes about the amateur status of college football players. At the close, the four protagonists carry the ball into the end zone on a horse-drawn garbage wagon. In 2008, ESPN rated this scene first among the top 11 scenes in football movie history.[27]

As the sociologist Margaret Thorpe pointed out in *America at the Movies* in 1939: "The movies are furnishing the nation with a common body of knowledge. What the classics once were in that respect, what the Bible once was, the cinema has become for the average man. Here are stories, names, phrases, points of view which are common national property. The man in Cedar Creek, Maine, and the man in Cedar Creek, Oregon, see the same movie in the same week."

When Thorpe wrote these words, Warner Brothers in Hollywood was hard at work on a film that would do much to permanently enshrine the scholar-athlete as an ideal in American popular culture. *Knute Rockne:*

All-American would tell the story of a man the College Football Hall of Fame could call, "without question, America's most renowned coach." In 1913, Rockne helped transform the game in a shocking 35–13 rout of highly regarded Army. The Irish used a deep downfield passing attack from quarterback Gus Dorais to Rockne, who became an All-American. The forward pass wasn't invented in that game, but it was the first time it was used so often in a major contest. In 13 seasons as head coach at Notre Dame (1918–1931), Rockne won three national championships and had five undefeated seasons.[28]

But late on the morning of March 31, 1931, a plane owned by Transcontinental and Western Air en route from Kansas City to Los Angeles crashed in a western Kansas wheat field, killing all eight aboard, including Rockne. The crash plunged the nation into grief and mourning, President Hoover termed it "a national loss," and Rockne's funeral was broadcast worldwide. His passing was treated much like the death of a president.

In the years that followed, Rockne's agent Christy Walsh pushed the idea of a biopic on his client's life. At least one script was sent to Warner Brothers, but it lacked the approval of Bonnie Rockne, the coach's widow, who, under then existing copyright law, had the rights to her husband's story.[29] Warner Brothers gave its green light to a Rockne biopic late in 1938, but would soon encounter headwinds from Bonnie and her lawyer. As Murray Sperber writes in *Onward to Victory*, during the 1939–40 production of the movie, she demanded that Warner Brothers "construct a fictitious portrait of her husband's academic career" by portraying him as "a brilliant scholar-athlete. . . ."

In doing so, Sperber writes, "Warner made a much more important film than it originally intended. Instead of a standard potboiler about an athlete-hero, the studio produced the first serious cinematic portrait of a scholar-athlete. In doing so, the filmmakers helped imprint this model on the American public and shaped the future of intercollegiate athletics."[30]

As a measure of how adamant Bonnie was about enhancing the academic side of her husband's accomplishments, in 1939 her attorney, Vitus Jones, sternly admonished Warner Brothers: "Now, Mrs. Rockne and myself will never be satisfied with this picture unless you develop the intellectual side of Rockne. If Rockne had not devoted his life to coaching, wherein he became famous, but had devoted it to chemistry, he would be an equally noted scientist."[31]

Rockne was a good student and graduated from Notre Dame with a degree in pharmacy—not chemistry. This might seem like a quibble, but not to Bonnie. In the shooting script, when a famous chemist pushes Rockne to become his full-time assistant, Notre Dame's President tells him he's been told ". . . you've got the best brain for chemistry of any man in the class." Later, the President, who is also a priest, praises Rockne's decision to coach football saying, "You're helping mankind and anyone who helps mankind helps God."

In terms of "stretches," the Rockne film went even further with its portrayal of the legendary Notre Dame quarterback George Gipp who died in 1920 two weeks after being named the school's first All-American. In the film, Gipp begins coughing during a visit to the Rockne home and ends up in the hospital with a severe case of pneumonia. He deteriorates fast, and after a priest administers last rites, Gipp utters lines to Rockne that will earn enduring fame: "I've got to go, Rock, but it's all right, I'm not afraid. Rock, some day when the team's up against it, the breaks are beating the boys. Ask them to go in there with all they've got and win just one for the Gipper. I don't know where I'll be then Rock—but I'll know about it—and I'll be happy."

In a screen test in one small California town before the film was released, the producer said when Gipp died, "I don't believe there was a dry eye in the theatre." No wonder Ronald Reagan campaigned so hard for the role and reprised it to great advantage in his political career.

But reality may have been sharply at odds with what the film portrayed. Gipp, indeed, did die of pneumonia, but South Bend locals held that he had passed out drunk in a doorway on a freezing cold night and died from exposure. Beyond that, Gipp was known to be a pool hustler and a heavy gambler, who, quite likely bet on his own games. As a measure of how myths often take on a life of their own, Reagan bragged in a 1940 speech to Notre Dame alumni in Los Angeles that he had spoken to Gipp when he was a radio announcer. It was quite a stretch because Reagan was only five years old when Gipp passed away, according to Sperber.

Were echoes of Frank Merriwell an undertone within the Knute Rockne biopic? Almost certainly they were. As Michael Oriard points out, a cliffhanger movie serial in 1936 and a radio series in the 1940s and 1950s made the Merriwell name "a touchstone" until mid-century: No matter what the ethnicity of star scholar-athletes, no matter what their abilities were, they still had to live up to Merriwellian values.[32]

Until mid-century, college All-Americans sat on a pedestal all their own—an aristocracy in which a place was not bequeathed but earned. Prior to 1950, their perch was secure, almost impregnable. From time to time, recruiting scandals caused a stir among reformers but not much more. But the year 1951 would not be so benign or forgiving, as we shall see in the next chapter.

CHAPTER FIVE

Shattered Ideals

The sports tip-off of the century—a warning that the high temple of big-time college basketball was being defiled—came in 1951 from the first black scholarship athlete at Manhattan College, a Jesuit school on the crest of a hill in the Bronx. The informant was Junius "Junie" Kellogg, a 23-year-old veteran of World War II attending college on the G.I. Bill and earning extra income working for minimum wage at a frozen custard shop near campus. His parents in Portsmouth, Virginia, were poor, but had faithfully churched their 11 kids.[1]

Junie was approached in his dorm room by Hank Poppe and John Byrnes, co-captains of the Manhattan team a year earlier, who were acting on behalf of professional gamblers. They offered him $1,000 to shave points in an upcoming game against DePaul University in Madison Square Garden.[2] They saw the 6-foot-8-inch center and team-leading scorer as a prime target to fix the outcome. Shocked that Poppe, Manhattan's second all-time leading scorer, could be part of such a blatant offer, Junie told him, "Get the hell out of my room." As the would-be fixers left, they urged Junie to "Just think it over" and offered to meet him again on Sunday at 9 p.m.[3]

Nervous and scared that he could lose his scholarship, Junie went straight to his coach, Ken Norton, and spilled the beans. Norton then informed Brother Bonaventure Thomas, the college president, and a decision was made to alert the district attorney's office to the fix offer. Junie spent the entire weekend answering detectives' questions and getting prepped to play along with the fixers on Sunday night.[4] He agreed to wear a concealed listening device.[5]

Poppe was alone when he picked Junie up and took him to a bar at Broadway and 242 St. for a beer. Junie quickly told him that he'd reconsidered and wanted to accept the offer. "Good. You won't be sorry," Poppe replied and then described the types of moves Junie should make to insure the right outcome at the sold-out Garden on Tuesday night. Poppe told Junie he'd see him at courtside just before tip-off "to let you know the final arrangements." His parting words were, "All you have to do is control the margin of victory. It's easy, Junie. Everybody's doing it. Everywhere. All over the country."[6]

It was well past midnight when Junie finished debriefing detectives from the DA's office on his meeting with Poppe.[7]

Junie was warming up with his teammates just before the game when Poppe signaled to him from courtside. "Manhattan is favored by 10 points," he told Junie. "So, make sure you win by less." He said he'd pay off after the game nearby at Gilhooley's Bar.

During the game, Junie was a nervous wreck, fumbling easy passes and missing rebounds time and time again. When the fans began calling him a fixer and yelling racial taunts, Coach Norton took him out; he could see that the pressure on Junie was becoming unbearable. He ended up scoring only four points, but his substitute made all eight of his attempts from the field, so Manhattan won by three points—well within the margin Poppe and the gamblers wanted.[8]

Poppe was a no-show at Gilhooley's, but the police arrested him at home in Queens at 3 a.m. Making no attempt to refute what Junie had told them, he admitted that he'd been in the gamblers' pockets since the 1949–50 season. The three gamblers who controlled Poppe were also arrested.[9]

In his "Sports of the Times" column, Arthur Daly of the *New York Times* praised Kellogg for having "the inherent decency, the high moral fiber, and the deep religious scruples to report the bribe offer."[10] Daley added that, "The personal preference here would be boiling in oil for all fixers."[11]

News of the January 17 arrests following the Manhattan-DePaul game was featured prominently in newspapers all over the country.[12] Junie became such a hero that a rally was held in his honor on the Manhattan campus. Students, professors, clergy and even maintenance workers gave him a loud ovation when he said, "I never gave that bribe offer a thought."[13]

While the sporting public saw the Manhattan-DePaul fix as an isolated incident, to New York's "Mr. District Attorney," Frank Hogan, it was the tip of an iceberg. Within days, he had set up a large sting operation that would lead to the arrest of 32 players from six colleges in addition to Manhattan: City College of New York (CCNY), Long Island University (LIU), New York University (NYU), Bradley University, University of Toledo and the University of Kentucky. The players admitted to taking bribes between 1947 and 1950 to fix 86 games in 17 states. The wider scandal broke on February 18, 1951, when Hogan made his highest profile arrests: three stars of a CCNY team that had won the National Invitational Tournament (NIT) and the NCAA Tournament in 1950, the only team ever to win both postseason events in the same year. The CCNY players were arrested at Penn Station after returning from a game against Temple in Philadelphia.[14]

Its fall from grace caused the school itself to land with a huge thud. The year before, at a campus celebration of its twin championships, CCNY's president, Harry N. Wright, had exulted: "This is one of the proudest days of my life. This team came here to study, not to play basketball. I am proud of the team and what it has done for the college. I want to emphasize that the players have been given no scholarships to play ball. They are not imported mercenaries."[15]

His disclaimer was entirely overwrought: CCNY was tuition-free and hard to get into because of its rigorous academic standards. It was widely praised for providing a first-rate education to a student body of working class commuters. In any event, no one had questioned the scholarship of the accused basketball players. En route to their championships, *Collier's* had touted them as scholar-athletes and "the few school-boy phenoms" who could get into CCNY.[16] Later, it would come to light that the transcripts of 14 players had been changed by the school's basketball office.[17] By then, New York media was calling the scandal at CCNY "City Dump."

CCNY and other offending schools had often played in double and even triple-headers at Madison Square Garden. The NCAA and the NIT postseason championship were both played at the Garden. Its image as the shrine of college basketball was apt: a swarm of "money-changers" or gamblers overran the place at big games. Once the fixes came to light, many schools brought big games back to campus to avoid the unseemly atmosphere of the Garden.

When news of Hogan's sting broke, the media rushed to query the architect of college basketball's greatest dynasty: where Kentucky's coach Adolph Rupp, fended them off with the absurd claim that gamblers ". . . couldn't touch my boys with a ten-foot pole." His Wildcats had won NCAA titles in 1948 and 1949 and were on the verge of a third such title a few weeks after CCNY stars were arrested. It was just a matter of time before Hogan's sting would nab three of Rupp's former stars—Ralph Beard, Alex Groza and Dale Barnstable. They were arrested on October 20 for accepting bribes to fix a game in the NIT at Madison Square Garden in 1949.[18]

Rupp's outlandish claim that his players were beyond reproach belied the fact that he had close ties to Ed Curb, a Lexington bookie with mafia connections, who ran one of the biggest gambling operations in the country. Curb often dined with Rupp and picked up the tab because Rupp was notoriously cheap. Rupp visited Curb's home, and they were involved in business and charities together. Curb often attended UK basketball practices and even traveled with the team.[19]

As much as anyone, Curb popularized the so-called "point spread" in gambling, a system that increased betting volumes exponentially. With the spread, bettors took the favorite and "gave" points, or took the underdog and "got" points. A spread set at 7–5 meant the favorite had to win by 7 or more for a payoff; the underdog had to lose by 5 or more to win the wager. A winning margin of six was a push, and the bookie won. Eventually, the system gravitated to a single point with a half-point tacked on to eliminate ties, or the so-called "push." Bookies adjusted the spread to balance betting volume on both sides of the offer. In effect, they "made" the market and in return collected 10 percent of what got bet—the so-called vigorish, or "vig." When amounts wagered on each side of the spread were balanced, the final score didn't matter to bookies; they got their vig, no matter what. The spread system's dramatic rise in the 1940s made it much easier to rig the outcome of games. Compromised players no longer had to "dump," or lose the game. Instead, they merely "shaved" points to beat the spread—a much more palatable outcome, which meant high poll rankings and winning streaks could be preserved.

Curb ran his public operations from the Clover Club above the Mayfair Bar in downtown Lexington. Western Union tickers provided up-to-date race results and game scores. It was estimated that Curb took in $50,000 per day there, a large sum at that time.[20] He often crowed about how many accounts he had with jockeys and notables. Curb's private operations were run from his opulent home next to the Lexington Country Club. It featured a secret room beneath the library accessed through a sliding panel with a secret button. The panel opened to a winding staircase leading down to a room with a phone bank and a bar.[21]

His connections to the New York City mob and Las Vegas casinos made Curb's point spread the official "line." He also served as the "layoff man" for smaller bookies with wagers too large for their own "book."[22]

Curb liked nothing better than rubbing elbows with the rich and famous. He and actor George Raft were seen at the races at Santa Anita, California, and he palled around Las Vegas with the gangsters Bugsy Siegel and Meyer Lansky. During testimony at a Senate crime investigation, New York mafia boss Frankie Costello stated that he bet on horse racing and basketball "with my little buddy Ed Curb from Lexington, Kentucky."[23]

Despite his close and open ties to Curb, and even though his was the most corrupt team caught shaving points, Rupp adamantly maintained that he knew nothing about what his players were doing. His most loyal supporters even insisted that he was a victim of greedy players who had let down their famous coach. But Rupp was far from alone in claiming ignorance of player misdeeds: None of the coaches whose teams rigged outcomes between 1947 and 1951 ever admitted to knowing that games had been fixed. To a man, they held that "a few rotten apples" were responsible and had no qualms about turning ruthlessly on players who had made them successful. Not a single coach or athletic administrator at schools where these misdeeds occurred got fired or disciplined. Nor did the media and public demand it. In contrast, many of the players went to prison, got probation or were banned from the game for life.[24] Coaches and college administrators alike said, "I can't believe our boys would do such a thing."

"But why not?" Yale basketball coach Howard Hobson asked rhetorically in a December 1951 article in *Collier's*. His answer was: "You paid them for campus jobs they didn't work at; you gave them passing grades for classes they didn't attend. You bribed them to play for you; the gamblers bribed them not to play too well. What's the difference?"[25]

Put another way, did standards still matter at all? For years, Rupp had offered his players a crip course called "Advanced Basketball." Cynically, he called himself the best professor at UK because all his students got A's.[26]

In *Onward to Victory*, Murray Sperber provides a telling explanation for why only the players suffered consequences for the point shaving fiasco:

> When the scandal exploded, this identification of Holman (CCNY's legendary coach) with the deepest American myths made it much easier for him and colleagues in similarly tight spots to defend their innocence. Could any fan possibly believe that the heirs of St. Knute [Rockne] would look the other way while their players rigged games? And just as the media had promulgated the myths about coaches, it now proclaimed their innocence. What's more, to expose their guilt would not have helped the promotion of college sports or the careers of individual sportswriters and broadcasters.[27]

But no matter how far the press and public had veered from true north on the moral compass, a sledgehammer blow was about to fall that no thinking American could ignore.

The country was still reeling from New York DA Hogan's first point shaving arrests when a massive cheating scandal began to unfold at the U.S. Military Academy at West Point. It would shake to the very foundations of a naïve public's faith in all that it held to be true and sacred. What made the scandal such a bitter pill to swallow was the Point's football team—the near-mythical Black Knights of the Hudson—had become "the Nation's team."[28] Generals trained there, like Eisenhower, MacArthur and Patton, had led the United States to victory in World War II, and no one had done more than they and the Black Knights of the gridiron to make America proud. And yet, 90 members of the cadet corps—37 of them on the football squad—had been dismissed. On August 4, 1951, the front page of the *New York Times* blared, "Corps Is Bitter at Guilty Men and Blow to Academy Honor."[29] Each of the accused had violated the academy's simple, profound and sacrosanct honor code: *A cadet will not lie, cheat, steal, or tolerate those who do.*

It made the scandal much worse that the cadets were not cheating on the field; they were cheating in the classroom, which gave the lie to their status as scholar-athletes, a classical ideal Americans had believed in for more than half a century. Incredibly, from 1944 through 1950, Army had lost only three football games under its legendary Coach Earl "Red" Blaik. Hardly anyone questioned how such a phenomenal record was possible at a school with a stiff entrance exam and a curriculum toughened up considerably during World War II. The public knew little or nothing of the changes wrought by Blaik in building his dynasty—a "cram" school for outstanding but academically deficient players; a tutoring system with thirty cadet tutors (Blaik called them "coaches"); an extensive alumni network that identified and helped recruit talented players; recruiting trips to the far reaches of the country by Blaik and his assistants; and expense-paid trips to the Point for top prospects.[30] Army football also benefited significantly from the draft-free status its players had during the war years.

Swift reactions to the dismissals were exacerbated by one harsh reality: once again, America was at war, this time in Korea. The conflict began not long after commencement at West Point, and many new graduates had been rushed into action. Just before the Navy game that fall, John Trent, Army's '49 team captain, was killed in the conflict. By mid-year in '51, more and more shavetails were coming home in coffins. Many had been killed during General MacArthur's disastrous retreat from the Yalu River after the Chinese communists entered the war.

Throughout the scandal's avalanche of negative news — at times it even rivaled in public disdain the television quiz shows of the time — the prideful Blaik took the same position as his counterparts in basketball: He was adamant that he had no idea his players were cheating. His denials were hard to believe because it was widely known at the Point that the 30 tutors he put in place were feeding "the poop" (answers to exam questions) to football players and other athletes. One mistake on the poop sheet for a chemistry test made clear just how extensive and sloppy the cheating got. The correct answer to one question was "concentration"; instead, the poop sheet gave it as "condensation." When many test-takers used the poop sheet answer, the fishy results were submitted to the superintendent as evidence of wrongdoing.[31] When one somewhat dim-witted football star suddenly began making perfect scores, his instructor brought the matter to Blaik's attention but got booted out of his office.[32]

One week after the scandal came to light, and with public reaction still white hot, Blaik invited about 40 reporters and columnists to dine at Mama Leone's, a famous Italian restaurant in New York. When Blaik informed his guests that he had no intention of resigning, they dropped all pretense of neutrality and gave him a rousing cheer. The outburst hardly reflected affection for Blaik, who for years had treated the press with cold disdain; instead, it expressed collective relief that their jobs in covering big-time football at Army would not be in jeopardy.[33]

The sports scandals of 1951 caused a profound loss of public and media trust. Never again would Americans believe unquestioningly in the classic ideal of the scholar-athlete or the purity of their games. Venerated ideals had been permanently shattered.

¤ ¤ ¤

The sense of loss at mid-century was compounded by the tragedy of Paul Robeson, who ranks with Byron "Whizzer" White in the pantheon of the greatest scholar-athletes ever. In 1915, Robeson became the third African American to gain admittance to Rutgers College after winning a statewide scholarship competition. In his career at Rutgers, he earned 15 varsity letters, became a two-time All-American in football and was valedictorian of his class.[34] He went on to earn a law degree from Columbia University while playing professional football. His brilliance had sparkled at every level of schooling—from winning oratorical prizes to stunning performances in all sorts of musical productions. Adding to his luster, there was no "grandstanding" and not the slightest hint of superiority for his abilities or achievements.

His remarkable father, William Drew Robeson, had been born a slave on a plantation near Williamston, North Carolina, but escaped in 1860 and then worked as a laborer for the Union Army. After getting a basic education, he earned two degrees from Lincoln University: a B.A. degree in 1873 and one in theology in 1876. He later became a much-admired minister in Princeton, New Jersey, where Paul grew up. Paul's mother, Louisa Bustill, was a woman of keen intellect but died, tragically, in 1904 when her long skirt caught fire in a kitchen blaze. That left her son, not yet six, to be raised by a 53-year-old father. Despite the age difference, Paul would be profoundly influenced by his father, who died at 73 during Paul's junior year at Rutgers. By then, the reverend had imbued his young son with the inner steel to be a trailblazer for his race, and to maintain calm and composure when subjected to the harshest of insults and even bodily harm—though he did, on occasion, respond in kind to violence on the football field. Above all, his father instilled an abhorrence of quitting as the ultimate shame, though "severe provocation" in adulthood would test the limits of his resolve. His aversion to quitting seemed to stoke a stubborn streak that did him great harm once he achieved fame.[35]

Few if any Americans, irrespective of race, ever soared to greater heights or fell to more abject lows. In many ways, his story became a cautionary tale for black Americans: If even the most talented among them could be completely broken, what chance did an ordinary soul—let alone the downtrodden—truly have?

Paul Leroy Robeson would never bask in greater glory than on the evening of April 16, 1944, at a mammoth five-hour 46th birthday gala at a packed Armory in midtown Manhattan; 12,000 attended and another 4,000 were turned away. The star-studded cast of performers included Count Basie, Jimmy Durante and Duke Ellington. Vice President Henry Wallace, Oscar Hammerstein II and Babe Ruth were among many who sent letters and telegrams.[36] Unnoticed among the revelers were U.S. Army Intelligence agents scanning the crowd for familiar "leftist" faces, intent on reporting what they saw to the FBI. Though he did not speak, Earl Browder, General Secretary of the U.S. Communist Party, was spotted in the front row.[37]

At the time, Robeson's face was so familiar he could be recognized on the streets of most American cities and overseas from London to Moscow and Cape Town to Beijing. His tall, athletic physique and his deep, rich voice—technically a bass-baritone[38]—made an indelible impression on most who saw him. He had drawn rave reviews for his performance in *Othello*, which was about to close its historic run on Broadway by shattering all-time box office records for a Shakespearian production. It was the first-time sexual attraction between a black man and a white woman had been shown on Broadway. That fall, the show would tour 45 U.S. cities in 17 states.[39] *Othello* was one of three stage plays, popular films and a broad repertoire of concert music, ranging from spirituals and Americana to classical and European folk, that made Robeson an international star. His performance in Eugene O'Neil's *The Emperor Jones* in 1925 had drawn rave reviews from critics, but three years later his starring role as Joe in

Paul Robeson, an all-time great scholar-athlete and entertainer

the London premier of *Show Boat* had been a sensation. The show got mixed reviews, but Robeson drew universal praise, and the British public fell in love with him. *Show Boat* was a big moneymaker, too, a financial windfall for its star, who drew the handsome sum of $600 per week for his performances and large sums in addition for giving private concerts for wealthy socialites.[40]

He and Essie, his wife and manager, a talented woman in her own right, settled into a comfortable life in London, which afforded easy access to the leading cities of Europe, where there were large audiences for his concerts. Despite the occasional restaurant that refused them a seat, they felt much less prejudice in England than America. As his fame and income rose, he and Essie lived more and more lavishly, accumulating debts that, at times, were burdensome.[41]

In 1934, the Robesons spent two weeks in the Soviet Union where Paul got a hero's welcome from ordinary Russians, the artistic community and Foreign Minister Maxim Litvinov and his English wife, Ivy, who hosted a large party in their honor on Christmas Eve. Paul astonished guests with near-fluent Russian.[42] His uncanny aptitude for quickly learning languages enabled him to sing in many tongues. But the couple got no inkling of the Soviet Union's "other side"—the police state arrests and detentions, its massive gulag network or the millions of deaths from famine caused by Stalin's forced collectivization of farms and large estates.

What they saw instead was a thin veneer of Soviet life—that of a tiny intelligentsia that served the state by producing works of art in the genre of socialist realism. As the tour was ending, Paul said he felt "like a human being for the first time since I grew up. Here I am not a negro but a human being. Before I came I could hardly believe that such a thing could be.... Here, for the first time in my life, I walk in full human dignity."[43] For the next two decades, he would maintain an unflinching, often uncritical conviction that the Soviet Union and its system offered the best hope for righting centuries of wrong.

While on tour in April 1947, Robeson caused a stir by saying, "It seems I must raise my voice, but not by singing pretty songs." The comment was noticed by FBI Director J. Edgar Hoover, who, by then, was trying to build a case against him. That same month, he and a thousand others were cited by the House Un-American Activities Committee as "invariably found supporting the Communist Party and its front organizations." Suddenly, virulent opposition arose to Robinson's concerts: one in Peoria, Illinois, was cancelled under heavy pressure from "patriot" groups.[44] More cancellations followed; even in Toronto a permit for Robeson to perform was issued with the stipulation that he not speak.[45] While the intense FBI surveillance turned up no evidence that Robeson was a communist, many rushed to label him a traitor. Even black leaders distanced themselves from what he had said, and his image was fatally damaged. [46]

In 1950, Robeson's passport was revoked on the eve of his departure for Europe, causing significant loss of concert income at a time when bookings at home had already dried up. His passport was not returned until June 1958 when the U.S. Supreme Court ruled that the State Department had no right to deny it because of his political views.[47]

By then, he was a broken man. He tried to commit suicide in 1961 and two years later received psychotherapy in East Berlin.[48] He and Essie, who had been his spokesperson through all these travails, returned to the United States later that year. He lived mostly in seclusion for the rest of his life. After Essie died in 1965,[49] he lived for a time with his son, Pauli, and his family in New York. In 1968, he moved in with his sister in Philadelphia and died in 1976.[50] His funeral was held in Mother Zion A.M.E. Church in Harlem, where his brother, Ben, had preached for 27 years. Thousands came in the rain to bid him farewell.[51]

Robeson's academic and athletic success at Rutgers and while he was in law school had proven to him that he could reach for the stars and grab a handful. His accomplishments as one of America's greatest scholar-athletes led him to heights few of any race would ever reach. His legacy is felt even today, more than half a century after he was broken and defeated. He remains an icon who uncompromisingly demanded that the American conscience embrace the worth and dignity of all its citizens. After he passed from the scene, nothing would express that sentiment quite so well as his towering song "All God's Chillun Got Wings."

CHAPTER SIX

Moral Collapse

Everybody's All-American—that described Derek Thomson
Sheely about as well as anything could. He was co-captain of
the football team at Frostburg State University (FSU) in Western Maryland, a two-time member of the Empire Eight Conference All-Academic team, every inch a leader and competitor and the boy next door who was handsome enough to set
cheerleader hearts aflutter over which one he'd end up asking
out.

In the shirt-soaking heat and humidity of that fateful
morning of Saturday, August 13, 2011, Derek and his Dad, Ken,
loaded the black Cadillac Escalade the family had owned for
eight plus years for the two-hour drive from their home in
Germantown, Maryland, to Frostburg. Derek had no idea his
parents had secretly agreed to give him the Escalade as a graduation present to reward his many accomplishments. He'd already earned a degree in history at FSU but was returning for
one last semester as a fifth-year senior to add a second major
in political science—*and* to play one last season of football,
a sport he'd loved since pee wee days for the camaraderie it
engendered.[1]

The summer had flown by for Derek. He'd won a competitive internship at the National Nuclear Security Administra-

tion in Washington, where his Dad was a top administrator. That experience had made him more determined than ever to follow in his Dad's footsteps and pursue a career in public service. He was fiercely proud of what his Dad had done in his thirties—how he helped to secure nuclear materials in the former Soviet Union after the Iron Curtain fell in 1989. That task—mainly to keep nukes from falling into the hands of terrorists—had taken Ken to Moscow and the far reaches of the former USSR for long stretches in the late 1990s. His team of experts had secured nuclear materials and nuclear weapons all across the former Soviet states to curtail a threat of appalling destruction. That summer, Derek got to meet a few veterans of that high stakes campaign and was impressed by their lack of pretense, by how they shrugged off their apocalyptic challenge as "Just doing our job."[2]

That summer, on their 80-minute commute each way, Derek often listened to hip-hop on his earphones as he and Ken rode the Metro. But they did discuss Derek's budding interest in a career with the CIA. Ken strongly encouraged him to give it a go, so in July he began filling out the lengthy first-round application required to enter the domain of foreign intelligence gathering. With help on weekends from his Mom, Kristen—an English major and editor—he felt he'd "nailed" the requirements and sent them off just before leaving for FSU. His supporting materials included several writing samples, among them a college paper on Russian history that Derek was especially proud of.

During that intense process, it dawned on Kristen that her 22-year-old son "suddenly was an adult. Ken and I were advising him—not telling him what to do."

Kristen had opted out of the FSU trip even though she very much wanted to go. The field hockey team she coached was scheduled to practice that same Saturday morning. She thought about rescheduling; but, ever the practical mom, she decided to stay to free up space in the car for Derek's high pile of gear.

Just before leaving for the match, Kristen went to Derek's room to wake him and say goodbye. As she often did, she turned off an oscillating fan that blew just enough air for comfortable sleeping. It was just how Derek liked to greet the day. As she turned to go, his eyes opened so she paused. He stretched out both arms and wiggled his fingers as if to say come hither. She went back and leaned down for a hug—

"Love you Mom," he drowsily rasped with his arms around her neck.

"I love you, too," she replied. And then she whispered the admonition every mother has for a departing child: "Have fun but please be safe." Those long-lingering words—*Love you, Mom*—would be the last she'd ever hear him say.[3]

Downstairs in their spacious home in Kingsview Village, Ken was already busy with preparations for the trip. It was their dream house, reflecting a strong affinity for openness and a welcoming feel. From its stone accents in front to its two-story foyer and open floor plan, they'd never grown tired of their home on Falconcrest Road. Derek had been in the sixth grade, his sister, Keyton, in second when they moved there in August 2000. Both were deeply attached to the place, too—a corner lot large enough for outdoor games and a porch that said "Howdy" to everyone passing by.[4]

As she hurried through the kitchen/family room combination en route to her field hockey practice, Kristen gave Ken a breezy, "See you tonight."

Not long after that, Derek and Ken loaded the car. They had to lower the backseat to get a widescreen TV and an indispensable Xbox inside. Clothes and gear stashed in plastic milk crates were stacked in the remaining backseat space and cargo area. One of the last items stowed was a Penn State pennant, a reminder of longstanding family ties to the school: Ken had majored in chemical engineering there; Kristen's father also had a Penn State degree; and Keyton would become a Nittany Lion freshman in just two weeks. Derek, too, had gone to Penn State for one year until the appeal of playing football with his old high school teammates had lured him to FSU. At 5'11" and 210 pounds, he was plenty good enough and big enough to play fullback at Division III FSU, but not at a perennial Division I contender like Penn State.

By 10 a.m. the car was crammed full. Later, Kristen couldn't forgive herself for not going, but as a practical matter, they were out of room. Which meant she'd miss the fun of being together, the keen anticipation for a season and semester to crown all the others. As Ken backed the Escalade out onto Falconcrest Road and Derek reached for his earphones, no one could have known that they were heading into a maelstrom, the worst the storm gods could ever brew, a catastrophe to be caused and made infinitely worse by the very authorities who were responsible for protecting Derek, for insuring his health, safety and wellbeing. These authorities—his football coaches and trainers, administrators at FSU and the NCAA and the company that made what it called a "concussion-proof" helmet—would later stand accused of "utter incompetence" and "egregious misconduct" in how they treated a young man who epitomized the best America's massive sports regime could offer. And yet, its crazed, win-at-all-cost mentality had caused him to be tossed aside like a spent tissue.[5]

Once they reached Frostburg, Ken helped Derek move his gear into a brand-new, two-bedroom apartment he was sharing with his best friend, Dwayne Washington, who'd been a high school football teammate back in Germantown. To the roomies, the apartment's standout feature was its balcony view of Bobcat Stadium on campus.

After saying goodbye to his son, Ken headed back to Germantown on I-68 through the spectacular cuts and gorges of the Appalachian Corridor. As he drove in solitude, Ken remembered Derek's early years: how small he'd been to play with so much heart; how, as a pee wee, he'd practiced broken-field running in the backyard by zig-zagging through a maze of plastic chairs; how he threw his arms up in triumph after each imaginary touchdown; and the Steve Young 49er's jersey he wore daily to practice—washed or not—hoping the coaches would notice him. The head coach had told Derek at the beginning of ninth grade, "If you keep working this hard, I can see you being pulled up to varsity by the end of the year." That same summer his growth spurt had kicked in: He shot up several inches and gained 20 or more pounds. He'd had a mythical sophomore season when the Northwest High School Jaguars won the state championship and Derek earned a ring to remember it by. The Jaguars had struggled his junior year but came within one win of playing for the state championship his senior year. At the season-ending banquet, Derek had received two coveted awards: the first for playing all four years and having the highest grade point average on the team; the second was the Jag Award "for excellence on the field, in the class and within the community."[6]

His intensity, vigor and derring-do belied a vexing vulnerability for Derek when football practice began at FSU on Monday, August 15. He'd suffered a concussion in practice the year before, one that an assistant athletic trainer still on staff had diagnosed. Medical evidence confirmed that a first concussion makes a player much more susceptible to a second. Despite that, the coaching staff ordered him to take part in what later was described as "virtually unlimited, full contact, helmet-to-helmet collisions"—and as more a "gladiatorial thrill for the coaches than learning sessions for the players." Their win-at-all-cost approach made little sense for a team that had won six and lost 24 games over the past three years.

Most of the hits occurred in a drill FSU players loathed as "ridiculously dangerous"—a so-called "concussion drill" in which halfbacks and fullbacks were smashed into by linebackers at top speed from six to ten yards away. Any attempts by the backs to defend themselves resulted in cursing rebukes from coaches and a rerun of the drill. Eventually, roles were reversed and the backs charged into linebackers in passive

Derek Sheely

mode. It was estimated that within a 15-minute period, each player took approximately 30 to 40 sub-concussive, or concussive, blows to the head.[7]

Coaches ordered the first such drills when two-a-day practice sessions began on Friday, August 19, 2011. They did so knowing that Derek and at least one other player had suffered a concussion while performing the drill during the 2010 season. Even so, players were ordered to hit "hat first"—i.e., to lead with the head—which increased the risk of injury significantly. Violence was stressed to such an extent that even the FSU Special Teams Playbook instructed players to "earhole" opponents—in effect, to deliver an illegal blindside hit which could induce violent rotational forces inside the cranium, leading to a concussion.[8]

That Friday's practice involved more than four hours of full contact drills. The next day, while participating in the concussion drill, Derek's forehead began bleeding profusely. Instead of investigating whether he was suffering from a concussion, the head trainer and staff merely bandaged his head and allowed him to keep practicing. Even though they knew he'd had a concussion the year before, coaches and trainers continued to allow Derek to play in violation of NCAA Rule 3, which requires that a bleeding participant "shall . . . be given appropriate medical treatment."[9]

When players broke for lunch on Saturday, his teammates noticed a large, protruding and discolored bruise on Derek's forehead. On Sunday, Derek and other backs were ordered again to engage in the concussion drill, and for the second time, Derek's head began bleeding. Once again, instead of performing a concussion evaluation, the trainers applied a bandage to Derek's forehead and sent him back into full contact drills. At lunch that day, players noticed, for the first time, a pronounced change in Derek's behavior: He was not his usual outgoing, high-spirited self and instead seemed morose and withdrawn. That afternoon, the same fiasco recurred: more bleeding at the forehead, no concussion evaluation, a band-aid treatment and swift return to a long, full contact practice.[10]

The trauma to Derek's brain passed the point of no return on Monday, August 22, during yet another session of full contact that included the loathsome concussion drill. After a heavy contact play, Derek walked back to the huddle and told an assistant coach he didn't feel right and had a headache. The coach responded by yelling, "Stop your bitching and moaning and quit acting like a pussy and get back out there, Sheely." A seven-on-seven drill simulating game-like conditions then continued, but, within moments, Derek collided with a defensive back in a hit of moderate intensity. And yet, it was forceful enough to trigger Second Impact Syndrome (SIS), which often causes explosive swelling of the brain. As he got up and walked toward the sidelines, Derek seemed lucid enough but collapsed seconds later.[11]

"Coach, look at Sheely," a teammate yelled. Instead of rushing to his aid, the head coach and a top assistant scoffed at Derek's plight and ordered him to get up. By then, tragically, their team co-captain was in the throes of what physicians describe as "brain herniation, an acute subdural hematoma and massive vascular engorgement."[12]

Derek had won a cheerleader's heart after all. He and Anna McFarland had met at an off-campus party and clicked from the start. She'd been captivated by his sparkling blue eyes, his muscular build and how smart and funny he was. He'd been smitten by her deep-dimpled smile, the jet black hair that fell well below her shoulders and by how outgoing she was.[13]

Anna and 20 or more cheerleaders were in the gym next to the football field that same Monday, practicing acrobatic routines to dazzle fans with in the coming season. It was so hot and stuffy inside that the outer doors of the gym had been opened to cool things off. Suddenly, through the open doors, the cheerleaders saw a helicopter hovering above the practice field. The sight of it caused one of Anna's friends to burst into tears and say she was sure her boyfriend, a member of the team, had been injured.

"Oh, no! I'm sure he's okay," Anna reassured her.

Just then, the football team trooped inside en route to the locker room. As he passed Anna, a player grimly advised, "Anna, you'd better go outside *right now!*"

With that, she ran outside and saw that the helicopter had landed and had a door open. She could hear the distinctive whop whop sound of the propeller blades and saw medics and players rushing with a stretcher toward the aircraft's open door. As she ran forward, she saw Derek lying on the stretcher with his eyes closed, a terrifying sight that made her burst into tears.[14]

Within moments, the helicopter took off and flew east about ten miles to the regional medical center in Cumberland, Maryland, where doctors performed an emergency craniotomy to relieve the pressure building up in Derek's brain. His physicians would later conclude with 90 percent certainty that the cause was Second Impact Syndrome (SIS), which can make the brain swell alarmingly.

As these foreboding events unfolded, Ken and Kristen had just dropped off their daughter, Keyton, at Penn State for the beginning of her freshman year. They'd driven only 30 minutes or so back toward Germantown when a number popped up on Kristen's cell phone. The signal was weak, so Ken pulled off the road as soon as it strengthened and dialed back on his phone. It was a message from a trainer at FSU saying it was urgent that he call the doctor at Cumberland Hospital who was treating Derek. Treating him for what? Ken and Kristen had no idea but got a devastating answer once they reached the doctor: Derek had suffered a traumatic brain injury and had undergone an emergency craniotomy. Prospects were not encouraging that the cranial pressure would abate enough for him to survive.[15]

With that grim assessment, they changed course and drove straight to Cumberland, about two and a half hours away. Soon after arriving, they were told Derek would be medevacked to the University of Maryland Shock Trauma Center in Baltimore, where the best available brain surgeons could treat him. Though bone-tired and grief-stricken, Ken and Kristen drove the two and a half hours to Baltimore, where they waited for hours before being allowed to see Derek. The following morning relatives picked up Keyton at Penn State and rushed her to her brother's side.

Early on, one of Derek's doctors asked Ken if his son had been in a car accident.

"No, it's football-related," Ken told him.

"Wasn't he was wearing a helmet?" the MD rejoined.

"Of course he was."

"I wondered because his injury is so traumatic," the MD concluded.[16]

When Ken, Kristen and Keyton finally saw Derek, he was upright, strapped vertically to his bed to use gravitational flow to reduce cranial pressure. He looked relaxed and serene to Kristen; only a red line on his forehead told of what happened; the rest of his head was bandaged. By then, all eyes were fixed on readings of an intracranial pressure (ICP) monitor physicians had inserted just inside his skull. It read millimeters of mercury (mmHg) at zero to 10 for a healthy adult; 20 or above for abnormal; 40 or above for deep dysfunction; and 60 for fatal.

First readings for Derek were not as high as expected—encouraging enough for Ken and Kristen to send Keyton back to Penn State. (Once she got back, she didn't go to class and couldn't eat or talk to anyone.) Physicians thought Derek's perilous swelling might subside, that prospects for survival were plausible, though he might not be the person his family, teammates and friends cared for so deeply. Then came a hugely deflating discovery: Somehow, the monitor had been incorrectly connected—the optimistic first readings were all false. Once the monitor was properly connected, the readings rose fourfold or more.[17]

By then, the hospital waiting room was swamped with distressed family, friends and members of the FSU community; even the coaches who'd ordered the concussion drill and the trainers who had failed to check Derek for a concussion came. Ken and Kristen consoled visitors as best they could, but no words could assuage the grief that enveloped the waiting room. More than once, Kristen found herself hugging a giant FSU lineman broken down in tears. Most knew Derek now faced a battle he couldn't win, but they came anyway—some simply to pay their respects, others to murmur a quiet and centering prayer and still others just to be among those reckoning with such a tragic loss. By Wednesday, with no visitor let-up in sight, nurses set aside a hospital conference room for Sheely visitors.[18]

Strange to say, but the maelstrom that had overwhelmed the Sheelys seemed to be driven, in part, by nature itself. Moments before 2 p.m. on Tuesday, August 23, an earthquake registering 5.8 on the Richter Scale hit Washington, DC, causing a crack in the Washington Monument and $20 million in damage to the National Cathedral. Its impact was felt as far away as New York City. Then, on Saturday, August 27, the eye of Hurricane Irene passed along the Maryland coast, uprooting trees, downing power lines and drenching the Baltimore area in rain. At the Sheelys' urging, close friends and family braved the elements that day to pay their last respects to Derek. His doctors no longer were offering hope, and his family had made the agonizing decision to let him go on Sunday, August 28.[19]

In the aftermath of Derek's death, the magnitude of his loss became more and more acute for Ken and Kristen. They were gravely worried about Keyton, who wanted to drop out of school. She was deeply depressed and cried in the only place she could be alone—the shower. She drank too much, and her grades suffered. Ken and Kristen began to feel alone and abandoned. Isolating seemed their only option—to such an extent that a trip to the grocery or drug store became a much-dreaded ordeal. Impromptu encounters with those who knew Derek often led to moments in which no one knew what to say. A cheery, "How's Derek?" from someone who hadn't heard the tragic news invited complete loss of control. To avoid such encounters, they did their grocery shopping at 6:30 a.m. on Sunday.

To make matters worse, they felt no one in authority was willing to help. Their appeals to FSU administrators and the NCAA to investigate Derek's death fell on deaf ears. Incredibly, the NCAA replied with the blithe suggestion that they consult the organization's safety website for more information. Being non-litigious by nature, all they wanted was to find out what happened and to share that information with others to push concussion awareness.

Several weeks after Derek died, they met with FSU Athletic Director Troy Dell to complete the paperwork for a catastrophic medical insurance claim. In offering his condolences, Dell assured them that Derek's death was an unavoidable accident. None of the actual circumstances—let alone any mention of the fatal concussion drill—were mentioned by Dell.[20]

The memorial service for Derek at Prince of Peace Lutheran Church on September 1 drew an overflow audience of more than 600 mourners. The FSU football and cheerleading squads were bused in from Frostburg. With a crowd too large to accommodate in the sanctuary, many were seated in an adjacent assembly hall. It was an open service at which teammates, friends and FSU President Jonathan Gibralter offered moving tributes—none more so than that given by Ken, who said, "During his hospital stay, we said we were praying for a miracle when we realized that Derek was the miracle—he so truly enriched so many lives and we are grateful for that. . . . Derek would want everyone to know this was an accident."[21]

Ken also said Derek's "loyal heart of a champion will beat on, Derek's warrior passion will help others live, and Derek's beautiful blue eyes will continue to see in the future." All because his son had become an organ donor. The sports blogging site, SB Nation, later reported that: "A man can play soccer thanks to Derek's ACL. Two men can see because they have Derek's corneas. Two men are alive because each has one of Derek's kidneys. . . ."[22]

The memorial service seemed to bring much-needed closure for Derek's friends, but not for Ken, Kristen and Keyton. Afterward, gradually, Ken and Kristen began to focus more and more on how to honor Derek's legacy in the widest possible way. By October, they had established a foundation in his name to promote concussion awareness.

Still, they had to face the daily pain and harsh reality of life without Derek. Nothing lifted their spirits more than reminiscing about Derek with his companions and closest friends. One staple of memory was Derek's spot-on impersonation of Marlon Brando's famous line, "I'll make him an offer he can't refuse" in his *Godfather* role as Don Corleone. After stuffing three peppermint candies in his mouth, he portrayed Corleone describing how a film studio executive would end up with a horsehead in his bed.

Other staples were Derek's stern warnings to any teammate with a roving eye that his younger sister, Keyton, was strictly off limits, and when Derek stood up to bullies in sixth grade soon after the family moved to Germantown. The first time Derek boarded the school bus he took a seat in back. Moments later, two larger boys boarded and told Derek he'd taken their seat. Derek got up, looked down and informed them, "I don't see a name on this seat" and sat back down. Derek got roughed up but refused to back down. Next day, the same thing happened, but this time the bus driver saw the incident and had the bullies kicked off the bus. It turned out that they'd been terrorizing kids on the bus for quite some time. Derek's willingness to stand up to the miscreants made him an instant hero on his bus route.[23]

Ken and Kristen couldn't come to terms with Derek's death, but they continued to believe fully in what they were told: that it had been an unavoidable accident. Seven months later, they were busy getting the newly formed Derek Sheely Foundation off the ground when their fragile sense of normalcy suddenly was shattered. On March 22, 2012, a person identified only as John Doe emailed info@thedereksheelyfoundation.org lamenting the loss of "a great spirited man" he proudly called his teammate.

Then, in graphic detail, the author of the John Doe email described the so-called concussion drill—the repeat head hits to defenseless players, the abusive language of coaches and the failure to heed and act on unmistakable concussion symptoms—that led to Derek's collapse on August 22 the previous year and to his death six days later. The author stressed that players "COULD NOT DEFEND THEMSELVES" and that an assistant coach often ordered a charging player to "KNOCK THE S**T OUT OF HIM" (meaning a defenseless player). The author concluded with, ". . . two coaches were aware that he (Derek) did have a headache and took NO precautions to ensure his safety as well as the safety of many other players."[24] The anonymous email was first seen by a volunteer who monitored website emails and told Ken right away. After his initial shock, he wondered if a disgruntled former player, someone with a grudge against the team, had sent it. But he called Kristen right away, telling her not to read the email, knowing it would devastate her.

Much later—after reading the email—Kristen would say, "It was like lightning struck; it was horrible. We were stupidly trusting people."[25] But they would trust no more—not after they knew how terribly Derek had been treated. For the first time, they discussed whether they should sue. Kristen had seen the website of a young Kansas City attorney named Paul D. Anderson, who had gathered a great deal of information on concussion-related cases, especially in football. She began following Anderson on Twitter and sent him a copy of the anonymous email. Anderson called the Sheelys soon after reading the John Doe email to say he thought they had strong grounds for suing. They agreed to move forward together, and Anderson began assembling a team of three law firms to develop a case against the coaches, the school, the helmet manufacturer and the NCAA. Formed in 1907 to guard against injuries in football, the NCAA still portrayed itself as a protector of player health and safety at member schools.[26]

Anderson's first and most urgent task was to identify who had written the John Doe email. It took him a year, but he finally found its author, Brandon Henderson, in North Dakota. Though younger, Brandon had been a teammate of Derek's, and Anderson secured his commitment to cooperate with the plaintiff side. Since Maryland was the proper jurisdiction for the case, Steve Nolan, a prominent Baltimore attorney who had represented several NFL players on work-related issues, was asked to join the plaintiff team.[27]

When the million-dollar lawsuit—defined in a highly detailed 66-page complaint—was filed on August 28, 2013, the second anniversary of Derek's death, it was covered by CNN, Good Morning America, Fox Sports, CBS Sports and many newspapers. The suit named as defendants two FSU coaches, an assistant athletic trainer, the manufacturer and distributor of the helmet Derek wore and the NCAA. As the lead defendant, the NCAA retained Latham and Watkins, one of largest law firms in the world, to mount its defense. In April 2016, Latham and Watkins made a motion for summary judgment to dismiss the case before Montgomery County Circuit Court Judge David Boynton. In denying the motion, Judge Boynton ruled that a jury could consider punitive damages and that the NCAA had a legal duty to warn student-athletes about the risks of SIS and to protect them from that threat. It was first time ever a judge judicially declared that the NCAA had this obligation. On June 20, just as the case was set to go to trial, the parties agreed to a $1.2 million settlement.[28]

It was a landmark settlement—the first the NCAA had ever agreed to for such a claim. Hosea Harvey, a Temple University law professor, predicted that the settlement could become a catalyst for how the NCAA and member schools handle concussions and other health risks for players. Prior to the settlement, NCAA President Mark Emmert told Congress the NCAA made a "terrible choice of words" when it contended in the

Sheely case that it had no legal duty to protect student-athletes.[29] Emmert knew the case could have far-reaching impact, and it did, especially in much broader awareness of the concussion risks in football. Five years later, a death with similarities to Derek's occurred. During an off-season workout on May 29, 2018, Jordan McNair, an offensive lineman at the University of Maryland, collapsed from extreme exhaustion. He had just run ten 100-meter wind sprints. McNair, too, was airlifted to a trauma center where he received an emergency liver transplant; he died 15 days later. A subsequent investigation found that the university's catastrophic incident guideline was not followed.

Ken and Kristen had the settlement funds placed directly in the foundation they'd formed and named for Derek to underwrite an annual leadership award and scholarship, to send concussion awareness kits to organizations across the country, to sponsor an annual run and other activities. The Foundation advocates a ban on dangerous drills (like the so-called concussion drill), limits on practices and suspensions for coaches violating rules to protect player health and safety. The two coaches named as defendants in the suit escaped financial consequences because the State of Maryland assumed their liability. The head coach left the school voluntarily three months after the Sheely suit was filed. The assistant who ran the concussion drill and berated Derek as he lay on the field unconscious remained employed by FSU until August 7, 2015.[30]

Despite the settlement, the Sheelys did not feel vindicated. Ken said he and Kristen "could never do enough" to perpetuate the memory of their son. "He was my best friend—so much so that I often wondered who was the dad and who was the son." It deepened the hurt that he was cut down on the threshold of adulthood and a life full of accomplishments, including giving back to society overall.

The Sheely tragedy was the perfect storm in which authority at every level broke down—a moral collapse on the part of coaches and trainers, administrators at the university and the NCAA. It has become a landmark case that should make coaches and administrators everywhere think long and hard about putting players in harm's way to gain a competitive edge.

Seven years after his death, Derek is still very much with his parents. His room looks much like it did the day he left for training camp. Kristen regrets tidying up his scattered things; otherwise it would be just the same. Cinnamon, the family's fawn-like Basenji, or sighthound, once slept on Derek's bed, but passed away in 2014 at age 16, missing her irreplaceable friend to the end. Kristen cannot bring herself to scatter or bury her son's ashes. Cinnamon's ashes sit beside them.[31] Three enlarged photos of Derek are prominently displayed on the dining room table where the blinds are drawn. His spirit still fills the home.

Centuries ago, the English playwright and poet laureate, John Dryden, wrote the soulful words: *And doomed to death, but fated not to die.* Those same words make a fitting epitaph for Everybody's All-American: Derek Thomson Sheely.

Part II

Character Formation

Seven essential qualities set the scholar-athlete archetype apart: passion, courage, empathy, discipline, intellect, faith and the capacity to lead a high-impact life. In Part II, John LeBar describes players he coached who exemplified these vital traits. The first chapter in Part II describes how the traits of a scholar-athlete are formed by coaches and teams dedicated to achieving outstanding performance.

CHAPTER SEVEN

Molding High Achievers

Chaim Arlosoroff (hi-uhm / are-LOS-soh-rof) was my first All-American and Duke's first, too, in tennis. During the '82 season, he defeated players ranked at Number 2, 4 and 13, and yet, he was ranked at Number 17 in the final national poll. That didn't bother him in the least, because he didn't have a big ego. And coming from Israel, where he played on the Davis Cup team, he attached scant importance to being an All-American or a top-ranked collegian. Universities in Israel didn't compete in athletics.

As a highly skilled player and a 23-year-old freshman, there was very little I could teach Chaim in the way of mechanics. What I could do was help him adjust to a strange new life by making the team his family. Early on, I set up several challenge matches for him to make sure the entire team knew how talented he was. His subsequent victories, self-effacing manner and gregarious nature enabled Chaim to bond quickly with his teammates and to feel a strong sense of belonging.

Before Chaim arrived, the prominent Duke alum who recruited him told me: "Just be aware that Chaim doesn't know how good he is." It turned out that he was even better than advance notices; so, Jim Bonk, my assistant coach, and I agreed to praise him and build him up in any way we could. Jim was a bachelor and popular chemistry professor who lived alone. We decided that because he was older, Chaim would be more comfortable at Jim's house than in a dorm. When Jim invited him, Chaim gladly accepted. The decision also made sense because Jim ran our tutoring program and could advise on just about any academic matter that might come up. In his first classes, Chaim took notes in Hebrew, a sight that bewildered students who sat nearby. His English-speaking skills were quite good, but his reading and writing were somewhat deficient, so Jim and I got him a tutor. Four years later, he graduated magna cum laude with a pre-med degree.

Chaim did not come from wealth and privilege but did come from a storied family. He was named for an iconic grandfather, a progressive leader in the Jewish community of Palestine until his tragic death in 1933. He was assassinated by radical right wing Jews while walking on a beach near Tel Aviv with his wife, Simi. The circumstances of his death would cast a shadow over the struggle for a Jewish homeland until its birth and beyond. Chaim's grandfather had asked what became an unending question: Can Jews and Arabs live in peace? He had warned, "If we do not find a way to deal peacefully with the Arabs, then unfortunately we will deal with them in war or on the battlefield."

When he made that warning, Chaim's grandfather was the de facto foreign minister of the Jewish Community in Palestine. His rise to prominence had been meteoric: At 24, he'd been elected as the Jewish community representative to the League of Nations and served in many high-level positions after that. In April 1933, he organized a historic meeting at the King David Hotel in Jerusalem that, for the first time, brought moderate Jews and Arabs together to explore options for cooperation and avoiding conflict. The meeting set off alarm bells with hard-line Zionists, who demanded that Arlosoroff resign his position as Political Director of the Jewish Agency for Palestine. Radical Arabs also were vehemently opposed to cooperation that might lead to a binational state.

Despite these objections, Arlosoroff was sent to Germany a few weeks later to negotiate with the newly installed Third Reich to permit German Jews to emigrate to Palestine without being stripped of their property. He came back with an agreement that eventually allowed more than 60,000 German Jews to emigrate and take with them $100 million that would finance the infrastructure of the emerging nation. At dusk on June 16, 1933, two days after he returned from Germany, Arlosoroff took his fateful stroll on the beach. Two members of a rightwing Jewish party with fascist tendencies shot him as his distraught wife watched. The assassins cited his efforts to foster ties between the Arabs and Jews as their reason. Arlosoroff's funeral drew an estimated 100,000 mourners, and his death caused long-lasting fissures in the Zionist Movement. I learned from Shaul, son of the elder Chaim and father of his namesake, that after independence, streets all over the country—even neighborhoods and kibbutzes—were named for Shaul's famous father. That made young Chaim something of a luminary in his tennis travels about the country; people were curious to see him and take his measure against a family patriarch and martyr of nationhood. That inheritance was a heavy burden to bear in a land still divided by the never-ending question for which the elder Arlosoroff became a martyr.

Shaul, who became a prominent water engineer in a water-starved country, told me that when Chaim was eight he was shy and mostly kept to himself. He said, "I finally dragged him to the tennis court to bring out his fighting spirit." At that point, neither father nor son could have imagined just how far young Chaim's competitive fires would take him.

In time, Chaim developed the qualities that characterize a scholar-athlete: the dedication to work hard, the toughness to cope with pressure, the selflessness to sacrifice for the team, efficiency in the use of time, an ability to set short-term and long-term goals and the grit to overcome adversity. These attributes bloomed in Chaim while he was at Duke. My role was to make sure the tennis environment helped to bring them out. Chaim didn't need a list of things to do, and I never gave him one. I did stress many times that sports teach us how to deal with success and failure and that failure often precedes success. I never saw Chaim gloat about a win or demean an opponent. On the rare occasions when he lost, he took the outcome in stride; his emotional highs and lows weren't very far apart. Achieving balance is the mark of a mature scholar-athlete, an attribute that will follow him or her for life. Sportsmanship is molded in the achiever's DNA, a rare quality in the win-at-all-cost era.

The widely-held impression that Duke is a rich man's school is far from reality. Like Chaim, most of my players did not come from wealth and privilege. Only two of 11 players written about extensively in this book came from well-to-do-families. A prime example of those who came from modest means is Ross Dubins, who was one month old when his father died during back surgery. When that disaster struck, his mother, Josie, was a stay-at-home mom with three children. As the wife of a veteran, she got a small benefit, but needed to find work. She moved everyone to Miami to be near family and found a job as a waitress and later worked in other low-pay jobs.

"Although our family means were limited, my Mom more than made up for that by giving us a home filled with love and a strong sense of belonging," Ross told me. He revered his Mom because she made him feel secure, that he never lacked for anything. She played on the A Team at the North Shore Tennis Center, and by the time Ross was seven, he was carrying a tennis racquet everywhere he went. A few years later, he was holding his own against older, advanced adults.

He came to Duke on a full needs scholarship, and, by the time he arrived, he was nearly 6'4" and deeply tanned by the South Florida sun. His chiseled good looks made him a great favorite with Duke co-eds. He played No. 5 singles as a freshman and won the ACC championship; he then became a stand-out in doubles, winning two ACC doubles championships at No. 2. Ross was a good student and one of the happiest, best-adjusted players I coached at Duke. His people skills were remarkable. Jim Bonk and I stressed to Ross, just as we did with Chaim, that Duke Tennis was his family; he, too, lived for a time with Jim. Looking back, Ross calls his Duke years the best of his life.

In 1989, Ross became the head tennis pro at the City of North Miami's tennis center and later became the city's Tennis Superintendent. The racquet Ross carried everywhere as a small boy was an extension of the family and the community that nurtured him, one that taught him to accept people for who they are, not for their financial or social status.

When fall practice began, I stressed to every player who went out for the team that academics had to come first, that I would monitor their grades on a continuing basis and would ask them to explain if they fell behind. I emphasized as strongly as I could that I would always treat them as adults unless they indulged in less than adult behavior. The last thing they wanted was a long, prescriptive list of "do's" and "don'ts," and I never gave them one.

Each semester, I got player grades from the Registrar's Office and reviewed them with Allison Holtom, my contact in the Admissions Office. I wanted Allison to know how players who'd been at or near the cutline for

From left to right: Ross Dubins, Coach LeBar and Chaim Arlosoroff

admission were performing academically. I couldn't do that today because federal regulations make student grades completely confidential. I feel strongly that this overregulated privacy protection undercuts a coach's ability—and that of others, including parents—to intervene when problems arise and to arrange for needed support.

In contrast to Ross, Joe Meir was nurtured by a doting father, who was a prominent engineer and businessman in the Research Triangle. Joe was the top high school player in North Carolina, and we had very high expectations of him when he came to Duke. When we started to get players with national rankings, Joe was playing at the 5th or 6th position and sometimes not at all. He understood the process to determine the lineup and did not complain, but always wanted the opportunity to work his way into the lineup. When this happens to some high school stars, they throw up their hands and quit. But Joe loved tennis and the tennis team enough to continue to work hard every day in practice. He understood that life does not always go as you would like but you do not give up, you continue to work hard. This is very difficult to do, but it is critical in sports and life. When he graduated, Joe was a sterling example of the scholar-athlete.

Joe Meir, 1981

The Meir family had an unforgettable story, too. Joe's father, Ezra, and his mother, Violet, were born in Baghdad at a time of rising anti-Semitism in the Middle East. In 1948, Violet was smuggled from Iraq to Israel on a school bus dressed as an Arab. She lived on a kibbutz for two years and finally, at age 12, was reunited with her family in New York. Ezra's family left Baghdad when he was five. A wealthy uncle sent him to schools in Beirut, Istanbul and the United States. He and Violet met for the first time at a party in New York.

By then, Ezra was studying and excelling in civil engineering at Yale, where he got undergraduate and graduate degrees. He chose Yale because he was a fan of textbooks on civil engineering written by Yale professor Hardy Cross. Two years after he finished there, a classmate convinced him to come to Durham to help build a big engineering firm. "He accepted that offer," Joe says, "and before long he'd established a reputation as the go to guy when a really tough problem arose." Ezra would go on to engineer many iconic structures throughout North Carolina, including Kenan Stadium and Carmichael Auditorium in Chapel Hill and parts of Duke Hospital in Durham.

While Joe was at Duke, Ezra called him on a bright spring day to say that he'd been asked to look at a problem near the hospital. He invited Joe to go to lunch and, after picking him up, said, "Before we eat, there's something I need to check on." They drove to Flowers Drive next to the hospital, where Ezra spotted a two-inch crack that was about 60 feet long in the street. He had a worried look, Joe says, when he said, "Let's skip lunch; there's someone I have to see right away . . . He knew instantly what was going on: a pond being dug in Duke Gardens was destabilizing the hospital walls." Ezra told the hospital administrators what he'd found and went back three days later for another look. By then, the fissure had widened and hairline cracks had appeared on an outer wall of the hospital. Ezra gave the administrators a grim report: Within a week the building would start to collapse and Duke would be out millions of dollars.

Joe says most engineers "wouldn't tackle a project like that today, because there's just too much liability." But Ezra went to work right away on a plan to save the structure. It involved driving 8 to 10 large caissons (a type of watertight column) made of steel and reinforced concrete beneath the hospital foundation. They had to be sunk to a depth of 50 feet, much of the way through rock, to shore up the walls and foundation. It took two months to complete the project, but Ezra's solution was permanent.

I've thought more than once that Ezra built, in other ways, on a rock-solid foundation. Joe wasn't surprised that his father's plan worked. Over and over he had urged Joe to plan, plan and plan some more. For the rest of his life, Ezra would warn his son with a favorite expression whenever Joe veered toward the rocks: "Full sail without a rudder." The foundation for all Ezra's planning was education. He'd gotten a superb education himself and urged all his children to get the same. Joe got an MBA from Duke and spent a year at MIT's Center for Real Estate Development, where he learned the fundamentals of preparing for recessions.

Because real estate is such a cyclical sector, that knowledge turned out to be a life-saver shortly after Ezra died in 2007. By then, he and Joe had built a large real estate development business, one of the most successful in the Research Triangle. Joe anticipated the real estate crash of 2008 when he saw "all this ridiculous lending in the housing sector." While his firm was not involved in the residential sector, he was sure the entire financial community would be affected, "because the banks shut down and you can't get money." The solution—one that had been stressed over and over in his classes at MIT—was to stockpile cash, which Joe did. That put him in a small minority: developers who came through the '08 crash largely unscathed.

I decided to include family background on Chaim, Ross and Joe because it provides all-important context for how they adapted at Duke and went on to become scholar-athletes. All three came from caring, nurturing homes that put them on the road to becoming true scholar-athletes.

My coaching was not primary in determining that outcome; my role was to encourage, to guide and to make sure they stayed on track. Players from less stable backgrounds require much more hands-on support, especially on the academic side. What a good coach can do, irrespective of a player's background, is cultivate a deep commitment to teamwork, fairness, planning, self-discipline and a continuing search for inspiration. Each of these dimensions of sterling character will have a direct bearing on what kind of life the player goes on to live.

In *The Game of Life*, former Princeton University President William Bowen and his co-author James L. Shulman wrote, "What you really want to know are the later life outcomes. What you want to focus on is not so much what students look like when they come. You want to look at when they go out and what they look like ten years later." Their Duke experience helped mold most of my players into high achievers.

Ten years out is a highly significant benchmark. In 1991, Anders Ericsson, a psychologist at Florida State University, and two colleagues made a remarkable discovery about outstanding performance: It's practice, not talent that ultimately matters.[1] They studied three groups of violinists at the famous Music Academy in West Berlin: first, those expected to become international soloists; second, those expected to play in the world's top orchestras; and third, those expected to become music teachers. The researchers found that native talent in all three groups was about the same. The major difference was that those in group one had practiced two thousand hours more than those in group two and six thousand hours more than those in group three.[2]

As Matthew Sayed writes in his fascinating book *Bounce: The Myth of Talent and the Power of Practice*, "From art to science and from board games to tennis, it has been found that a minimum of ten years is required to reach world-class status in any complex task."[3]

Sayed found this same phenomenon to be true in his own life. A former British No. 1 table tennis player, Sayed had taken up the game at age eight, played endlessly with an older brother who won three national titles before retiring due to injury and had access to a facility where he could play 24 hours a day.[4] By age 18, Sayed had gained his ten years and ten thousand hours of practice. I'm confident that by the same age, Chaim Arlosoroff had done the same. And by then, he was competing successfully against some of the world's best tennis players as a member of the Israeli Davis Cup team.

Diversity is another important factor for developing scholar-athletes who become great teammates and high-achieving adults. We got players from all over the map, even others like Chaim from abroad. Their diversity kept us from engaging in group think, helped us understand and accept different perspectives and improved our problem solving. Jewish guys like Chaim, Ross and Joe brought a remarkable sense of history, sharp humor and a determination to become scholar athletes. So did Marc Fleur, who came from Vermont and made All-American the same year as Chaim. Marc got his MBA at Duke and became a successful financial planner in Durham. You'll read more about him in Chapter Sixteen.

Once introductions were made, no one cared where a teammate came from or what ethnic or religious affiliation he had. Such differences quickly faded as we melded into a tennis family bent on winning. That family would have been greatly diminished without our Jewish stars: I would include in that group Ruby Porges, an Israeli who played from 1976 to 1979, went to med school and built a large medical practice in Miami.

Despite our success in recruiting Jewish players, I struck out in luring African Americans, mainly because there were so few who played tennis in the seventies and eighties. I almost got John Lucas, a phenom in basketball and tennis at Durham's Hillside High School. Jim Bonk and I had coached him as a middle grader because he was already an extraordinary athlete by then. After making an all-out effort to recruit him, he called with very polite but firm turndown. "Coach," he told me, "I've decided to go to Maryland where I'm going to accomplish four things: first, win a national championship in basketball; second, become an All-American in basketball; third, become an All-American in tennis; and last, become the NBA's number one draft pick." His decision was a huge disappointment, because I knew Lucas would have great success at the collegiate and professional. As it turned out, John achieved the last three goals on his list but not the first, though he came very close to achieving that one as well.

Most of my players came from the South and most formed friendships with their Jewish teammates that have lasted a lifetime. They took them home on holidays and adjusted to each other's quirks in a myriad of ways.

Bloopers, such as small miscues in pronunciation, were prized for the great laughs they gave us. "Grab some tissues as you leave," Russell Gache once told Chaim as they packed for a trip. Hearing "T-shirts" instead of "tissues," Chaim threw several T-shirts into a suitcase. They laughed about that for days.

A good coach nurtures indispensable values for well-rounded growth. He or she teaches that selfless effort for the good of the whole is a prerequisite for winning; that progress and improvement only come through hard and frequent practice. They ingrain good habits and instinctive decision-making in an indispensable way. Players also must learn that losing is never fatal if it leads to improvement; and that competitiveness should focus on maximizing strengths and never on vanquishing a foe.

In all my years of coaching, I never met a coach, player or fan who liked to lose. Everyone wants to win, but not everyone thinks about what it takes to be a winner: the drudgery of conditioning, the boredom of drills and the endless practicing that high-level competition requires. Like it or not, losing teaches us to work harder, to improve strategy and to control emotions. Many people aren't willing to make the effort these lessons teach; hard work is indispensable if excellence is your goal.

I used to keep a large banner on the wall behind my cluttered desk in Card Gym. It featured horn-rimmed glasses with a bloodshot eyeball peering out from each lens. A caption below the eyeballs proclaimed: "Pain is good!" That banner was my warning to the faint of heart that winning does not come easy, that an athlete's journey always involves two types of pain, one harmful and one beneficial. The harmful type causes suffering that can be destructive; the beneficial type tells the athlete that he or she is getting the desired result. The legendary coach Vince Lombardi once said, "Fatigue makes cowards of us all." I stressed to all my players that knowing the difference between good and bad pain is crucial.

High achievers never just happen; they are molded by coaches, by parents and teachers, by fellow players and by entire communities; they understand and fully embrace the value of being a scholar-athlete. I'm proud that every player I coached earned an undergraduate degree and nearly half got advanced degrees. But I didn't do it alone; it takes a cohesive community deeply committed to excellence to accomplish that.

CHAPTER EIGHT

The Passionate Professional

I still remember my deep apprehension and sense of unease one spring morning in 1979 when David Robinson, our Number 3 singles player and one of Duke's all-time great scholar-athletes, faced the toughest choice of his young life: whether to play for an ACC singles championship or take the medical school entrance exam scheduled on the same day.

His dilemma arose just moments after he took a seat in a Duke Biology Building classroom with fifteen others taking the MCAT, or Medical College Admissions Test. David, a good-looking six-footer with a mop of hair growing below his ears, wore shorts and flip-flops, opting for comfort on what promised to be a long and arduous day.

As he fiddled with his pencils, the proctor came over and asked,

"David Robinson, right?"

David nodded yes.

"The tennis player?"

"That's me."

"Read about you in the Morning Herald."

"How so?"

"The Sports Section has a write-up on the raw deal you've gotten in the ACC Tennis Championship."

"You mean my default?"

"Apparently so. Seems that taking the MCAT is going to cost you a chance to win the championship."

David nodded ruefully, then told the proctor: "My coach—Coach LeBar—did everything he could to reschedule the match, but the Clemson coach said no. Claimed his player will be too tired to play late today, even though I'm the one taking an all-day exam."

"Sounds like you really want to play that match."

"Absolutely. I'd been pointing for it all year."

The proctor then advised David that, after reading the story at six a.m., he'd called an official in Iowa in charge of the MCAT exam nationally to request permission to excuse David from the test's second morning session beginning at 11 a.m. That would give him just enough time to get to the tournament in Chapel Hill, play the match and get back to Duke in time for the MCAT afternoon session beginning at 1:45 p.m. With the big boss's approval, the proctor would then permit David to make up the morning session once the MCAT afternoon session ended at 5 p.m.

"In the history of the MCAT," the proctor noted with pride, "this has never been done before. Guess what—I got the head guy out of bed, but he gave me the go-ahead anyway."

Without a second thought, David jumped at the chance to play.

"You're sure?" the proctor asked. "You've got a lot riding on this exam; you know you can't go to med school without it. If you're late for the 1:45 session, I'll have no choice but to disqualify you."

David said, "I understand the risk, but I'll take that chance." As he rose from his desk, he fished about in his pockets. "I've gotta go call Coach LeBar right now and ask him to reschedule the match for 11 a.m.—that's when we were supposed to play all along." Having found both pockets empty, he sheepishly asked, "Can you loan me a quarter to make the call?"

The proctor handed him the coin, and David hurried to a hall pay phone. My wife, Carole, answered and told him I'd just left for Chapel Hill to get the lower round matches started. Once David explained his reprieve, Carole told him she'd pick him up at 10:30 sharp in front the Biology Building at the end of the first MCAT session.

"Can you come a bit early?" David asked. "The first session is mostly physics; I can zip through that fast."

Instead, it turned out to be one of the toughest tests he'd ever taken. He finished at 10:29 and dashed out the door—thirty minutes before match time, forty-five counting the fifteen-minute grace period. He remembered as he ran that a Carolina player had been defaulted the day before for showing up twenty minutes late.

Carole was waiting out-front in her brown Corolla station wagon, but complications were waiting too. First, David had to go to the locker room to change from street clothes into a tennis outfit. At 10:45, or thereabouts, they finally departed for Chapel Hill, but half a mile or so en route, David exclaimed, "My racquets! I forgot my racquets—they're in my dorm room." Carole wheeled the wagon around and drove straight to the Quad near Duke Chapel—as close as she could get to David's dorm. He jumped out, ran to the dorm, up four flights and grabbed three racquets he'd put away the day before, thinking his season was over.

At last they were off to Chapel Hill, eight miles away in light Sunday morning traffic. It was 10:50 a.m., twenty-five minutes before default time, more than enough to get there, or so they thought.

But half a mile from the tennis courts, traffic came to a complete stop. Cars had backed up getting into the Tennis Center. With five minutes left, David jumped out of the car and began running down the median of the highway toward the courts. Reaching the crest of Hinton James Hill, a long, gradual slope leading down to the courts, he saw a thousand or more spectators seated on the hillside. With a minute to spare, he spied Coach LeBar, Clemson Coach Chuck Kriese and Pender Murphy, his opponent, in a huddle at the check-in tent. With default imminent, David waved frantically for their attention and ran straight to the court for the match—the ACC championship for Number 2 singles. Later, David and I had a huge laugh at the look of deflation and surprise on Kriese's face at David's last-minute arrival. Kriese, who could be quite temperamental, was sure he and Pender Murphy had the match already won.

During warm-up, I took David aside and told him he was cutting things way too close. If it turned out to be a long match, he couldn't possibly get back to Duke by 1:45 p.m. His reply was, "If I can't beat this guy in two hours, I'll just quit and go take the MCAT."

"David," I rebutted, "this guy knows about the MCAT; he's going to play slow and drag out every point. Just remember, this match is for one season; the MCAT's for the rest of your life."

But David was adamant: He aimed to take the risk come hell or high water.

Pender Murphy, a formidable opponent by any measure, stood waiting on the other side of the net. He was one of Clemson's best players. By the time his collegiate career would end, he'd be named an All-American four times. The next year, he would win 29 consecutive matches, still the Clemson record. It was a heavyweight match in every respect because David had won 22 of 23 matches his freshman year.

In the early going, the match went David's way. He won the first set handily but lost the second. He ran up a 5–1 lead in the third with the time just past 1 p.m. All David had to do was win one more game to become champion. Then, he could get back to Duke to finish his MCAT exam with plenty of time to spare. But suddenly, complications set in. Murphy held serve to make it 5–2 and then broke David's serve to make it 5–3. I knew David was struggling to stay calm, but Murphy held serve and the match stood at 5–4. It was 1:20 and David faced a stark dilemma: either hold serve and win the match, or lose and have it tied 5–5. Then, he'd have to quit with barely enough time to get back to Duke by 1:45. Glancing at the top of Hinton James Hill, David could see Carole's brown Corolla wagon waiting.

At that point, the points all became a blur. I kept muttering to myself, *first serve David, first server, you've got to get your first serve in.* Somehow he did that: he held serve and closed out the match to win at 6–4. By then, he barely had time to shake Murphy's hand. He dropped his racquets and gear in a heap and ran to the gate where a swarm of reporters and cameramen waited.

"Sorry guys," David told them, flashing a broad grin: "Can't talk now. I've got an exam to take in just twenty minutes."

As he dashed out the gate, I handed him a brown paper bag with two cheeseburgers and a can of Coke. He sprinted up the hill to Carole's car. On the way back, David polished off the cheeseburgers, then took off his sneakers and socks. His feet were sore from the long match; going barefoot felt good. Carole got him back to the Biology Building without a moment to spare; and he walked into the classroom barefoot, shoes and socks in hand.

As he took his seat, the proctor asked expectantly, "Well . . . how'd the match turn out?"

"I won!" David exclaimed.

Coach LeBar and David Robinson in 1979

The proctor and David's fellow test-takers rose *en mass* to give him a standing ovation. The proctor later surmised that it had to be the only standing ovation in MCAT history.

Years later, David told me: "I've never forgotten what you did: how you released me emotionally to take that exam and not to feel that I was letting you or the team down."

I couldn't begin to explain how the turmoil of that decision churned in my gut. I must have mumbled, "It's never about the coach; it's always about the player."

"You said the MCAT was for the rest of my life," David reminded.

"Yes. Around here, the stakes don't get any higher than that," I replied.

"I'm never going to forget that. Not many coaches would have done what you did."

He had no idea what I'd said to myself, over and over, as the match teetered back and forth: *For Christ's sake David, forfeit the damn match, get your butt back to Durham and take your MCAT exam.*

It was 7 p.m. when he finished taking it. Before leaving the exam room, he thanked the proctor with great appreciation for his gutsy, early morning call to the big boss of MCAT. The sun was fading as David walked barefoot back across the quad to his dorm. Later he told me how good it felt to wiggle his toes in the grass, to know he had won the ACC championship and was on his way to med school. He was certain he'd done well on the exam—that the career he'd always dreamed of was his to grasp. His confidence soared in the fullness of youth, and the future sprawled before him like a million summer suns.

David Robinson went on to become a prominent eye surgeon, one of the best in the country and one of the most passionate professionals I've ever known. There was nothing superficial about his passion because it led to a future few could have predicted, and the mastery of challenging, sometimes ornery details that had to be handled correctly. Becoming an eye surgeon had been his goal—a burning ambition, actually—since his first year in high school. When I recruited him to play tennis for Duke, he and his dad drove to Durham after visiting the University of Virginia in Charlottesville and arrived at Duke almost certain that he'd go to UVA. I badly wanted him to sign with us because he was the 30th-ranked player in the nation. Despite his strong leanings toward UVA, fate intervened in a way I could never have planned.

During our tour of the campus, David asked me what I knew about the Duke Eye Center. In nearly a decade, I'd never gotten a question like that from a prospective player. I told him: "As a matter of fact, I've got a tennis buddy over there, Art Chandler, who's on the faculty."

"Could we to drive by and see the place?"

"We can do better than that," I enthused. "I'll call Art and see if he can arrange a tour."

As luck would have it, Art gave David the cook's tour himself and even arranged for him to burn his name on a piece of paper through a microscopic laser used in eye surgery.

Suffice it to say when David left Durham, he was 100 percent certain that he'd take my full scholarship offer and come to Duke. He would spend 11 of the next 12 years in Durham: four as an undergrad, four in med school and three in a residency in ophthalmology at the Duke Eye Center. Between med school and his residency, he interned for a year in general medicine and surgery at the University of Hawaii. He was an A student as an undergraduate and near the top of his class in med school.

In the spring of his senior year, David ran into an eye-catching classmate, Roberta Fuccella, at an off-campus party. They eventually ended up at a fraternity party where a friend was spinning perfect tunes to dance by. By the time the crowd started drifting away, David and Roberta were in a trance and not about to let go. Their friend kept spinning and so did the room. The wee hours melded into dawn—just the two of them, dancing all alone on a beer-soaked frat house dance floor.

"We knew that night that we were meant for each other," Roberta recalls. "David was such a good dancer—I mean a *really* good dancer. All that athleticism, I suppose. It was a moment we never forgot."

Both earned degrees that spring at commencement: Roberta got a B.S. in nursing and David got a B.A. in comparative religions. The following year at Christmas, they got married in Roberta's hometown, Doylestown, Pennsylvania. While David was in med school, Roberta worked as a nurse. They have two daughters, Jessica, or "Jess," and Julie, both of whom were outstanding scholar-athletes coached early on, naturally, by their father. Jess co-captained Duke's 2009 national championship tennis team. She and her husband, Alan, live only 10 minutes away from David and Roberta. Julie won the Delaware State Junior Golf Championships at ages 13 and 15 and later played for Brown University. She lives in New York City.

When I visited David and Roberta in their Rehoboth Beach home in October 2016, we sat in the living room, just off a deck with a stunning view of the Atlantic Ocean. I was struck by how young they looked 30 years after leaving Duke. Roberta wore a cream-colored turtleneck. Her spice brown hair fell just below her shoulders. She had the same wide deep-dimpled smile I remembered from their undergrad days. David wore blue jeans and a Duke blue shirt with collar buttons. He had an arm draped around Roberta's shoulders as we talked. His short mocha-colored hair was brushed straight back—nothing like his shaggy look in MCAT days. His hairline may have receded a bit but that merely accentuated his high forehead—what I took as one of many signs of his intelligence.

In effect, the two of them had tossed a dart at the map in deciding on life after Duke. Their relocation criteria had been vague at best: find a nice community near the coast that needed an eye surgeon—that was it. Lady Luck had guided their dart to the Delaware coast. As David puts it today: "What we didn't realize was that it was a resort community that was turning into a retirement destination—one of the leading retirement centers for people from the surrounding states of Maryland, New Jersey, Pennsylvania and even Northern Virginia. They all came to Delaware to retire. And it just so happens that my specialty, ophthalmology, is very often needed the most when people get to an age where they develop cataracts."

In choosing Lewes, Delaware, David and Roberta started out in a quaint beach town equidistant (about 115 miles) from Baltimore, Philadelphia and Washington, DC. He joined the staff of Beebe Hospital, founded in 1916, where emergency surgeries were first performed on a kitchen table. David knew right away that they'd landed in clover—that the demand for his specialty bordered on unlimited. His vision became to build one of the largest eye centers in the country.

He started out in a 2,000 square foot office and began operating at Beebe Hospital where he first met Joyce Hargraves, the nurse who would end up at his side in the operating room for the next 30 years. She could anticipate his needs for assistance and instruments so well they eventually could operate in complete silence. Soon after he opened the practice, David was seeing 60 to 70 patients a day and was booked six months in advance. After 15 years of operating at Beebe Hospital, David decided to build a freestanding outpatient eye surgery center and asked Joyce to join him as head nurse. When I visited in 2016, he had just given up surgery the year before after having performed 20,000 operations overall. Joyce had been at his side all that time and was still working with him.

David has a gift not often found in physicians—what I'd call a helluva head for business, for building an enterprise that will last long after he's gone, I'm sure. That gift didn't come from Duke; he was born with it—and with the good sense to know Lady Luck had smiled on his decision to practice on the Delaware Coast. He seized that opportunity and ran with it hard. Today, the Delaware Eye Institute he founded has 12 physicians and 100 employees; each year it sees about 40,000 patients for routine and comprehensive eye care and performs over 5,000 surgical procedures. It occupies ten times the space David's first office did with its own 28,500 square foot building facing a main highway in Rehoboth Beach. David planned and oversaw all aspects of construction when it was built in 2001 and three new wings since then. The practice also has eye centers in Dover and Millsboro.

His strategy all along was to offer patients all the subspecialists that, for years, weren't available on the Delaware coast. "You can only do that in one way," he told me. "You have to allow those subspecialists to be as successful as you were." His dream had been to build a Duke Eye Center North; and while he couldn't possibly replicate Duke's research capabilities, he could—and did—replicate most of the same clinical capabilities. To do that he had to attract and keep the best possible talent. The continuity reflected in the tenure of his scrub nurse was reflected throughout the organization: people loved its beach location, loved the work environment and especially loved David's "share the wealth" philosophy.

"We've got a handful of employees who've been with us 20 or 25 years and lots who've been here 10 or 15 years," David says. "It's really the strength of the organization. If you treat people the way you want to be treated, it works really well. Working together as a team was the only way to achieve our dream of the Delaware Eye Institute for the community. Finding dedicated doctors and staff has made all the difference."

In 2007, an Ethiopian woman named Tali, who worked at Whole Foods in Durham, asked my wife, Carole, to help bring her brother, an attorney in Addis Ababa, to the United States for an operation to cure his blindness. Carole has a big heart, so she agreed to make a few inquiries. The operation would have to be performed pro bono, which complicated the request a lot. Carole first approached the Duke Eye Center and got turned down cold; they wanted $15,000 to perform the operation. Her entreaties to several private practices fell on deaf ears.

Then one night she bolted upright in bed and blurted: "David Robinson! Why didn't I think of him sooner?" First thing next morning, she called David, who agreed to talk to Tali. She told him her brother, Fikreyohanas—Fik for short—had been blind in his right eye at birth and had gotten a puncture wound with a stick that left him blind in his left eye at age six or seven. Coming from a family of some means, he'd had two surgeries in Ethiopia—both unsuccessful—to repair the damaged eye. Because braille was not readily available, Fik's education had come through "readers"—companions who read his written assignments to him aloud all through secondary school, high school, college and law school. He'd done remarkably well—enough so to become a practicing lawyer.

By coincidence, Carole told David that Fik lived in Addis Ababa, just as he read about a clinic being opened there by the American Cataract Refractive Surgery Society (ACRSS). Through ACRSS, David arranged for Fik to be examined by a visiting doctor using a slit-lamp, a type of microscope that provides a 3-D image of the eye. Unfortunately, the only bulb for the slit-lamp burned out midway through the exam, but the physician told David, "There is potential." His brief look wasn't enough to tell whether the left retina was healthy, but he had discovered that an artificial lens implanted in that eye years earlier during one of Fik's surgeries had been removed. That worried David, but he still gave Tali, through Carole, the go-ahead to bring her brother over. David had to write a letter to the State Department confirming that all medical expenses would be covered by the Delaware Eye Institute. It was peak summer, so he told Tali to delay until after Labor Day when accommodations wouldn't be so expensive. Somehow, that recommendation got overlooked: Tali, her husband, their two children and her brother, Fik, arrived in Rehoboth Beach the very next week.

David asked one of his retinal specialists to come in on Sunday to examine Fik. After looking in the back of his left eye, the specialist told David the entire retina was scarred. That meant putting an implant in wouldn't help at all. David's first thought when he heard that was: *Geez, this guy and his family came halfway around the world and here we are on Sunday telling them, 'Sorry, there's nothing we can do.'*

Fik and Tali were distraught, but David wasn't ready to give up hope. Fik's right eye *did* look healthy but that didn't mean much: In general, no matter how normal it might look, a patient blind in an eye since birth has little or no chance to see with it. That said, it was still unclear what was wrong with Fik's right eye. When David checked it with a light, the pupil still worked, which made him wonder even more why Fik couldn't see anything at all. David thought his optic nerve might have atrophied; if so, that would keep it from sending images to the brain, but it could also cause glaucoma or another eye disease. The eye was too normal, which made it highly unusual to David.

At that point, he sent Fik and Tali back to their hotel, telling them: "Don't lose heart. I'll take another look in the morning. We aren't out of options yet." That night, David kept thinking how Fik's right pupil had responded to light. He recalled Fik telling him he'd gotten very thick glasses before the puncture wound and might have seen some light with his right eye. But with the glasses on, he saw nothing with his good eye. *That's it—he's nearsighted!* David told himself in a eureka moment. *This guy may be more nearsighted than anybody I've ever seen.* A person who is extremely nearsighted might be able to read large lettering on a card at the end of their nose or thereabouts. But when David held a card near Fik's nose, he could read nothing. David held the card marginally closer—still nothing. Then, he put the card on Fik's brow and shined a penlight beneath it. Suddenly, Fik could read a few letters on the reading card. David told himself *Oh my God, we've got an eye that's in focus just millimeters—not inches or feet—from the cornea* (the outermost lens of the eye and the window that controls and focuses the entry of light). It was so myopic David's equipment couldn't read the extent of Fik's myopia. At that point, by trial and error, he put multiple sets of lenses on top of each other and tried different combinations of them on Fik. He then read a few letters. Finally, David had a definitive answer: Fik was minus 28 myopia, a condition he had never seen before.

But there was no easy solution to giving Fik the miracle of reading, driving or going to the movies. Glasses were out of the question—the lenses would be thicker than coke bottles. Contact lenses for someone living in Ethiopia weren't an option either. Fik didn't have a cataract in his right eye, but David could perform an artificial lens implant with the correct power to bring the eye into focus. He decided to do that, but when he ran the calculations, David found that the power of the lens would have to be minus eight diopters. Did the supplier even make minus implants, he wondered? When he called, he was told, "Yes, we make them, but they are rarely used. We have some available."

"Okay," he replied, "but do me a favor and overnight the order." That was Monday; the new lens arrived as promised on Wednesday.

"I had no idea what I was in for in performing that lensectomy," David told me. "Obviously, it was an unusual eye with much thinner tissue. If I encountered a retinal detachment, that could cause all sorts of complications." The operation required a small incision much like a cataract procedure and took about 45 minutes to perform. David was elated that nothing went wrong. Once the operation was over, he put a patch over Fik's eye and sent him back to the hotel with instructions to come back at 10 the next morning.

By the time Fik and Tali came back on Thursday, word of the operation had spread to every nook and cranny of the Delaware Eye Institute. The entire staff knew what was at stake when the patch came off: If Fik could read the letters on the eye chart, Dr. Robinson had done something miraculous; if he couldn't, the operation was a bust.

When the patient and his sister and her entire family arrived at the reception area with great excitement and hope on Wednesday and were escorted to an exam room, a crowd was already waiting. Nurses, technicians and doctors were jammed like sardines into the tiny space. After Fik took his seat, a few moments passed before David came in.

"My word," he chuckled. "I could have charged admission for this." That drew nervous laughs, but no one spoke or moved as David reached for Fik's eye patch. "Well, let's see what we have," he said, swabbing and cleaning the eye area. Then, pointing to an eye chart on the far wall some eight feet away, he asked Fik, "Can you read those letters?"

"F . . . Z . . . B . . . D . . . 4": Fik could read the fourth line from the bottom of the chart—good enough to pass a U.S. driver's license exam. His face bore a look of shock, but he grasped David's hand and asked: "How can I ever thank you?" Then Tali threw her arms around Fik's neck and held him in a long embrace. Next she rushed to give David a hug. Pent-up emotions were impossible to contain; tears streamed down nearly every face in the exam room as family and staff hugged in celebrating that moment of joy.

It was a life-changing moment for Fik *and* for David too. It opened his eyes to the heart-rending need for eye care in places like Ethiopia, a country of 80 million with only 80 ophthalmologists. He got back in touch with ACRSS and volunteered to help at the clinic in Addis Ababa. The next year, he went there at his own expense to perform surgery to help train doctors for ten days. He took $100,000 worth of donated equipment with him but got a rude awakening to callow Third World bureaucracy when he tried to bring the equipment into the country. It was stopped cold on the shipping docks because government officials had to be bribed at roughly 100 percent of the value of the equipment to allow it to come in.

He was shocked that so many Ethiopians had nothing—"Dirt floors, no running water, cooking over an open flame. But they were the happiest people I'd ever seen. I worked all week without an anesthesiologist. The guy helping me just told patients to hold still while I put a needle behind an eye to numb them up. The whole week I heard nothing—not a complaint, not a moan, not a groan. Then, examining my very first patient coming back stateside, a middle-aged woman, recoiled and said, 'Oh my God, that's killing me' when I simply shined a light to look in her eye. I excused myself and walked out of the exam room to calm myself before saying something I'd regret. I took a deep breath and told myself I was home again and went back inside and told the patient as pleasantly as I could, 'Okay, let's try that again.'"

David continued his involvement with the clinic in Addis Ababa for several years, raising funds and urging physicians to lend their services. In that time, the clinic tripled in size and saw thousands of patients in one of the poorest neighborhoods in Addis Ababa. While he helped spearhead that growth, he is quick to dismiss his work in there as "a very small part in the overall success."

And yet he has done much the same thing elsewhere. In Guatemala, he was part of a team that rode three to four hours by bus into the hills to a small convent to perform surgeries ten hours a day for six days. They took many tons of free supplies but had to wait for hours at the airport while someone figured out who had to be bribed to get the cargo in country. No one told him beforehand that men armed with machine guns riding in jeeps would ride in front and behind the bus en route to the convent and back to the airport.

Each morning when the doors to the convent's surgical waiting room opened, David and his colleagues looked out on an endless sea of faces. "We knew if we didn't do as many as we could, they were going to be blind for another year," he told me. "Sadly, in a place like that, blindness takes the lives of two people because the blind person has to have a caretaker. So, the operation frees up two people to be productive." Most of the operations he performed there were for advanced cataracts, which had rendered the patient totally blind. David also has done pro bono work in Panama, where he performed surgeries to train 40 to 50 ophthalmologists on new technology and procedures.

David Robinson's life provides an authentic template for the career path of a scholar-athlete. Passion and drive have always been at the heart of his success. His decision to take the MCAT exam and play for an ACC championship on the same day epitomizes what a scholar-athlete is all about. I doubted that he could do both—even feared that it would ruin his career prospects—but he never doubted he could. I hope I'm not indulging overweening pride when I say one of the best decisions he ever made was coming to Duke. He took advantage of everything an outstanding school can offer—academically, athletically and socially. And I would never undervalue the latter because he and Roberta met at Duke. Their values meshed and were a major factor in how they built a happy and highly productive life together.

I've asked myself more than once: What would have happened had my friend at the Duke Eye Center not invited David to sign his name with that laser? We might have lost him to a worthy rival, the University of Virginia. It seems especially important for me to make that clear because many wonderful American colleges and universities graduate outstanding scholar-athletes year after year. We just need more of them—as many as we can get.

CHAPTER NINE

The Gold Standard of Courage

Nancy Hogshead-Makar was born to swim. As a child in Jacksonville, Florida, she knew she wanted to be the world's best swimmer and set out in relentless pursuit of that goal. By age 12, she was breaking national age group records and at 14 was No. 1-ranked in the world in the 200-meter butterfly. In high school, she won three national butterfly championships and left home toward the end of her sophomore year to train for the 1980 Olympics with the University of Florida swim team. That experience helped her qualify for the U.S. team and become an odds-on favorite to win a fistful of medals at the Moscow games. But her prospects vanished overnight when the U.S. government decided to boycott the 1980 Olympics because of the Russian invasion of Afghanistan. She was so disgusted with that outcome that she didn't even watch the games on television. As she explained to me in 2019: "I was brainwashed into believing my swimming would help my country avoid World War Three."[1]

Nancy went to Duke that fall on the school's first swimming scholarship and left no doubt that she deserved it, setting school records in eight different events and going undefeated in dual meets. She also became that year's ACC Champion and an All-American.

As an undergraduate, she had striking good looks: blonde, shoulder-length hair parted just right of center and J-shaped curls framing a heart-shaped face that tapered toward a very firm chin. When relaxed, she seemed quite feminine, not muscular at all. But when she dove into the pool for a 100-yard freestyle, taut muscles rippled across her entire frame to form a capital "L" turned 45 degrees to the right: her head, arms and hands pointing perfectly down and her feet, legs and torso yardstick straight.

She faced much tougher competition the summer after her freshman year at the U.S. Nationals, coming in second in the 200-meter butterfly. "I really thought that it wouldn't bother me to not win . . . [but] it just ate me up inside," she told *Deadspin,* an ESPN website, in an interview when she turned 50.[2]

Unfortunately, a year of nonstop swimming, following a year in which she barely went to high school, had cost her academically: Nancy's first-semester grade point average at Duke was a disappointing 2.3. But after that, her GPA never fell below 3.0, and she excelled in her major, political science. She'd gotten off to a promising start her sophomore year when calamity struck.

Just before Thanksgiving break in 1981, on a routine run between Duke's East and West Campus, she noticed a guy running slowly toward her. Suddenly—"I had every bell going off in my head, but I told myself to be quiet. And I started running in the street. My bells were going off. And he grabbed me and pulled me. There were like three giant evergreen trees where the branches went down low, and we fought inside of those for probably, I'm guessing, 40 minutes. You know, wrestling and battling. And I lost. And he didn't even have a weapon. And I was strong. Trust me. At the time, I was in great shape. And I lost . . . I was very lucky that he let me live."[3]

During that desperate struggle, she remembered something she'd read in *Seventeen Magazine* long before: "Try to make him see you as a person!" Fighting frantically to forestall panic, she described how much her mother loved her. Then came, "I'm pregnant" . . . and after that, "I've got VD."[4] But nothing she said gave pause to her attacker. In the dark and cold, her clothes ripped, she began to shiver. Her assailant warned that he'd kill her if she kept shaking, so she forced herself to stop. But soon she felt her body temperature begin to fall.

Then came a terrible fear that she might pass out. On occasion, that had happened after swim meets—a feeling of blackness closing into a tiny vortex. An inner voice warned: *Don't you dare pass out, because you are totally gone if you pass out.* But the sensation would not go away. *This is it,* she told herself: *You have done everything. You don't have any more tricks up your sleeve here.* She began to cry.

At that instant, a dramatic change seemed to come over her attacker. He became quiet and listened. She noticed and began to cry harder.

"You know, I really respect you," he rasped at last.

Respect—riiight. Just don't do this to anybody else.

His reply—"I won't"—sounded sincere and slightly apologetic, though she found it impossible to believe.

Then, as suddenly as he'd attacked, he was gone. The rape lasted over two hours, but not two minutes had elapsed since she began to cry.

If only I'd cried sooner, she thought in the cold and the dark.

Touching her face, she felt one eye closed and lips so swollen she could hardly close her mouth.

Before heading into the police station, an inner voice scolded: *Don't let anyone see you cry. They won't believe you if you're hysterical. You've got to make the police believe you.*

But the police, the doctors and nurses at the hospital couldn't have been more sympathetic. So was Duke University.

But there was one decision she wanted to take back. It was a conversation she had with herself in the hospital: "This was a horrible night, but you're not going to let it affect you. You're going to continue a great life." Much later, those words would come to haunt her. She would feel they prevented her from grieving, from healing, from being human.

It seemed that friends, even people she barely knew, were reaching out with open arms to embrace her. But she was guarded, even backed away, mainly because she didn't want them to see just how damaged she felt inside. It was hard to accept and internalize what had happened: *Are you kidding me? A victim? Give me a break. That's just not who I am.* And yet, her emotions were very victim-like. In retrospect, she would come to see how misplaced that decision was: It had delayed her healing by many years.

Her Duke swimming coach insisted that she redshirt (sit out for a year) and predicted she'd still be a big winner at the 1984 Olympics. "When he said that, I thought he was off his rocker," Nancy recalls. "I thought I was quitting for good." But her coach knew if she sat out for a while, she'd regain her will to win.

While its manifestations already had appeared, Nancy had no idea at the time that she was deep in the grips of post-traumatic stress disorder (PTSD). One sign was that her extraordinary ability to focus and concentrate was deeply impaired. Shortly after the rape, her studied attempts at a cool façade crumbled. She found herself obsessively checking to make sure her outside doors were locked. She often felt that danger lurked just around the corner. Then she had two accidents in two weeks (her first ever). After one, she'd left the scene and went to the airport without packing. It didn't help that, despite an all-out search by the Durham police, her attacker was never found.

At 19 years of age, Nancy's world had been shattered. "I felt forsaken. I felt unloved and unlovable. I knew my thoughts and feelings were not normal, but I couldn't stop them with the force of my personality. I didn't know how to heal, or even if healing was possible. I didn't see great women thriving who admitted to having been raped."[5]

How she recovered and went on to become a superstar and to lead such a high-impact life is truly astonishing. In all my years of coaching, I never encountered a more inspiring comeback or a scholar-athlete who proved more courageously to have the heart of a great champion.

For me, no sport would be easier to quit than swimming. The thought of getting up in the dark at 4:45 a.m., entering a cold pool and swimming four hours or more a day and as many as 800 laps would do me in. No wonder Nancy told herself to quit during the worst of her despondency. When she returned to Duke for her junior year, her coach, Bob Thompson, offered to continue her scholarship if she just participated in team swim meets. No, he assured her, she didn't have to come to practice, didn't have to lift weights, didn't have to swim laps, didn't have to do anything other than show up, swim her events and cheer for her Duke teammates.

That was a wise offer, but Thompson sensed that she couldn't just sit and watch—or compete at less than her best either. At the first swim meet, she was so out of shape she could hardly warm up. But she won—which made her think she'd just attend enough practices to warm up properly. At the next meet, she didn't just win, she swam to top 10 in the country. She progressed from there to twice-a-day practices and lifting weights; after that, her old hunger for competition returned quickly.

After getting back in the water, she began to experience something shocking: She imagined herself battling her rapist to a different outcome, one in which she overpowered him and won. Using a machete, she chopped him to pieces, relished being strong and got stronger every day. As she vented and released her rage for her assailant, her times began to improve. That thrilled her, and she told herself: *Oh, God, I can actually use this.*

Before long she had posted the third fastest time in the country. It psyched her up to know she could swim that fast having trained for such a short time. With her competitive fires stoked, it left no doubt that she had to compete for a spot on the '84 U.S. Olympic Team.

When she went home that Thanksgiving, she told her parents she wanted to drop out of Duke at the spring semester to train full-time for the Olympics. Her father, an orthopedic surgeon and founder of Jacksonville Orthopedic Institute, was incredulous: "You want drop out of college, not work and take a year and a half to train for one swim meet?"

"That's exactly what I want to do."[6]

Her mother didn't like the idea either; she felt strongly it was high time for Nancy to move beyond swimming and begin preparing for the next chapter of her life. But even though they disagreed with her choice, her parents relented and agreed to help financially for her to pursue her Olympic dreams.

In January 1983, Nancy took a leave of absence from Duke and devoted herself to training. Her stamina was discouraging at first, but she regained it quickly. Her emotions were still raw, but swimming was giving her the feeling that she was regaining control of her life. "I was really proud of what I was doing. Even though I was just swimming back and forth in a pool, I was living with dignity. Being strong, feeling gifted, taking control of the course of my life all contributed to healing."

She came in second in the '83 Nationals and won the Comeback Swimmer of the Year. Award. But the biggest reward for all her hard work and dedication came the next year at the Olympic trials in the 100-meter freestyle event. At the halfway mark, she was convinced that she wasn't doing well at all. Closing with a furious rush, she touched the wall having no idea where she'd placed. She recalls turning around—"and there was a one after my name. Somebody took a picture. . . . It was the biggest smile I think I have ever had in my entire life. It's just joy rising."

Nancy's greatest triumph came in the 1984 Summer Olympics in Los Angeles at the McDonald's Olympic Swim Stadium at the University of Southern California. Built for the 1984 games, the cavernous outdoor venue seated 2,500 spectators. The games occurred amid international tensions caused by a Soviet Union and East German boycott retaliating for the U.S. withdrawal, four years earlier, from the Moscow games.

Nancy was one of just three competitors to win four gold medals. Her medals included the gold for the 100-meter freestyle, the 4 x 100-meter freestyle relay and the 4 x 100-meter medley relay; she also won a silver for the 200-meter individual medley. She missed winning a bronze, fifth medal by a microscopic 7/100th of a second. Her spectacular performance earned her recognition as the most decorated swimmer at the '84 games.

But something shocking had occurred as she raced for all those medals: Nancy had suffered a bronchial spasm caused by asthma. Her first reaction to the diagnosis was, "Impossible!" But the diagnosis made sense: she'd always struggled to breathe in cold or dry air. Capitalizing on her Olympic fame, she soon launched a public campaign on managing asthma. At one point, a leading drug manufacturer, GlaxoSmithKline, was sponsoring many of her hundred or more per year public appearances. In 1990, her first book, *Asthma and Exercise,* was published by Henry Holt and Company. It examined the condition's impact on health and sports, featuring stories of great athletes who had asthma.

After the '84 games, Nancy had returned to Duke, where she graduated with honors. Next came a degree in 1997 from the Georgetown University Law Center, followed by an invitation to join Holland and Knight, a large international law firm in her hometown. She then taught law for 12 years at Florida Coastal School of Law in Jacksonville, where she became a tenured professor teaching torts, sports law and a course on "Gender Equity in Athletics."

A passion for advocacy has marked her entire professional life. Building a successful law practice and teaching law set the stage for Nancy to become a national authority and leading advocate on Title IX, gender equity and sexual abuse. Sterling contacts in the Olympic Movement and from many years of competitive swimming contributed much to her stature. A good example was her 30-year history with the Women's Sports

Foundation: She started there in 1985 as an intern and by 1992 had become its fourth president. Another was being inducted into eleven halls of fame, including the International Women's Sports Hall of Fame. Other honors included the 2011 "Courage Award" of the National Organization for Women, and being named by ESPN in 2012 one of 40 women who'd changed how sports are played. She'd been asked to serve on the editorial board of the *Journal of Collegiate Sport* in 2009 and, in 2011, she joined the board of the prestigious Aspen Institute and still serves in that position. Her standing as a national authority on gender equity and other issues has made Nancy a frequent guest on CNN, ESPN, MSNBC, Fox and network news. The camera couldn't seem to get enough of her because she'd kept a youthful look and was always prepared for concise and clear discussion.

In 2009, during the worst economic downturn since the Great Depression, the Florida state legislature made drastic cuts to high school athletic programs, but the cuts were not evenly applied: Programs for girl's were cut 100 percent, while boy's football was untouched. Nancy moved swiftly to form a coalition that filed suit and won 100 percent restoration of funding for girl's athletic programs.

Another major legislative victory came during the administration of President George W. Bush. In 2002, the President assembled a task force, which attempted to weaken Title IX legislation passed by Congress in 1972 that opened doors for millions of girls and women to play school-sponsored sports. Nancy was part of a team that helped organize and lead a coalition of sports and civil rights organizations to block proposed changes to weaken the law and thereby greatly diminish opportunities for girls and women. The coalition generated enough grassroots pressure to convince the Bush Administration to back off; the landmark legislative framework of Title IX has remained intact to this day. In such legislative battles, Nancy testified often before various House and Senate committees and built strong Capitol Hill allies who were willing to stand up for gender equity and women's sports.

Seven years before the Harvey Weinstein case, Nancy began pushing to end widespread sexual abuse in club sports and the Olympic movement. While public schools have insurance and other protections for kids who get abused, sports clubs don't, nor do participants in Olympic events. After years of pushing, Nancy helped convince the U.S. Olympic Committee to establish the U.S. Center for SafeSport, which finally opened in

Nancy Hogshead-Makar in 2017.
Courtesy of Wikimedia Commons.

2017. Nancy served as an expert witness at the trial of Larry Nassar who was convicted in 2018 of molesting young girls—many of them Olympians—while serving as a medical doctor at Michigan State University.

Champion Women, a non-profit Nancy organized in 2014, gathered sports leaders, elite players and coaches, as well as organizations protecting against sexual abuse and assault, to pass federal legislation forcing the Olympic Movement to protect children and athletes from physical, emotional and sexual abuse. The law was signed on February 13, 2018.[7]

Her demanding schedule notwithstanding, Nancy still has found time for an active family life. Her husband, Scott, is an appellate judge. They have twin daughters, Helen-Clare and Millicent, and a son, Aaron, who became a Duke freshman in the fall of 2019.

I could go on about Nancy's glittering accomplishments. Instead, I want to focus on her most admirable character trait: the sheer courage she has displayed on so many occasions from that terrible ordeal in 1981 under the evergreen limbs near the Duke campus, to her greatest victories, years later, in the courts and in the public square. It would be a mistake to attribute her courage, mainly, to moments of great crisis in which she exerted the will to prevail. Most of all, I believe, her courage is derived from hard work—the sheer effort required to get up day after day at 4:45 a.m. knowing a cold pool is waiting, in pressing onward, day in and day out, when muscles are sore and bones ache, in finding the will to go on when no one would know if she didn't.

Her courage also comes from a huge and caring heart. She often speaks about her 1981 attack to audiences of young girl, who are mesmerized by her candor and courage. Having suffered great pain has given her empathy, I suspect, that victims of abuse sense on a deep level and are comfortably drawn to. And finally, her courage comes from the intellectual prowess and firepower to shape an epic and just cause—a rare attribute, indeed, but one that is much more than a gift, one that only comes about through hard work and deep caring.

Nancy's thoughtfulness has never been more evident than in the highly conflicted debate about reforming our deeply flawed athletic system. Years ago, the late William C. Friday, a former President of the University of North Carolina and a co-founder of the Knight Commission on Intercollegiate Athletics, remarked: "We are trying to superimpose an entertainment industry on top of an academic structure, and it won't work. It never has worked. What you are seeing on the college scene right now is the consequence of not controlling that very enterprise."

¤ ¤ ¤

Each year "brings more scandals and more incidents calling into question the compatibility of universities and a gargantuan entertainment industry."[8] To that she has added that our collegiate sports have reached "a tipping point" in which they will either return "to the soul of higher education . . . [or] become more professional." As she noted in 2011, 80 percent of big-time football programs had a net operating loss of nearly $10 million. "That's money coming from academics to athletics, not the other way around."

She set forth her reform agenda in an article in the influential *Chronicle of Higher Education* in 2011. She was one of the first to call on Congress to pass a narrow antitrust exemption that would help preserve amateurism by containing program costs and enabling more colleges and universities to share in television revenues. That view was informed by one of her heroes, Supreme Court Justice Byron White's prescient 1984 dissent in *NCAA v. Oklahoma Board of Regents* predicting that the majority opinion would lead to the commercialization and professionalism of college sports on a vast scale—which it has. (Note: White's opinion is discussed in Chapter Two.) In that same article, Nancy also urged that the NCAA stop distributing television revenues based on won-lost records and use educational values instead. The values she advocated include higher graduation rates, improved academic performance, diversity of all kinds and gender equity.

"I swam during the era of true 'amateurism' in the Olympics," she says, "and I cannot imagine training harder if a first-string NFL contract had been waiting for me at the finish line. But linking winning to economic viability is the surest pathway to its overemphasis." She has aptly summarized the meaning of her own life: "I am altered by the Olympic experience not because I stood on a victory platform, but because I went for it without holding anything in reserve. There was no 'What if?' because I knew I had gone through the struggle and had done everything I could do.

"Throughout this journey of years of workouts and competitions, there were moments of true mastery, of bliss, of a oneness with myself and the world. All the splashing and chaos of workout life were muted and my soul was very still. Truly effortless. During these times, it felt like my soul hovered about two feet above my body and it condensed into a sliver, a needle. These were my shared moments with God."

That powerful thought should make us mindful of First Corinthians 13:12: "For now, we see through a glass, darkly; but then face to face: now I know in part; but then shall I know even as also I am known."

CHAPTER TEN

Miracles in Guatemala

I've never known anyone with a greater commitment to the disarmingly simple creed *actions speak louder than words* than Clinton B. Davis II—"Chip" to teammates and friends—who played for me between 1974 and 1977 and went on to become a prominent orthopedic surgeon in the Tampa-St. Petersburg area. One of the first to perform life-saving surgeries in poverty-stricken Guatemala, Chip has performed pro bono operations there for the past 22 years. Such accomplishments are norms in the high-impact lives of scholar-athletes. Chip exemplifies the indispensable character trait of empathy more than any scholar-athlete I coached.

There was nothing subtle at all in Chip's game: An imposing six-foot three-inches tall, he had a cannonball serve that could unnerve opponents. His volley was flawed, but he got away with that because his serve produced weak returns he could "kill" with his second-best shot—a powerful forehand. That arsenal had been honed in his own backyard on a tennis court his Dad, Cecil, had put in when Chip was 12. It quickly became a mecca for Orlando prodigies: At one point, four nationally-ranked phenoms practiced and played there almost daily.

Cecil was a large and imposing man, stern and tough. He

and Chip's Mom, Helen, had a traditional marriage, but Helen was not unwilling to put a foot down when Cecil became overbearing. His parents imbued Chip from an early age with the "show me" principle he would come to live by. Cecil, himself, was a natural athlete—good enough to play tailback on offense and linebacker on defense at the University of Georgia, where teammates called him "Goose" because of his long, arching neck. As a troubled youth, Cecil got sent to military school for a strong dose of discipline. It strongly influenced how he raised Chip and his three siblings: Life plans were mapped for each. Chip's was to make good grades, parlay his tennis skills into a scholarship at a good school and become a doctor. It worked out that way, in part, because Cecil knew how to read aptitude and wasn't shy about enforcing his mandates. He was dead serious about his plans, knowing his income as a realtor would not be enough to underwrite a first-class education for all four kids.

That said, toeing the mark was never easy for Chip. After he rose to a lofty No. 4 among Florida juniors, I invited him up for a campus visit. When he went home, as blasé teens are prone to do, he gave his Dad a ho-hum reaction to Duke. "Well get used to it," Cecil tartly advised his son. "If they'll have you, that's where you're going to go."

Such emphatic assertions didn't mean Cecil was always right. Through much of junior tennis, Chip had worked hard to develop a two-handed backhand at a time when few players, other than Jimmy Connors, had one. Slowly, the shot had improved, but never stood out like his serve or forehand. In a major 14-and-under tournament in Orlando, his best friend and backyard practice partner, Scott Smith, who later became one of America's top teaching pros, exploited a glaring weakness by hitting low and short to Chip's backhand side. "Scott was relentless," Chip recalls. "For the life of me, I just couldn't stop netting my returns." After Chip lost to Scott, Cecil was so upset he declared "enough" and ordered Chip to shelve his two-handed shot. "My backhand was defensive for the rest of my career," Chip notes. "It definitely limited my success." While he questioned the mandate, he still did what Cecil said.

That same year, Chip played in a national 14-and-under tournament in Chattanooga, Tennessee, where he advanced to a late-round match against the number one seed, Billy Martin, who'd later star and coach at UCLA and win several tournaments on tour. Chip won the first set and had two match points before losing the second set. At the break before the third set, a reporter for the *Chattanooga Times* asked Chip to stick around afterward for an interview. As he turned to go, the reporter asked in bafflement, "You do realize who you're about to knock off out there? This guy hasn't lost in three years."

"Holy cow!" Chip blurted. The reporter's question proved deflating: He promptly lost the third set 6–0.

Years later, Chip would tell me his match against Billy Martin was one of the most memorable he ever played. He said the same thing about a match he lost in the Southern Open the summer after his outstanding freshman year. It was his first night match and drew the largest crowd he'd ever played before to the Raleigh Racquet Club. His opponent was another number one seed, Chico Hagey, who'd played at No. 1 and 2 on Stanford teams that won national championships in '73 and '74. Chip pushed Hagey to the brink before a late service break cost him the match. He still fondly remembers the raucous shouts of friends as the match tightened.

Why were close losses Chip's most memorable moments in tennis? Despite his disappointing sophomore year, his cumulative record by the end of his junior year was 40 wins and 26 losses. That put him in the top third of those who played for me. Was he overindulging "What ifs?" Much later, I heard him say much the same about his surgeries. In 30 years as a spine surgeon, he averaged 350 operations a year, a total of more than 10,000. "Strange, but I hardly remember any of the successes," he would say. "I remember the one or two that weren't." My hunch was that something deep inside goaded him with *show me—show me just how good you can be.*

Not too long after his cliffhanger at the Raleigh Racquet Club, the good times began to crater for Chip. Playing tennis six to eight hours a day all summer had taken a toll. He first felt a twinge of pain, then a no doubt strain, in his right knee. He came limping back to Duke hoping to build on his strong freshman year, but his limited mobility was so obvious at fall practice I told him he had to get the knee examined. A cruel sentence soon followed: he had a meniscus tear that required surgery, which meant he couldn't play tennis for the first time in his life. His GPA fell from 3.9 to 3.2 due to a follow-on bout of depression. And to make matters worse, Cecil was riding him hard, warning that his tennis scholarship and med school chances were vaporizing.

In all his years at Duke—from freshman year in '74 to finishing his residency in '87—Chip recalls that period as "the absolute low. I was under so much pressure I could hardly think."

Chip was still rehabbing his knee when the spring season began. He tried playing again at No. 3, but the results were mediocre. Fortunately for the team, promising new recruits picked up the slack. That summer he laid off tennis and worked in construction and delivered furniture. That fall, his junior year, he was still uncertain and unfocused; his quiet confidence and strength clearly were missing. So, I asked him to come in for a heart-to-heart talk. Somewhat to my surprise, a litany of miseries came pouring out: He was worried that he'd never regain his form, that poor play would cost him his scholarship, that the decline in his GPA meant he'd never get into med school.

"Whoa . . . Whoa," I told him at one point. "Let's get a handle on this. We've still got some options."

"We do?" was his incredulous reply.

"Of course! What if I dropped you from No. 3 to No. 6? Wouldn't that tamp down some of the pressure?"

Chip stewed on that a bit, then asked: "You'd really do that? A lot of coaches will accuse you of stacking the lineup."

"The hell with what a bunch of coaches say; this is just between the two of us."

"Gosh coach, if I could play at six, that would really help."

"Then consider it done."

After our talk, Chip slowly but surely turned things around: His GPA went back up, he began dominating play at No. 6 and his confidence got renewed. After a summer job teaching tennis to kids, he posted a sensational senior year in which he lost only two matches. Playing at No. 6, he was nearly unbeatable. No one worked harder, so good things were bound to happen. At the ACC Tennis Tournament in Charlottesville in the late spring of '78, I got a call from a friend on the Duke Med School Admissions Committee. "I'm calling with some good news," he said. "Your guy Chip got in."

When I told Chip, he had to squint hard to hold back the tears. "You're sure? You're absolutely sure?" he asked anxiously. I nodded and gave him a grin: "Yes, you're in. They've already posted the results."

"My God, Coach, I can hardly believe it." Once the news had sunk in a bit more, he excused himself to go call his parents. I could only imagine how elated they'd be.

Good things kept coming Chip's way. During the second week of med school, he and a friend went to the cafeteria for lunch. After sitting down, the friend spied his girlfriend and two other women a few tables away.

"Let's join them," the friend proposed, "my girl has got someone she wants you to meet."

Introductions and lunch ensued. Afterward, Chip's friend asked, "Well, how you like her?"

"Which one?"

"The one my girlfriend had picked out."

"Actually, not so much. But I really liked the other one—the one named Susie Beck."

A short time later, Chip called Susie to invite her to a Duke football game. She accepted, but they barely watched the game; they spent the whole time in an animated tête-à-tête. It turned out that Susie had graduated in the same class as Chip with a degree in nursing. They knew a lot of the same people, but had never met each other. A two-year courtship preceded a large and happy wedding amid the soaring arches of Duke Chapel. Nothing could be more quintessentially Duke, which is exactly how Chip and Susie wanted it.

By the time Chip finished his residency, Susie had gotten into med school too. A daughter, Kristen, had been born in '87 just before they moved to St. Petersburg. Twins—Charlie and Becky—arrived in '92. By then, Susie had become a pathologist but had opted to be a stay-at-home mom.

When the twins were three, Susie asked Chip to take them to a birthday party in the neighborhood. Little did she know that her chance request would lead to a dramatic change in their lives. Chip was one of two dads at the party, the other being Chuck Jones, an assistant pastor at First Presbyterian Church, where he and Susie were members. Amid the shouts and hijinks of amped up three-year-olds, Chip and Chuck struck up a conversation. At one point, Chuck asked, "Have you ever considered going on a medical mission abroad?"

"Not really," Chip replied. "Why do you ask?"

"Because a couple I know—Joe and Vera Wiatt—from the church I served in Houston are organizing a mission to Guatemala. They have a critical need for surgeons. Would you be interested in going?"

Chuck's directness took Chip aback somewhat. He couldn't imagine going to a place he couldn't find on a map. It was so out-of-the-box, and Chip was, decidedly, an in-the-box guy.

"Would you consider meeting with this couple—Joe and Vera?" the minister persisted.

"Well . . . maybe. Let me give it some thought."

Chip left the party with no intention of meeting the couple. Why, he wondered, would a St. Pete spine surgeon go to a place like that? The conditions for operating were bound to be primitive.

He'd have been shocked to know that Chuck had already called Joe and Vera. "I think I've found just the man you're looking for," he told them. Two weeks later, Joe and Vera arrived and called to invite Chip to lunch.

What could he say? This is a colossal waste of time. That didn't seem right. No harm in meeting, after all. He decided he should hear Joe and Vera out since they were coming under the aegis of the church he and Susie attended.

The lunch was unlike anything Chip had expected. Joe and Vera were humble, open and honest—not churchified in the least. He was impressed that they had run a successful hardware business, which they were selling to devote full time to a medical mission in Antigua, Guatemala—a place where there were almost no surgeons despite a heartbreaking level of need. Joe and Vera did not press Chip, did not play guilt cards; they simply explained their dire need for an "ice-breaker"—an orthopedic surgeon who would agree to go and work in conditions a good bit less than optimum. "By going, you'd help us attract others and put the place in good working order."

The more Joe and Vera explained, the more intriguing their proposition became. It was obvious to Chip that they were making an incredible commitment—devoting their lives, in fact, to this unusual cause. By the end of the lunch, Chip was ready to commit except for one reservation: He wanted to talk to Ernie Rehnke, a physician and friend who'd been on several medical missions to Central America. He did that right away, and at the end of the conversation, Rehnke told him, "Let's do it."

At one point, Joe or Vera had told Chip, "It's a gift to put your faith in something much greater than yourself."

But how do you do that? he'd asked.

Their answer was through "Faith in Practice," which happened to be the name of their organization. The name came from James 2:18: *Yea, a man may say, Thou hast faith, and I have works: shew me thy faith without thy works, and I will shew thee my faith by my works.* The verse resonated deeply with Chip, who strongly believed that actions—not words—mattered most.

¤ ¤ ¤

In the spring of 1995, Chip and a small group he'd later call "a band of miracle workers" flew to Antigua, a city founded in 1543 by Spanish conquistadores as the colonial capital of Guatemala. Nestled in a natural bowl formed by a ring of volcanoes, he found its natural beauty stunning. Plumes of ash were rising from a few active volcanoes. On the drive from the airport to La Quinta de las Flores (House of Flowers), where Faith in Practice (FIP) teams stayed, he passed ancient ruins of churches, palaces and government buildings destroyed in 1773 by a devastating earthquake and never rebuilt. Eventually, the capital was moved to Guatemala City, where it remains today.

Conditions for surgery were so primitive that Chip first used a makeshift operating room set up in a garage-like setting. It had no back-up power and certain supplies—stainless steel screws, a drill and a mallet—were procured by Joe from a nearby hardware store.

Showing Chip several screw types and sizes, Joe had asked, "Will any of these do?"

Chip told him, "The small ones will work fine once they're sterilized."

One of his first operations was a late-night laminectomy—decompression surgery to relieve nerve pressure by enlarging the spinal canal—on a large Guatemalan man. Midway through the procedure, the power went out, plunging the garage into total darkness. Having no generator meant there was no back-up power. Within minutes, several men standing high up on ladders were beaming large flashlights on the area of incision. They gave off enough light for Chip to close the wound. He then stood in silence waiting for the power to come back on. An animated murmuring followed among the men on ladders.

Chip asked a nurse to translate what they were saying.

"They're asking each other why you're waiting."

"I'm waiting for the lights to come back on."

When she translated, the men all laughed.

"What's that all about?" Chip demanded sharply.

"They say you'll be waiting all night—that we'll be lucky to get power by morning."

Early the next morning, Chip hurried from La Quinta to the makeshift clinic to check on his patient and finish the laminectomy. But an unexpected obstacle arose: His patient said it would be wrong for him to push someone else off the morning schedule. Chip adamantly insisted that he had to finish, but the patient would not agree until Chip said he'd stay until everyone on the schedule that day got taken care of. The patient was typical of the stoic Guatemalans who felt surgery was more than a life-changing event; for them, it was a true miracle. After his successful laminectomy, the patient went to remote villages, spreading the word about how Faith in Practice had changed his life.

Early on Chip began making two trips each year to Obras Sociales del Santo Hermano Pedro (Obras for short), the place where the Faith in Practice's clinic and operating room ultimately were located. It was a hybrid institution that served as a hospital, orphanage and old folks home. His first trip was a triage visit in early winter to evaluate and schedule surgeries; the second trip was in May to perform scheduled surgeries. More than once, strange things happened—things he could not explain.

On one of his first trips, four kids in their early teens with scoliosis, or curvature of the spine, had been scheduled for corrective surgery. The origins of scoliosis can be genetic but are generally unknown. It causes the spine to curve or twist abnormally into the shape of the letter C. In advanced stages, excruciating pain occurs as pulmonary function began to shut down. Death may follow in a very short time. As always, Chip had patiently explained to the parents how he planned to proceed and why the operation couldn't be delayed another year without the deformity getting much worse. He was set to begin on a Sunday afternoon when he learned that the two available anesthesiologists had refused to join him because they'd never had a pediatric case.

He found them right away and told them they had to help because, "Everything's all set to go."

"No way," they replied. "We're not doing big cases like these with equipment that's no good. We're not going to risk killing a kid."

"Look, I've already spoken to their parents and more or less given them hope. They'll be devastated if I tell them the whole thing's off." But the specialists refused to budge.

"If you can't do this," Chip seethed, "why the hell would you come down here?"

"I was mad as all get-out," Chip now recalls, "and things really started to get hot."

Finally, Vera stepped in and told Chip he needed to take a break.

To cool off, he walked to nearby Frieda's, a popular pizza restaurant named for Frieda Kahlo, the iconic Mexican artist of the 1920s and '30s. He took a table near the bar and ordered a slice of pizza. When the waitress brought it, he began telling her his woes. The place was almost empty, but Chip noticed a man with a beard at the bar wearing camouflage and a big straw hat—another gringo like himself, the only two in the place. The fellow at the bar kept glancing over at Chip, who gave him a good-natured nod. In a moment or so, he wandered over and asked—

"Mind if I sit down?"

"By all means," Chip replied.

"Couldn't help hearing what you're up against. I'd be pretty upset myself."

"I guess my luck's run out," Chip lamented.

"Mighty tough for the kids and their parents."

Sensing a note of warmth and concern, Chip asked, "What kind of work do you do?"

A wide grin spread slowly across the man's face. "I'm a pediatric anesthesiologist," he said.

Chip was dumbstruck. He couldn't believe what he'd just heard. "You're what?" he finally mustered.

"I'm in charge of pediatric anesthesiology at the biggest hospital in Houston."

"You've got to be kidding me." Chip replied.

"No. Been doing it for quite some time."

"You wouldn't consider helping me with these cases, would you?" Chip ventured.

"You bet I would."

Chip and Jim Street got the stalled operations underway that afternoon and had them all done by midweek. Street turned out to be an impressive specialist—one of the best Chip had ever encountered. At the end of the week, Chip told him, "Jim, that was a very timely intervention. I still can't believe you were down here, but thank God you were."

"Glad I was. What time next year?"

Thus began a close friendship and collaboration at Obras that would last until Jim Street retired. Together, they performed countless scoliosis surgeries on kids who otherwise would not have gotten that life-changing surgery. Chip often wondered how Jim Street came to be sitting at the bar at Friedas that Sunday when he was so sure his luck had run out. No matter how he tried, he couldn't explain the unseen hand that seemingly had intervened. Joe and Vera had no doubt that the unseen hand was God's—that it was a miracle. As time went by, Chip was less inclined toward doubt and more inclined to believe Joe and Vera were right.

He marveled that two other phenomena at the clinic in Antigua had no scientific explanation at all. The first involved the intense pain scoliosis surgery could cause when the spine canal is opened, implants are inserted and screws get screwed into bone. His American patients required a lot of pain medication, but his patients in Guatemala asked for none—they expected to have pain and bore it stoically. On his daily rounds, Chip always asked, "Are you hurting?" Nearly all would nod *yes*, but seemed to say, *Of course I'm hurting but surgery is a wonderful thing, I wanted it, now I'm not going to be deformed, now I'm going to be normal.* Chip knew joy was a powerful pain medication, but it couldn't be prescribed.

The second phenomenon was even more mysterious. Chip's post-op results in the United States for scoliosis included the standard 5 percent rate for complications—everything from infections to pneumonia and excess bleeding. For those operations, he always had full access to the most advanced medical technologies, including portable X-ray machines (fluoroscopes), which provide real time images during surgery, CT scans and advanced ventilators. In Guatemala, none of these machines were available. Yet, incredibly, his complication rate in Guatemala was zero—not one complication had occurred in the 22 years he had operated there. Once again, it seemed that an unseen hand was at work, but, long ago he'd quit trying to fathom the how or why.

From a purely human perspective, the surgery trips were not nearly as emotionally draining as the triage trips when patients were evaluated and scheduled for surgery. Year by year, the ripple effect of surgical success at the Faith in Practice clinic at Obras had spread far and wide in Guatemala. Not everyone could be fixed—which meant parents faced a Sophie's Choice moment at evaluation time. Kids were chosen using risk/benefit analysis to select cases in which the greatest benefit could be achieved at the lowest possible risk. While that process was underway, parents often begged in tears for an operation for their child. Some even fell on their knees and threw their arms around the surgeon's ankles. Triage turned Chip into an emotional wreck—nothing he could say or do would assuage the tears of a parent whose kid wasn't chosen.

"To do something for human beings that would not otherwise be done is a powerful thing," Chip once told the *Tampa Bay Medical News*. "That doesn't really happen here. We try to take good care of people here, but the truth is that if we don't do it, someone else will. Down there, if you don't fix them, their lives will be awful. . . . You make a difference that is hard to equate to anything else we do here."

Over the years, his work at Obras had caused his values to change so much that Chip wanted Susie and the children to share the experience as fully as possible. He began taking them there, one by one, and they went together in 2011. He insisted that each kid and Susie take on real responsibilities: a gourmet cook, Susie prepared evening meals for the entire team; Kristen served as journalist supplying blogs to the FIP website; Becky worked in triage gathering patient background information; and Charlie helped patients with physical rehab.

It was an eye-opening experience for each: For the first time, they saw up close what Chip did in his daily routine, even watching him operate, something they'd never done back in St. Pete. Kristen later wrote a paper about that experience entitled "Mystery in My Bones" for a class on spiritual autobiography at Duke. Witnessing an operation in scrubs, a cap and mask, she was shocked by the physical force her Dad used on a 12-year-old girl with advanced scoliosis. Kristen had taken the girl's photo not thirty minutes earlier, capturing the terrified look on her face. Only a small rectangle of flesh along the girl's spine was visible beneath her blue gown. As Chip hammered screws into place along her vertebra, he seemed to be using all the force he had, impervious to blood spattering on his gown, even his glasses. Before the operation began, the girl's spine was shaped like a question mark; when Chip finished, her spine appeared to be entirely straight. The only way Kristen could tell she was alive during

Chip Davis with patient

the operation was the rhythmic rise and fall of her torso as a ventilator forced air into her lungs.

Three or four days later, Kristen was present when the young girl's bulky bandages came off. It was a moment her father never grew tired of: a celebratory milestone with parents, the patient's closest friends and hospital staff when results of the surgery were laid bare for all to see. When the last of the tape and gauze came off, there she stood, ramrod straight. Tears of joy glistened in her parents' eyes, knowing she'd now lead a normal life. They thanked Chip profusely for performing such a miracle; Chip, in turn, insisted that it was just his job.

In her interview for admission at Duke, Becky had described her trips to Guatemala as her favorite week of the year. Their time together at Obras had accomplished exactly what Chip and Susie had hoped: They had shared profoundly in giving to the less fortunate, and it made the family much closer than ever before.

Those ties would be put to severe test in 2013 when Kristen was nearly overcome by debilitating depression. After fighting the disease through much of high school, she began to fear that she'd fall apart completely. Eventually, Dr. Christopher Caston, a psychiatrist at CooperRiis Therapy Farm near Asheville, found that her brain was producing far too little serotonin, a neurotransmitter that can cause chronic depression. He was able to prescribe an anti-depressant that restored her serotonin to a proper level. After taking it for a few weeks she felt a great relief and improvement. She credits Dr. Caston with saving her life.

Just as Joe and Vera Wiatt had hoped, dozens of surgeons would follow Chip to Guatemala. They came as word spread in the U.S. about the remarkable work Faith in Practice was doing at Obras. During that same period, FIP became one of the largest medical providers in the small Central American country. It was treating 25,000 people a year, and its annual operating budget rose to $10 million when the value of the time its medical teams were contributing was included. From its origins in a garage-like setting, FIP's surgical facilities became the best in the country. Today, twenty-five physicians, nurses and medical technicians—most of them recruited by Chip—travel from St. Petersburg to Guatemala each year to staff the clinic. In many respects, the organization itself was a miracle.

Their role in planting FIP's deep roots could not have been more personal. Joe had been awakened at 2 a.m. from a deep sleep one night in 1991 with the clear sensation that God was telling him to make a profound change in his life—to sell the hardware business and devote his time to serving others. He and Vera had discussed this in detail the next day, and she agreed that they should both open their hearts to God's will. They decided to put their hardware business on the market, but the economy was not good and it didn't sell until 1996. Early in their transition, a friend called to ask if they'd help organize a medical mission to Guatemala. They agreed and became more and more engaged once they saw how great the need was to help what they called "the castaways of society."

For many years, I felt Chip had an ineffable quality I couldn't quite fathom. I knew he had a kind and giving heart. Something Joe and Vera said clarified what that quality was: "Chip's empathy toward his patients is beyond description." Empathy was just the word I'd been missing all along. In Chip, it was the opposite of a saccharine, feel-good emotion.

Linda amplified on this very point. She recalls telling Chip, "We've got to have more spine surgeons."

"You're right," he replied, "but we have to be very intentional about who they are. They can have good hands, but if they don't have a good heart, it won't work."

Linda correctly points out, "Surgeons make the biggest 'fixes' of all—to the heart, the spine, the neurological system. Often they are godlike to their patients. People hold them in that place, so they tend to believe their press. Part of it is self-protection, a way of dealing with duties in which there is so little margin of error. As a man of deep faith, Chip sees that sense of responsibility differently. He looks at it as a great gift; he stands in awe of it—it is not something that belongs to him. That's why I think he's so special. We're in the healing business, not the medical business after all."

In the decade after Chip left Duke, he established himself as one of the top orthopedic surgeons in the Tampa–St. Petersburg area. He was named chief of orthopedic surgery at Bayfront Medical Center in 1997 and chief of surgery at Edward White Hospital a decade later. He credits much of his success to the work ethic he learned at Duke. "I was 17 years old when I got there and 32 years old when I left. The difference between what I was when I arrived and what I was when I left is something I'm incredibly grateful for to Duke and to my Coach. That ethic was central to becoming successful and achieving something worthwhile in life. You can only do that by working hard and doing your best. You can't bluff your way to success in life or tennis."

Chip's connections had enabled him to recruit many top surgeons and medical professionals on behalf of Faith in Practice. His experience there had changed his life. In all their years of going to Guatemala, Chip and Susie still marveled at the simple faith of the Guatemalan people, how they treated each other so kindly despite having so little—the lives of quiet dignity and deep faith they lived.

Susie still remembers Chip and the team disembarking from the plane after his very first mission to Guatemala. "It was clear to me from how they interacted that they'd had a transformational experience. In many ways, Chip hasn't stopped changing since. That, too, has been a beautiful thing to see. I think God just grabbed him by the collar and told him: 'Chip, have I got something for you.'"

She will never forget a painting that used to hang on the wall of the operating room at Obras and was later moved to the break room. It depicts a surgeon and nurses in masks leaning over a patient on an operating table. Jesus is standing behind the surgeon with a hand lightly touching his arm.

To Susie, more than anything, that painting expresses what Faith in Practice stands for. For her, Chip, Kristen, Becky and Charlie, it will always mean that faith without works is dead, but empathy nearly always comes first.

CHAPTER ELEVEN

The Spartan Way

Going way back, I'm sure his Momma must have spotted a flaw or two but I never could. It takes an extraordinary man to orchestrate a mid-sized empire from the palm of his hand. With three construction projects underway at any given time, operations in six states, 130 full-time employees, ongoing negotiations with banks and private investors and more than 4,000 apartment units to manage and keep 99 percent occupied, as they generally are, you'd think Will White would be on a hot seat without a minute to call his own. And yet, he's relaxed, unflappable and, always, on point. Somehow, he coordinates a geyser of detail without a personal secretary, an executive assistant or even a gatekeeper, despite the open-door policy he steadfastly maintains. Instead of a palace guard, he employs an iPhone, which he wields with the speed and efficiency of a light saber to cut through clutter and bring order to his day.

Small wonder that Will White is my exemplar of discipline, the fourth of six essential character traits that set scholar-athletes apart—a trait that cannot be bequeathed by birth, one that can only be developed through hard work and mental toughness. I liken Will to the Spartans in the sense that he acquired discipline in roughly the same time span, from age seven to his mid-twenties. Young Spartans between the 7th and 6th centuries BC became full citizens after a long training period; when ready for command, they were pledged never to throw down their arms. That same finely honed instinct to never quit was instilled in Will from childhood to early adulthood.

An especially strong mother, Elizabeth Heard White—"Betty" in the family—set Will on a path that would make discipline and organization paramount in his life. A tragic event—the death of her father when she was only 23—had made them important in Betty's too. Her father had left her a third of his business—land that could be developed and apartments. She decided to manage these assets herself and began rehabbing the apartments with a crew she managed on her own. By then, she'd learned the value of hard work through tennis having become the ninth-ranked woman in the nation in the mid-1930s. Will's father, Kenneth Eugene White, was good at the game too and played on the Auburn University team.

By the time he was seven, Will was hitting balls, and his parents could see he had an aptitude for the game. Betty took him to a well-known Columbus pro, Fred Berl, who had a no-nonsense reputation and an unusual approach.

"I wanted him to develop good habits, to respect his opponents and knew Fred Berl didn't put up with any foolishness." She liked the fact that Fred had Will keep a goal book and daily diary to organize his time. He'd review Will's entries and point out how to become more efficient.

Betty was like a Spartan mother in her willingness to let go. She came to a few of Will's early matches, but soon stopped. Trusting Fred's methods and approach, she felt, "The last thing they needed was to have his Momma hanging around the courts. Will needed to learn to be on his own."

When I observed that she'd given him "quite a start," she quickly countered, "I didn't give him anything. He did what he needed to do, but I think his coaches—you and Fred—made a big difference in his life."

Even in advancing years, Betty puts a high premium on continuing to learn. She calls herself "a perpetual student" and clearly has eclectic tastes. At Hollins in Hollins, Virginia, one of the country's oldest colleges for women, she majored in Russian history, an unusual choice, by any measure for a young woman from South Georgia. She later earned a PhD in epidemiology from Emory University in Atlanta.

Her broad worldview convinced her that Will should attend a northern prep school. "I wanted him to see that there are a lot of smart people in the world and that some of them would be smarter than he was." He stoutly resisted her decision because he was having more and more success on the junior tennis circuit. Pointing out that very few top tennis players came from the northeast, Will held that going north could kill his prospects for earning a national ranking. But that argument did not dissuade his mother, so, in the fall of 1976, he went to the Choate School in Wallingford, Connecticut. It turned out not to be a good fit: He transferred two years later to the Lawrenceville School in New Jersey and finished high school there. Lawrenceville had no indoor courts, but Will managed to play enough on holidays and in summers to become 10th-ranked in the United States in the 16-and-under age bracket.

That impressed me enough to invite him in January 1979 for a campus visit. I also invited his best friend in junior tennis, Jim Latham, who was highly ranked too. We rolled out the red carpet with a party at the home of Dr. Jim Bonk. Will and Jim got to rub elbows with members of the '79 team and could sense our high confidence that Duke was ready to take a big step up in the Atlantic Coast Conference. Arrangements also were made for them to attend a basketball game between Duke and Marquette at wild and wooly Cameron Indoor Stadium. That was the clincher. Will later told me, "I fell in love with the atmosphere that night and knew Duke was the place for me." Ultimately, Will and Jim both accepted my offer of a full scholarship.

I can say without reservation that Will was, by far, the most disciplined player I ever coached. By the time he arrived at Duke, the attributes of hard work and mental toughness were already deeply ingrained in his character. I had developed a highly structured practice routine based on any number of drills designed to improve players in all phases of the game. I also emphasized wind sprints six days a week and long cross-country runs on Sundays. Will seemed to thrive on my methodical approach and never complained about running one last wind sprint or anything else I asked the players to do. As time went on, he proved to be the consummate teammate because he never put himself first and always kept a positive frame of mind. He was not our best player—a status he willingly accepted—but he was a holy terror at No. 3 singles and doubles; and, his linebacker build quickly made him the team's "enforcer" when conflicts arose that could get out of hand.

I'd like to think what Will learned on the tennis court at Duke factored in a meaningful way into his subsequent success. More than anything, I think he had a solid foundation early on and has built on that at every stage of life. The best evidence of his unwavering commitment to discipline is the daily regime he has followed for years.

His typical day begins at 4:30 a.m. when he gets up and listens to headline radio while getting ready for work. He scans the newspaper over coffee, then drives two miles to his office at Greystone Properties, usually arriving at 5:45 a.m. on the dot. Until 8 a.m., he hosts a series of 10-minute, highly focused "check-in" meetings with construction supervisors and project coordinators. He asks managers whose projects are running smoothly to let him know that.

From 8:30 to 11:30 a.m., he works on pro formas and other paperwork for banks and private investors. He sets time aside during this period to review architectural designs and other matters that require concentrated thought.

Over the years, he's gotten a "second wind" from a mid-day workout at the fitness center of one of the apartment complexes he owns. Between noon and 1 p.m., he lifts weights, runs on a treadmill or gets another type of cardio workout. He sweats in relative anonymity, having found it a practical way to get unfiltered feedback from tenants on all sorts of concerns.

He avoids "sit-down" lunches as time-wasters. A quick sandwich at his desk or downing a handful of almonds on the fly is usually enough. He spends the entire afternoon, from 1:30 to 6:15 p.m., visiting job sites and holding out-of-office meetings. At 6:30 p.m., he wraps up his day and heads home for dinner with Amy, his wife of 33 years. They prefer quiet evenings alone with their dogs, Milli, a Boykin Spaniel, and Red, a Chocolate Lab. Will rarely watches television; instead, he reads books on corporate finance, marketing and management. Over the years, he's taken many classes on business subjects at Emory University in Atlanta about 100 miles north. When the hours are all added up, Will typically puts in a 65-hour week.

He and Amy first took note of each other in junior tennis at age nine in Sewanee, Tennessee. "We didn't really talk," she recalls. "Girls didn't really talk to boys at that age. I remember noticing him after our freshman year and thinking, 'Gosh, he's gotten really cute.'" She was on the tennis team at the University of Alabama at the time. They started going out together soon after that and got married at age 24. She says so many of Will's friends came to their wedding in her hometown of Louisville, Kentucky, "It seemed like a college reunion."

A longstanding relationship with his most successful protégé tells a lot about Will's approach to business. In 2001, with a newly minted law degree from Mercer University in Macon, Georgia, Austin Gower volunteered for the re-election campaign of his friend, Tom Buck, at the time the longest-serving member of the Georgia House of Representatives. Buck sent Austin to see Will to ask if Buck campaign literature could be passed out at Will's apartment complexes. "I'd never met Will or heard of him," Austin recalls.

Will was in his office (with the door open, of course) and overheard someone ask, "Is Mr. White in?" Before the question could be answered, a voice from nearby rang out, "I'm here—come on back."

Austin was dumbfounded that he'd gained entry to the President's office at Greystone Properties without an appointment and was further surprised that, without hesitation, Will readily agreed to Tom Buck's request. Will then asked, "You're from Columbus, aren't you?" Austin explained that he was, that he'd just earned his law degree, had an undergraduate degree from Auburn in civil engineering and had come back to explore career options.

"Your dad has a couple of apartment complexes in Columbus, doesn't he?"

"He does."

Will explained that Greystone's primary business was building apartments and told Austin a bit about his approach. He ended by saying, "If you come across a project that's not a fit for your Dad, please give me a call and maybe we can work on it together."

Together? Once again, Austin was dumfounded—this time that, with hardly a spare dollar to call his own, and without a track record in business, an established pro was treating him like a peer. Austin readily agreed to keep his eyes open but doubted an opportunity would surface anytime soon. A month or so later, something did. Austin discovered that a 160-unit apartment complex in Columbus was in foreclosure. After fully researching the case, his analysis made clear that the best approach would be to acquire $7 million in outstanding debt, but not the complex. Once his fact-gathering was complete, Austin asked his Dad if he'd like to pursue the project. His Dad said *no*—mainly because he was obligated to other partners and wanted his son to find one on his own. "You just met Will White," he told Austin. "Why don't you take the project to him?"

Austin called Will right away and asked to see him. The answer: "Come today at 1 p.m."

"That's vintage Will," Austin observes. "He jumps on everything right away and never procrastinates. You'll never get a waffling 'Let me see if I can work you in later.'"

Will already had some familiarity with the project, but he liked Austin's analysis. Once he'd looked it over carefully, he asked, "How would you like to structure the partnership?" It was yet another surprise for Austin. "I didn't have a red cent to lay on the line, so I told him: 'If you're putting in the money, you should make the rules.'"

"Then, what about 50–50?" Will replied. "You do the work, and I'll put in the money." That seemed more than generous to Austin, so he readily accepted.

The paperwork for the project had to be signed in Atlanta, so Will and Austin drove to Atlanta the next day. En route, Austin started feeling sick in his stomach. *What if this thing doesn't work out?* he asked himself. *This guy's going to think I'm an idiot.*

But the deal did work out, and it led to a close, continuing relationship in which Will now relies on Austin to help identify projects outside Columbus, where the apartment market is now quite mature. Austin rewarded Will's confidence by finding attractive projects in Pensacola, Knoxville, Albany, Georgia, and elsewhere. He freely admits, "I've modeled myself, as closely as I could, after Will." Over the past 17 years, Austin has become a successful plaintiff's lawyer, taking a wide assortment of cases on a contingency basis. Will puts a high value on Austin's ability to handle legal transactions that don't fit cookie-cutter norms. After that first joint project, they've taken on many more together. They've operated the entire time on a simple handshake.

"People ask me all the time—'How come he's so successful?' A lot of them have the misconception that it all came easy because his family had a certain level of means. But that doesn't begin to tell the full story. Yes, Will started with some financial backing, but he works hard; I've seen a lot of people with financing and smarts, who just didn't put in the effort. Will's got the whole package and the amazing thing to me is that he never takes shortcuts. He is as steady as you'll ever see."

Will has formed many close and enduring friendships, some dating as far back as junior tennis, others from his Duke years. One who bridges both periods is Jim Latham, who roomed with Will all four years at Duke and played with him in the 10-and-under age bracket on the junior circuit. Two years after he finished at Duke, Jim went to Europe and stayed. He worked for General Motors for a decade and currently is a senior marketing executive for Adidas.

Rarely a fortnight goes by in which Will and Jim fail to talk to each other. They used to do it by phone but now use Facetime. Their exchanges don't involve weighty matters; mostly they catch up on what's going on in their respective lives. About the only time they see each other is at class reunions that occur at five-year intervals.

Jim has known Amy almost as long as he's known Will. "I don't know too many couples who are as harmonious as they are. It doesn't happen unless you're aligned on life, love, priorities and character. She has a naturalness and seamlessness that complements their relationship in such a positive way."

When Will lost his father about five years ago, Jim says he could sense an increased sense of obligation within Will to his family's legacy—"to pass on the family business and family name better than when he came on the scene. That may sound like a cliché, but clichés are there for a reason."

During their senior year at Duke, George W. "Skip" Finkbohner from Mobile, Alabama, roomed with Will and Jim. Today, he's a partner with Cunningham Bounds in Mobile and was named the state's top trial attorney in 2017. He and Will call each other every week or so to discuss matters they'd bring up with very few others. A hard-nosed plaintiff's attorney, Finkbohner has won some of the highest legal settlements ever granted in the Southeast. His feelings about Will are unabashedly strong: "Listen. I love the guy. Okay?" Will engenders that kind of loyalty within a close circle he's cultivated for more than thirty years. It's the antithesis of a "backslapping" business network; at heart, it's about continuity of friendships based on shared experience that could never be forgotten. Every December, Will hosts many of these friends at a second home he and Amy have on Sea Island, Georgia.

Skip played on our practice squad at Duke but never played in matches. He says Will "had ability that I'd never see in five lifetimes. He was fast, strong and intense. I was intense, but slow and not particularly strong, although I was a big kid. In tennis, pressure brings out cracks in character. I never saw Will crack. There was no pretense about him. He just happened to be good without having an ego about it. I don't think he ever made a bad line call in his life, but if he did, he'd have reversed it."

In a sense, Will was old school in his approach to the game. He once sized it up for me in words far beyond his years: "I want to win, but I want to do it in a way that doesn't make an opponent suffer."

Not long ago, Will told Skip: "What I do is not that hard." Skip says he rolled his eyes and replied: "Okay dude, make that pitch to somebody else. Maybe it's not that hard for you, but I've looked at the spreadsheets on your jobs, the amount of detail you cost out and how you project an outcome. Look, you've been doing it for thirty years; very few others could do what you do."

There are times when a good friend can splash a little cold water when no one else—except, maybe, a wife or mom—would be so bold.

Will has little or no interest in the limelight. He's well-known and widely respected in the Columbus business community but might stroll, without being noticed, from the corner of Main and Whittlesey to the nearby entrance to Greystone Apartments, a lovely community of garden apartments he developed and owns. Columbus can be a bit quirky that way. Coca-Cola grew to maturity in Atlanta, but a Columbus pharmacist, Dr. John Pemberton, began tinkering with the secret formula for the famous soft drink in Columbus not long after the Civil War. A good bit of the company's early investment and management came from there, and Coke's success created substantial wealth in Columbus. The town is justly proud of that success and tends to feel no one is likely to top it.

For years, Will has given back to the community in meaningful ways, not quite in anonymity but close. For twenty years, or thereabouts, he has been a leading donor and served on the board of the Columbus Regional Tennis Association (CORTA), which has made tennis the city's most popular adult sport. Will raised a lot of the money for CORTA's state-of-the-art Cooper Creek facility, a leading site for state and regional tournaments. CORTA has been nationally recognized for its innovations and leadership in popularizing the sport.

Its energetic Executive Director, Judy Pearce, has known Will since the third grade. She says, "Will's the last person you'll ever see engaged in self-promotion. He could have been president of CORTA on many occasions but preferred to remain as a member of the board. He is the only Expansion Project Chairman we've ever had, and the Cooper Creek project would never have gotten off the ground without his leadership."

Will also serves as a trustee or director of Brookstone School, a private school he once attended, the Chattahoochee Land Valley Trust, Columbus Regional Health Care and the Columbus Boys and Girls Club.

Ken Henson, a Columbus attorney and one of Will's longtime business associates, says Will usually "focuses in depth on one or two causes at the time. I know when Brookstone School needed four new buildings, there wasn't anybody else who could take that on. Will did it, even though it took a lot of time. It turned out well; in fact, I can't think of a project he's ever done that didn't turn out that way."

One primary reason, Ken says, is Will's confidence in his own judgment and instincts. "I remember when he was just starting out, he'd just developed a subdivision and wanted to build some apartments. He decided to commission a market study but when the results came back, the study said Columbus didn't need any new apartments. His response was, 'There's something wrong with this data.' He decided to build the Main Street Apartments anyway—probably 150 units—and once they were built, they all leased out right away."

Ken makes an interesting observation about Betty's side of the family. When her father died, he left her land suitable for development and apartments that were somewhat outdated. He left Will's uncle, Bill Heard, a large Chevrolet dealership. "They represented two very different approaches. On Betty and Will's side, you have a cautious, analytical and incremental approach. On Bill's side, you had high levels of risk and an extravagant lifestyle. At one time, his GM franchise here was probably the biggest in the country. Bill's nickname was 'Big Volume.' He had two jets, and dealerships in Atlanta, Phoenix and Dallas. But when the '08 recession came along, it just tanked him; he had too much debt. In contrast, Will had very little debt. Demand for apartments soared when the single-family home loans dried up. He was in the right business at the right time.

"I think he and Amy live a very balanced life. They have a nice setting, a nice house. I don't consider them extravagant. Amy doesn't go out and spend a lot of money on jewelry or foolish things. They are very well centered people." Amy has a good sense of what's going on in the business because she furnishes its corporate apartments, clubhouses and recreation centers.

It's a small thing, but it says a lot that Will doesn't carry a wallet. Austin Gower, his protégé, says, "When I travel with him, he'll carry maybe a five and a few ones, a driver's license and a credit card—that's all. He's the last guy you'd ever see flashing a wad of bills."

That unpretentious ethos carries over to the office as well. Terri Smith, the Comptroller, went to work at Greystone Properties at 23. A co-worker there introduced her to the man she married. When she was pregnant, Will insisted that she stay home and not think about work for the last two and a half weeks before her daughter, Emerson, arrived. Will's mother, Betty, gave Emerson a crib as a baby gift. When she has a daycare problem, Terri doesn't hesitate to bring Emerson, now a preschooler, to work. "We have a very close-knit office, a family atmosphere," Terri observes. "Will has this knack of pulling us outside our routines to think about each other. The turnover here is incredibly low. I know I'd never want to work anywhere else."

What all this reflects, Austin points out, is that "The guy gives a damn about people. One of our project managers got cancer and had to quit work. He got paid until the day he died." Austin cites another instance when a laborer without insurance lost his home in a fire. Will moved him into a Greystone apartment rent-free until he could get back on his feet, and his co-workers chipped in items to furnish the new place.

"That year at our Christmas party, that man got up to speak," Austin recalls. "I'm sure he'd never spoken to a group of a hundred in his entire life. Will had no idea what he was going to say. But when he got finished, it was a pretty tearful crowd for lack of better words."

The highlight of every Greystone Christmas party is when everyone gets $50 in cash and is encouraged to give that money to someone they're not related to and don't know. "It could be the guy under the bridge or the

Will White and Russ Gache

lady at the fast-food drive-through," Austin notes. "I think Will just wants to put the focus where it belongs—on giving to others, especially those in need, and not thinking so much about our own little world."

A freak accident in his sophomore year ingrained discipline in Will on an even deeper level than before. He and a bunch of his buddies were engaged in a foolish, if good-natured, late-night fracas: a wrestling match—throwing each other around, I'd imagine, among a lot of sharply angled objects like chairs, steel-framed beds and the like. Lady Luck took revenge: Will tore his medial collateral ligament and a lateral collateral ligament and suffered cartilage damage as well. His tennis season was over in an instant: The accident meant he had to undergo a serious operation with a long recovery process—eight months as it turned out. He was fortunate that Dr. Jack Hughston, who was widely known as the Father of Sports Medicine, could put his knee back together.

Will was also faced with a long and difficult rehab, involving countless leg lifts and lifting heavy weights. He was also faced with the fact that he'd let the team down. His coaches and teammates had counted on him as an almost "sure win" at the No. 3 singles position. Instead, he was out for the entire season in the spring of '81 and couldn't even hit tennis balls.

But I'll have to say he faced up to his mistake and rectified it in the only way that truly mattered: by putting in all the boring "reps" that made his injured knee stronger than ever. That takes discipline and tough-mindedness at a very basic level.

Without that discipline, his terrific comeback in 1982 would never have happened—a season in which he went 29–7 at No. 3 singles, won the ACC championship for No. 3 doubles with Russell Gache and was runner-up ACC Champion at No. 3 singles. To top it off, Will, who majored in economics, a demanding subject area, made the ACC All-Academic team.

He was a true scholar-athlete and the only real flaw I ever found was wrestling late at night when he should have been in bed.

CHAPTER TWELVE

The Public Intellectual

Somehow, the students filing into Room 202 of Harvard Hall on January 31, 2002, had the look of mannequins in a department store window. So much so that an article in *Harvard Magazine* had asked, "Don't you, you undergraduates—so convinced of your individuality—get tired of looking the same?"[1] Their informal dress code was described, in part, as denim from Diesel, a button-down shirt from J. Crew, name brand sneakers or Timberland hiking boots and a fleece from North Face or EMS Apparel[2]—all label-conscious choices, what an article in *The New Yorker* had called "nobrow culture."[3]

Such arrant conformists seemed unlikely prospects for evangelization, but evangelizing was precisely what John Stauffer, their boyish-looking professor in sports coat and slacks had in mind with a new lecture course he'd called, "American Protest Literature." At 27, Stauffer had recently given up a lucrative career in finance at Paine Webber and Company to become an apostle for the humanities, earning a PhD from Yale in American studies in 1998 and becoming, the following year, an assistant professor of English, history and literature at Harvard. He'd been promoted to associate professor of English and American civilization two years later, and, in 2004, became the second person in 30 years to be granted tenure from within the university.[4] By then, he was well on his way to becoming a public intellectual with influence far beyond the lecture halls of America's oldest university.

As they entered Room 202, a thought-provoking ambience greeted the 50-plus students who'd signed up for Stauffer's course. The stirring strains of the "Battle Hymn of the Republic" filled the room, and a large screen down front displayed the 1831 masthead of William Lloyd Garrison's newspaper, *The Liberator,* depicting a slave auction in the foreground and a slave tied to a whipping post in front of the U.S. Capitol in the background.[5] The students were about to be immersed in one of the first multimedia courses offered at Harvard. A few colleagues had been dismissive of John's surprising departure from the standard lecture format, but he'd gone forward anyway, bent on finding an approach to broaden the appeal of the humanities.[6] It had worked surprisingly well: In time, the course became one of the most popular on campus, attracting more than 300 students to three classes each week—two sessions en masse and a third in seminars of 15 or so students, where graduate fellows honed their writing skills on a one-on-one basis. Stauffer taught the course for the last time in 2016; by then, its run had been about the same as the Broadway shows *Beauty and the Beast* and *Mama Mia.* Jazzing up content had never been his aim, but he'd made his point: True, the humanities were under siege, but they could be enlivened, could be presented in a way the modern student would find relevant, even riveting. His ever-evolving course title said as much: "American Protest Literature from Tom Paine to Tupac Shakur." In Tupac, AKA 2Pac or Makaveli, Stauffer had opted for the au courant: a famous rapper, who'd been murdered in a drive-by shooting in 1996, a figure many of the millennials he was proselytizing to were more familiar with than Tom Paine.

He continues to evangelize for the humanities with as much fervor as ever. "Students today don't see the humanities as practical, but the humanities can change the world," John recently told me. In 2017, he launched yet another "big" lecture course—"Is the Civil War Still Being Fought?"; it, too, has 300-plus students,[7] many of whom are attracted by his reputation as one of America's leading authorities on the Abolition Movement, Frederick Douglass and the Civil War period.

In a sense, his early life made John something of a loner and forced

John Stauffer in the classroom

him to entertain himself. His father, Bill, was a small-town newspaper editor in the upper Midwest, who moved the family often until he joined Northwestern Bell and moved his household permanently to Des Moines. John finished high school there, but by then, he'd attended nine different schools and had formed few close friendships. That void was partially offset by the bonds of a close-knit, nurturing family—parents whose constancy he could always count on and two doting sisters. Growing up, he was awestruck by the athletic exploits of his father, Bill, who'd been an All-American basketball player at the University of Missouri and got drafted by Red Auerbach, coach of the Boston Celtics. Having majored in journalism, Bill had chosen a newspaper career instead and moved his family from town to town as he progressed up the ladder of success to become a widely respected editor.

Frequent moves made it difficult for John to develop close friendships; thus, his retreat within led to a great passion for reading. By the time he got to high school, he'd progressed to serious history and fiction, voraciously reading classics like *Uncle Tom's Cabin*, *Little Women* and *The Red Badge of Courage*. They had opened his eyes to America's tortured past. Revelation of its terrible pain came from *Narrative of the Life of Frederick Douglass, an American Slave*, a book an African American friend gave him his junior year. Learning about Douglass whetted his appetite to know more about Lincoln and his generation of writers: Whitman, Stowe, Thoreau, Dickinson, Hawthorne and others. Gradually, his grasp became three-dimensional: he could absorb, deconstruct and interpret content rapidly, a skill that provided a strong foundation for the academic career he'd one day pursue.

The other constant in John's formative years was tennis. His Mom first introduced him to swimming and then, at age nine or ten, had put him in a tennis clinic with an excellent teacher. He liked the game, and it was soon apparent that his talent would take him far. His Mom then began driving him and his doubles partner to tournaments throughout the Upper Midwest. During down time between matches, he and his partner both read instead of watching other matches. As a teen, he was a scrawny kid, five feet, five inches tall and 145 pounds, but he kept climbing steadily in the national rankings for the 12-, 14- and 16-and-under age categories. By the time he finished high school, he was 39th in the nation in the 18-and-under age group.

That fall, he and Bill took a trip to Duke to see the school and meet me. I knew about his high national ranking, but I'd already awarded all the scholarships we had for his freshman year. I told him if he became a starter in his first year, I'd award him a full scholarship for the next three years. Little did I know that he'd become a Most Valuable Player, but I saw very early on that he'd strengthen the team significantly. He started at No. 6 singles as a freshman, advanced to No. 3 singles as a sophomore and played at No. 1 his junior and senior years.

I developed a great affection for our talented young whiz with the Beatles style mop top and boy band good looks; he was square-jawed, trim and taut, with a deep-crease smile that lit his face like a lantern. By the time he got to Duke, he was five feet, ten inches and a bit more than 150 pounds—about the same size he is today. I could see right away how hungry he was, how eager to learn. He lacked that one big shot—a thundering serve or knee-buckling crosscourt—that most stars can always count on. Instead, he won with keen anticipation, great quickness and unusual tenacity. I was always impressed with John's analytical side: his sound match strategy, how seldom sloppy thinking cost him a point.

That same mental acuity animated his passion for literature *and* mathematics, twin aptitudes I'd rarely seen in other players. While literature

John Stauffer on the tennis court

was his first love, he shied away from an English degree, thinking he might not write well enough. He opted, instead, to get an engineering degree because solving problem sets—a big part of the engineering curriculum—came easy. He also was influenced by his Dad, who kept stressing that engineers were the most sought after majors on college campuses. "You won't earn nearly as much with an English degree," Bill had advised, "but you'll get a lot more offers and a lot more lucrative ones, too."

John recalls that: "I felt it would be easier to budget my time, devoting 30 hours a week or more to tennis and the same to my engineering studies. Writing a 10-page essay was just too open-ended; I had no idea then—and even now—how long that might take."

He earned a degree in mechanical engineering and worked briefly for American Hospital Supply in Southern California, then as a weapons designer for Ford Aerospace in Newport Beach, where he had a top security clearance. He got lots of overtime at Ford, which enabled him to start saving and investing. He began by reading about stocks and bonds, the history and theory of investing. But his growing disenchantment with defense industry bureaucracy and the sameness of Southern California weather made a job change seem attractive. Friends advised that his skills in math and engineering would make him attractive in the financial sector, so he began exploring options there. An offer soon came from E.F. Hutton to become an institutional manager in New York, Boston or Hartford. He chose Hartford, thinking he'd face less competition in a smaller city. For the first nine months, he was sent to what he calls a "superb" training program. At the end, he took an examination that only half the trainees passed; those who failed were out of a job. Success meant he got several institutional accounts—mainly small and medium business relationships—to manage and quickly established himself as a workhorse, putting in 10- to 12-hour days, six days a week. I'm sure the same boundless energy that made him a No. 1 in tennis served him well at E.F. Hutton, where financial rewards came quickly. His income soon rose to six figures and, then, a good bit beyond.

On the down side, he had no social life at all. Reading, again, was his only outlet in the meager spare time his typical day afforded. The more he read, the more aware he became of his passion for literature. Several years after he joined E.F. Hutton (and the company had become Paine Webber), Joel Fleishman, a professor he'd played squash with at Duke and kept in touch with, asked John: "Have you thought about taking an English seminar at Wesleyan? I think you'd love it. You'd be in a community of book lovers."

John took that suggestion, and it led to a complete change in career trajectory. He enrolled in "Masterworks of Fiction," a course that featured the works of James Joyce, Virginia Woolf and D.H. Lawrence, among others, at Wesleyan University, a short drive from the center of Hartford. The spirited class discussions were exciting and whetted his appetite for more. The writing assignments, too, were challenging, nothing like the hard slog he'd feared. While taking a second seminar at Wesleyan, a not-so-subtle change occurred at work. His boss at Paine Webber had noticed that John wasn't quite the workhorse he'd been, that he was putting in fewer hours and late nights. He began pressing John to return to his old schedule and that engendered guilt. It also forced a fundamental reassessment: At 27, still single, his first post-Duke decade more than half gone, had he found the right profession after all?

The answer he got was an emphatic, No! He now says the seminars at Wesleyan clarified something he desperately needed to know: "I realized that making a lot of money did not make me happy. That was a real revelation; it freed me up to spend the rest of my life doing something I loved." Ultimately, he wanted to earn a PhD and to pursue a career in academe. He knew he'd make a lot less money, but fortunately he'd saved enough to pay for a master of arts degree in liberal studies at Wesleyan. After that, he'd be on his own, but his entrepreneurial instincts told him that he could find enough fellowships and grants to pay for a PhD.

When he broke the news to his family "My Dad literally thought I'd gone crazy. I was quitting a job that paid $250,000 a year for a mere prospect that would pay me nothing to begin with. It was a scary step to take, but I was absolutely sure it was the right thing to do."

After earning a master of arts degree at Wesleyan in 1991, John got a second master's in American studies from Perdue University. By then, he'd sold his house in Hartford and was living in a graduate dorm room—a step backward that very few, even scholars, would be willing to take. But the degree at Purdue helped him get into Yale University, where he earned a PhD in American studies in 1999. As one of the older PhD students at Yale, John says, "I felt like I was playing catch-up." Despite that, he soon was being mentored by one of America's most prominent public intellectuals, David Brion Davis, who directed his work on a PhD. Best known for his seminal work on the history of slavery and abolitionism, Davis won the Pulitzer Prize for general nonfiction in 1967 for his book *The Problem of Slavery in Western Culture.* He later won the Bancroft Prize and the National Book Award for a sequel, *The Problem of Slavery in the Age of Revolution.* Davis profoundly influenced John, whose academic career, in many ways, has mirrored that of his oft-awarded advisor. The dissertation John wrote under Davis's guidance would soon become an influential book, *The Black Hearts of Men,* published by Harvard University Press.

John's impact with *Black Hearts*—which he dedicated to Davis—and other work has been greatly magnified by an uncanny ability to explain difficult, often highly complex subjects to the general reader and lay audiences. He made his mark soon after joining the faculty at Harvard by reviving interest in a near-forgotten Frederick Douglass, who'd been one of the most influential and most photographed men of the 19th century. Douglass had gone into virtual eclipse after reconstruction when many white southerners began glorifying the "Lost Cause" and when black Americans were being marginalized with Jim Crow laws and a spate of lynchings that continued to the eve of World War II. Few academics bothered to study or write about Douglass, even though he and other abolitionists had helped transform the world in the 19th century. In *Black Hearts,* which was published in 2001, John explained that phenomenon, writing that: "For centuries, slavery had been unquestioned in the New World. In 1770, hardly an acre existed in that vast expanse that was not tended by slaves. The institution of slavery was practiced everywhere in that sphere. It was thought that city-state civilization would not exist without slaves—that they were indispensable. And yet, a century after the idea of abolition took root, the will to end slavery was victorious. It was truly heroic, one of the great successes in world history."[8]

Black Hearts was one of the first books to develop this argument, and many books followed that explored variations of it. The book earned a host of admiring reviews and three major awards: co-winner of the Frederick Douglass Book Prize; second place for the Lincoln Book Prize; and winner of the Avery Craven Book Award. In addition to Douglass, *Black Hearts* focused widespread attention on three other antislavery leaders: James McCune Smith, a black physician, who held that white Americans had to acquire black hearts to understand race in America; Gerrit Smith, a wealthy white land baron who brought the others together; and John Brown, who led the famous raid at Harper's Ferry. This quartet overcame social barriers and mistrust to form an alliance to reconcile ideals of justice with the reality of slavery and oppression.

John's first big breakthrough with the general reader and the public at large came in 2008 with the publication of *Giants: The Parallel Lives of Abraham Lincoln and Frederick Douglass.* A bestseller, it was reviewed in more than 100 newspapers. Overall, the reviews were quite positive, but *Giants* was criticized for inflating Douglass's impact and overstating the importance of the Lincoln-Douglass friendship. Speculation in the book that Lincoln and his close friend, Joshua Speed, may have had a homosexual relationship provoked some negative reactions. Despite the criticisms, the book stimulated lively discussion and debate. His clear writing and original research established John, for the first time, as a public intellectual who would be heard from often.

John followed *Giants* a year later with a second bestseller, *The State of Jones: The Small Southern County that Seceded from the Confederacy,* co-written with Sally Jenkins, a popular sportswriter with the *Washington Post* and author of several other well regarded books. *The State of Jones* describes the 1863 revolt in a rural Mississippi county against the Confederacy, thereby challenging the popular notion that southerners offered monolithic opposition to the Union. Based on a true story, the book describes a guerrilla band led by Newton Knight, a dirt-poor farmer and likely deserter from the rebel army. Living off the land and hiding in the swamps, Knight and his guerrilla band skirmished, from time to time, with Confederate troops as the war wound down, but never got captured. Knight had a mixed-race family and, after the war, aided with Reconstruction. The paucity of sources on Knight's deeds prompted criticism that the authors embellished the facts, but most reviewers credited them with producing a highly readable account that challenged the near-universal belief that all southerners supported the Confederacy.

In 2016, a major motion picture, *The Free State of Jones,* was brought to the screen by director Gary Ross, whose box office hits include *Seabiscuit, Lassie* and *Dave.* Ross asked John to serve as a historical consultant on the film. It was not the first time he'd had such a role: In 2012, John had served as a historical consultant to Quentin Tarantino, who directed the hit film *Django Unchained*. Assignments like these reflected John's recognition as a leading authority on abolitionism and the Civil War.

His two bestsellers are merely the best-known part of John's prodigious writing output: He has written four other books on the Civil War and the Abolition Movement; written five books of limited edition photography;[9] edited and co-edited eight books with others like his prominent friend and colleague at Harvard, Henry Louis Gates; and written dozens of magazine and newspaper articles.

Even more enthusiastic than the accolades for his books are those of the PhD candidates he's mentored and other graduate students he's advised. After getting her undergraduate degree at Cambridge, Zoe Trodd went to Harvard, expecting to earn a master's in history and then return to England for her PhD. John hired her as a teaching assistant for his big lecture course on American Protest Movements; and she stayed on to pursue a PhD at Harvard with John as her mentor. They ended up writing three books together: two on John Brown's raid at Harper's Ferry and another on Frederick Douglass.

Trodd returned to England as a superstar among antislavery scholars; for a brief time, she was the country's youngest professor. Today, she is Director of the Rights Lab at Nottingham University, a part of the Faculty of Social Sciences, where she is developing strategies for ending slavery worldwide by 2030. She nominated John for the Harvard Mentoring Award, which he won.

She calls John a leading scholar of American antislavery and American protest and says he has done more than anyone to fuse the subjects of antislavery, race, protest and photography. "He pioneered the study of protest literature which is at the heart of all great protest movements. Before John, they [protest movement leaders] were being marginalized, dismissed as rabble rousers and propagandists. He's made it a serious field and has had many imitators for the big course he launched in 2002 on American Protest Literature."

Trodd also offers a personal insight about John's relationship with those he mentors and advises: "He wants you to improve your life. He was very attuned to whether we were happy and healthy, whether we had good relationships with our family, even whether I was homesick in being away from England for such a long time."[10]

That view is confirmed by Manisha Sinha, author of *The Slave's Cause: A History of Abolition*, which won the Frederick Douglass Book Prize in 2016. She credits John with "incredible generosity" in advising her on how to improve her writing once she had a draft of *The Slave's Cause*. She says, "He has a public presence beyond academia with the reviews he writes for the popular press and where his books are widely read and published by commercial houses. Those are things very few scholars attain." Moreover, her basic assessment is, "I think he is a good human being. That for me is the highest compliment."[11]

When John joined the faculty at Harvard in 1999, it was the first time he'd lived in a large metropolitan area. Pouring himself into his work left no time for a social life; soon he began to feel lonelier than he'd ever been. Not long after he got tenure in 2004, a chance meeting at Primary Sources, a Boston-based organization that develops curricula for secondary school teachers, changed all that. He was being interviewed for a seat on its board when a young woman—one of three persons conducting the interview—asked if he'd assess a course she was developing on the Civil War and the Gilded Age. A few days later, he and Deborah Cunningham met at a nearby coffee shop, where he quickly learned that she'd earned a PhD in education at Yale in 1993, the year he began his studies there. While they never met at Yale, John had gotten to know Deb's closest friend; it was soon clear that they had similar interests and a lot to talk about. Not long after that, Deb invited him home to Bennington, Vermont, to meet her parents.

When they got married in 2005, Deb was in her mid-thirties and John in his mid-forties. She wanted kids and was afraid she might not be able to have them. "I was ambivalent," John recalls. "I told her 'I'd love to have you for a year all to myself. But if you insist on having a kid, we'll have one.'"

It was a big step John says in retrospect. "I'd rarely been around kids and didn't really know what to expect. Kids change you; you quickly learn that they come first. I'd have to say it's all worked out beautifully." Today, he and Deb have two sons: Erik, age 12, and Nicholas, age 9. He can draw on deep and successful experience in guiding them forward. No aspect of John's career has been more impactful than the high achievers he's taught—students who went on to become successful teachers, lawyers, journalists and even protest leaders. He is emphatic that the bricks and mortar of his career were the experiences he gained as a scholar-athlete.

He has thought more deeply about the ideal of the scholar-athlete than anyone I know. He has been incredibly helpful to me in shaping my ideas for this book; in fact, his ideas and deep experience have informed and improved the narrative remarkably. He worries that "few people, and virtually no major public voices, are calling for a return to the scholar-athlete ideal. Most see varsity athletes—certainly those in the big revenue sports—as gladiators. We reward them for their athletic talent because they draw crowds. Now, nearly everyone seems to be arguing, 'Just pay them and be done with it.' But that would leave us with a bankrupt system that may never become solvent again."

To that I heartily add, "Amen!"

John and I strongly agree that we must develop and carry out policies that nurture more scholar-athletes. If we do that, we can transform our colleges and universities and reestablish learning and excellence in education as their highest priority. We have long felt that revival of the scholar-athlete ideal will play an indispensable part in achieving that goal. He points to the fact that "scholars and athletes are both essentially crafts people. It requires an immense amount of knowledge, dedication and repetition whether you're preparing for the big game or to become a scientist, chemist, biologist, engineer or music critic. To compete at the highest level in sport, or even at the varsity level, requires much the same thing: a caring coach who helps with motivation and training, who critiques your progress and cultivates a competitive attitude and mental toughness to make you successful."

In his superb bestseller *Shop Class as Soulcraft,* Matthew B. Crawford writes, ". . . creativity is a by-product of mastery of the sort that is cultivated through long practice. It seems to be built up through the *submission* (think of a musician practicing scales, or Einstein learning tensor algebra)." Or think of a tennis player spending hours practicing to master his craft. Crawford's point here is reminiscent of Matthew Sayed's assertion (see Chapter Seven) that, no matter what the activity, performers at the highest level have had 10,000 hours of practice.

Stauffer is certain that "Before anything gets done, there first has to be a growing awareness of the importance and value of the scholar-athlete. There is no way anything is going to get done unless educational leaders come to embrace this ideal."

The English writer H.G. Wells once warned that we are in a race between education and disaster. George Orwell feared those who would ban books, while Aldous Huxley feared that no one would want to read one. In 1985, Neil Postman, an end-of-century philosopher king and a prominent public intellectual, pointed out both these fears in his widely-read book, *Amusing Ourselves to Death*. All by way of saying it will not be easy to build awareness and gain the public commitment needed to restore the scholar-athlete ideal. Huxley feared that "the truth would be drowned in a sea of irrelevance," that we'd become "a trivial culture, preoccupied with some equivalent of the feelies, the orgy porgy, and the centrifugal bumblepuppy."[12]

In short, Huxley feared that what we love will ruin us. And so it is that on any given Saturday 100,000 full-throated fans gather to cheer pale images of the student-athlete in settings as raucous as a Mad Max Thunderdome. The featured song in that 1985 film, ironically, was Tina Turner's "We Don't Need Another Hero."

Alas, three decades on and counting, we still don't need another hero who can carry the pigskin; we need more scholar-athletes to lead America back to educational greatness. John Stauffer's path to many accomplishments as a scholar-athlete offer me great hope that we can accomplish that much-to-be-cherished goal.

CHAPTER THIRTEEN

A Life in Full

Mark Meyers was my first scholarship player, the best recruiting decision I ever made, a great competitor who still holds the highest winning percentage of any player who ever toted a tennis racquet for Duke. He was singularly observant, thoughtful, self-possessed and, without a doubt, remarkably understated. Most memorably, his corkscrew backhand was so good it became a powerful offensive weapon; among all the players I coached, his backhand was the strongest and most consistent, among the very best I ever saw. That said, I would venture to say his career path had more than a hint of predictability: a corporate man through and through; a trusted attorney at Shell Oil who negotiated high-value ocean drilling rights with foreign governments from the Gulf of Mexico to the South China Sea; a man of the world with somewhat ordinary tastes. Was his ultra-unorthodox corkscrew backhand—that long, graceful flowing motion up and over the ball, imparting such explosive topspin—in any way the harbinger of the about turn his somewhat staid life one day would take? Did that extraordinary stroke—which he practiced so long and hard—foretell of the iconoclast who would come to follow, in a biblical sense, a pillar of cloud by day and a pillar of fire by night?

To explore these questions, I must first describe Mark's early life and certain influences that profoundly shaped his worldview and character.

Mark grew up playing at the oldest tennis club in America, founded in 1876—the New Orleans Lawn Tennis Club, whose pro, Emmett Paré, had starred on the early pro tour as a playing companion of the legendary Bill Tilden. When his playing days ended, Paré took two jobs: head pro at the New Orleans Club and tennis coach at Tulane University, where he soon built a national powerhouse. During his long career at Tulane, Paré's teams would win 18 Southeastern Conference championships and one national championship and boast eight NCAA singles and two NCAA doubles champions. His forte was teaching classic stokes and mental toughness; and at 9 a.m. every Saturday, Paré gave a lesson to young Mark Meyers on the finer points of the game, including tactics and strategy. Learning from Paré on the Club's clay courts, where the pacing was much slower than on hard courts, forced the young comer to develop flawless ground strokes. No wonder, then, that by age 12, Mark was the seventh-ranked junior in the nation, or that by the time he got to Duke, he was second-ranked in the South and ninth-ranked nationally in his age category.

He and his brother, Bill, who was four years older, traveled widely and alone by train to play in junior tournaments in places like Atlanta, Jackson and Chattanooga. Bill would go on to become a tennis star at Northwestern University. He finished first in his medical school class at Louisiana State University and is considered one of the leading gastroenterologists in the South today.

It was always a longshot for Mark to come to Duke; his high national ranking made him a prime target for many schools with high profile tennis programs. Alabama, LSU, Michigan and Virginia all offered him a full scholarship. In taking the reins at Duke in '71, I inherited a team that won six matches and lost 12 the year before. Duke had never offered a tennis scholarship, not even a partial one, even though its powerhouse competitors—UNC, NC State and Clemson—all offered what we called "a full ride" to the best players. As I began recruiting for the '72 team, I picked up a useful piece of intelligence: Mark's dad, Bill, was dead set on his son choosing a school with high academic standards. That gave us a chance if we could come up with a scholarship.

Even though I'd been in the job barely a year, I decided to approach Duke's baronial Athletic Director, Eddie Cameron, to request a scholarship for Mark. I liked Eddie because there was nothing counterfeit about him and he always stuck to his word. But Eddie was crusty and could be gruff. He was focused almost entirely on football and basketball—both of which he'd coached with great success at Duke—and had little time for the non-revenue sports like tennis. Just before he interviewed me to be tennis coach, I'd heard a worrisome rumor that Eddie's counterpart at NC State was bragging about not paying his tennis coach anything at all. I badly wanted the job but couldn't help thinking about the NC State rumor when I entered Eddie's spacious office near the main entrance of Duke Indoor Stadium (later renamed Cameron Indoor Stadium for Eddie). Had he been in uniform, the man who rose to greet me easily could have been mistaken for the Chairman of the Joint Chiefs of Staff. A high forehead and arching eyebrows reinforced his imposing look. Eddie had little time for small talk, so our conversation went something like—

"As you may know, I've got an opening over on the tennis courts. Duke needs a new head tennis coach and I wonder if you'd like to be considered?"

"Sure I would. I think I could turn tennis into a strong program."

"My concern is that you already have a job as fencing coach."

"Actually, two jobs: I'm teaching courses in PE too."

"Then tennis would make three. Can you can handle three? You know what they say about tennis—it's a bit on the sissy side and not that demanding."

I was completely flummoxed. At the time, tennis often *did* get dismissed as a lightweight sport. I fumbled back: "You'd be surprised how much a good tennis player has to sweat. Takes that to improve. I'm sure we can put athletes out there who will make Duke proud."

A faint smile flickered, but I sensed a no pay offer coming. To head it off, I blurted: "I'd get a boost in pay, right?"

"Not much," Eddie rejoined with the look of a sphinx.

I must have seemed crestfallen during another eon-like pause. Finally, Eddie said: "What about $500 bucks? That should be enough to put us on the road to a championship."

Eddie had big expectations, but so what? I was convinced the job had great potential. So, we shook hands; that was the kind of agreement you got back then because the Athletic Department was still a mom and pop operation. When I went back to see Eddie the following year to ask for a scholarship, I stressed winning and not much else. Knowing that he was all about winning, I stressed that I had my eye on a player who was good enough to attract others—that given time Duke *would* have a tennis championship. That's what he needed to hear, so I got his somewhat grudging support. A Duke Athletic Director had only so many scholarships to give, but I had my first and was determined to get more.

Ironically, the suitors recruiting Mark were chasing a scrawny kid weighing 140 pounds and only five feet eight inches tall. None of us could foresee that, as a freshman, he'd grow like a weed, adding 30 pounds and six inches of height—gains which, naturally, made him far stronger. When he got to Duke, his serve was a tad weak, but it soon became a major strength. His improved all-around power was magnified further by a change in surfaces: Instead of clay, he'd be playing on acrylic-topped hard courts that favored a faster, more explosive game. Still, the long and patient tutelage of Emmett Paré paid great dividends: Mark had all the shots, almost never made unforced errors and stood out most as a tactician, who could quickly identify and attack an opponent's weaknesses. Moreover, once the match got underway, he was completely unflappable; I never saw him lose focus over a bad shot or a bad call. Most admirably, he never let himself get distracted by the last point and had the mental toughness to accept winning or losing with the same even-keeled demeanor.

I remember well what he said when I praised his cool in a very tense match: "Getting mad at myself takes too much energy." I seem to recall he won that match in a tiebreaker.

In 1971, my first year, the team won 10 matches and lost eight. Mark came in '72, and we improved slightly to 12–9; but individually, Mark had a phenomenal year, going 19–2 in his individual matches. That fall—the beginning of his sophomore year—he won the prestigious Southern Intercollegiate Championship in Athens, Georgia, which attracted nearly all the South's best players, a huge accomplishment. Mark remains the only Duke player ever to win it. And what a start! In barely six months, he'd entirely changed team expectations.

Though we regressed a bit in '73 to a team record of 10–8, Mark continued his dominance at No. 1 singles. That year's season-ending ACC championship was played on very fast courts at Wake Forest. Mark entered the tournament with only one loss—to UNC All-American Freddie McNair on a slow clay court in Chapel Hill. McNair would later become a French

Open Grand Slam champion in doubles and one of the world's top-ranked doubles players. Mark expected to get revenge in a rematch with McNair after winning a close semi-final match over Audley Bell of Wake Forest. But Clemson's streaky Bhanu Nunna, a terrific player from India, scored a stunning upset of McNair in the other ACC semi-final. Earlier in the year at Clemson, Mark had squeaked by Nunna in a three-set thriller. Their rematch in the championship was much the same with Mark pressing point after point with strong serves and crisp volleys. Mark finally won 7–5, 7–5 to become the first Duke player to win an ACC singles title—a huge milestone for us because it clearly showed we could win and win big! After that, the team psychology became *we can beat anybody.*

The expectations of top-ranked juniors everywhere changed too. Between 1972 and 1975, top-ranked players like Ted Daniel of Tulsa, David Robinson of Westfield, New Jersey, Chip Davis of Orlando and Niels Rathlev of Denmark, learned about the winning atmosphere at Duke and wanted to be a part of it. They were all strongly influenced by Mark's decision to come to Duke—and by the fact that I *did* get more scholarships.

The following year (1974), Mark added an exclamation point to his ACC championship in a herculean battle against UNC's Rich McKee, one of Carolina's all-time greats, a three-time All-American ('72–'74) and a three-time ACC champion. The match turned on a single point in a tie-breaker at the end of the third set. (At that time, tennis tiebreakers were first to win five points.) Leading at 4–2, McKee needed only one point to win the match. Mark served a bomb into the backhand court right down the "T" to McKee's forehand. His return was a funky double hit that somehow fluttered over Mark's head and landed short of the baseline. McKee quickly came toward the net as if to shake hands after winning match point.

"Richard, wasn't that a double hit?" Mark politely asked. "I thought it banged around on your racquet two or three times before it came off."

McKee forthrightly replied: "I think you're right, Mark. It *was* a double hit."

That made the tiebreaker score 4–3 in McKee's favor. Mark won the next point to force match point at 4–4. He served another bomb to McKee's backhand, again in the backhand court, but this time it was returned low and hard down the line to Mark's forehand. Mark lunged and somehow managed to volley a crosscourt winner. It was the first-time in

Mark Meyers in 1972

the modern era Duke had won a No. 1 singles match against UNC since the Tar Heels had established a dynasty in the early 1900s. In his four years at Duke, Mark only lost 11 matches.

After graduating, Mark spent the remainder of '75 and the Spring of '76 playing pro satellite tournaments and ATP (Association of Tennis Professionals) qualifying events and earned his way into tour events in Barcelona, Madrid and Tehran. The Tehran event was played at the Imperial Country Club, which seemed to epitomize a new and highly westernized Iran. Little did he, or anyone else, know how adamantly the Iranian Revolution would reject western ways four years later.

By the end of June 1976, Mark had accumulated wins against players like Brian Teacher, a future Australian Open champion; Peter Fleming, who would win seven Grand Prix doubles titles with John McEnroe; Tom Gullikson, a future U.S. Davis Cup captain; Hank Pfister, who would defeat Arthur Ashe, Roscoe Tanner and Jimmy Connors at the Alan King Tennis Classic in Las Vegas in '81; and Steve Docherty, who would defeat Arthur Ashe at Wimbledon in '81. Along the way, Mark collected enough ATP points to rank just outside the world's top 100 players. That made him a direct entrant (i.e., no qualifying) for 1976 ATP tour events. In Cincinnati, the first event of the year, he partnered with NCAA singles champion Bill Scanlon in doubles to reach the quarter-finals where they got knocked out by the eventual winners, Eddie Dibbs and Harold Solomon. Unfortunately, Mark suffered a shoulder injury in Cincinnati that sidelined him for several months.

After consulting with a Duke orthopedist on possible surgery, Mark had a long talk with his dad, who strongly suggested that it might be time to move on from professional tennis. He was proud that Mark had earned his way onto the ATP tour, but they both knew he'd have to be a top 30 player to make serious money and that was a very high hill to climb. Mark decided to quit the tour and go to law school at LSU and accepted an invitation to serve as assistant tennis coach that spring. Even so, his ATP ranking was still high enough to make him a direct entrant in the '75 U.S. Open and the Australian Open in early '76. He played in both events even though he had already begun law school and had stopped playing competitive tennis due to his shoulder injury.

Unlike many who played at the highest level, Mark never suffered tennis burnout and has had lifelong success in the game. Between 2009 and 2018, he won the men's national clay court championships for age 55, 60 and 65-and-under. These championships brought Mark's tennis full circle: it was played at the New Orleans Lawn Tennis Club, where Emmett Paré gave him his first lesson at age eight.

My greatest regret as Duke tennis coach was that Mark wasn't named an All-American despite defeating many who were. At the end of his senior year, he got invited to the NCAA National Championships in Athens, Georgia. Carl James, who'd taken Eddie's place as Athletic Director, agreed to pay Mark's travel expenses to Athens but not mine. When coaches made up the seedings for the championship flight of 16 players, Mark got left out. It was a double slight—and a terrible one at that—because the top 16 seeds automatically became All-Americans. When I got the news, I knew instantly I'd made a bad mistake: I should have gone to Athens at my own expense. The case for Mark being named an All-American was overwhelming; all he needed was an advocate when the seedings were made, and I'd failed him by not being there. And yet, there were no recriminations from Mark. When I apologized, he told me: "Everybody believes you've had our best interests at heart and I know you've given me and everybody else a fair shake." That meant the world to me, because Mark never expected special treatment, even though he was our greatest star.

For Mark, tennis was only one part of the balanced life. He epitomized the type of player I was determined to get: a scholar-athlete with a four-year GPA of 3.2 (equivalent to 3.5 today), a double major in economics and political science and splendidly prepared for law school.

Mark came from a family of four boys and two girls—all of them super achievers—that first settled in Louisiana in the late 1800s and would eventually develop strong ties on both sides to LSU and Shell Oil. Their Dad, William Morrison Meyers, was the perfect role model: He'd supervised the 16-inch guns as a Marine lieutenant aboard the battleship U.S.S. Washington in the Battle of Leyte Gulf, the largest naval engagement of World War II and a devastating defeat for the Imperial Navy of Japan. After the war, Bill went to law school at LSU, finished third in the class of '48 and embarked on what would be a highly successful legal career, first with Shell and later in private practice. He died at age 90 in 2013. The year before he died, the Meyers family was named to the Louisiana Tennis Hall of Fame. Mark's mother, Lorraine Holleman Meyers, also graduated from LSU and remains in good health at 92.

While Mark's siblings have all become highly successful professionals, his youngest sister, Mary Meyers Howard, is a world-famous set designer in Brooklyn. Her firm, Mary Howard Studios, builds glitzy sets for cover shoots by famous photographers like Annie Leibovitz for *Vogue*, *Vanity Fair* and other big-name magazines.

Mark's three children are also high achievers. Brent, 30, is a magna cum laude graduate of Washington and Lee University and in 2015 got a divinity degree from Westminster Theological Seminary in San Diego. He is an evangelist church "planter" in Barcelona, Spain. Holly, 27, majored in theater arts at Texas Christian University and works for Athletes in Action in Houston, the athlete-focused affiliate of Cru, formerly Campus Crusade for Christ. Anna, 25, got a degree in agriculture from LSU and assists at Mary Howard Studios with set construction.

Mark's wife, Susan, got her law degree at LSU and practiced for five years with the prestigious Milling Benson law firm in New Orleans before becoming a stay-at-home mom. She now has her own business advising students on undergraduate and graduate school admissions.

After several years as a litigator at Phelps Dunbar, a large New Orleans-based firm with oil and gas, London insurers and other commercial clients, Mark began a 28-year career with Shell in New Orleans, where he negotiated commercial deals in the hundreds of millions to the billion or more dollar range. He first worked on joint venture, acquisition and divestiture projects in the Gulf of Mexico.

But in 2008, Shell offered Mark a job as one of the top transactional attorneys at company headquarters in The Hague, the capital city of the Netherlands. He and Susan jumped at the chance to expose their kids to the Old World's cultural riches. Their home on Van Ouwenlaan Straat was three hours from Paris by train, and even closer to Brussels and other capitals. The family was soon thriving on a lifestyle few Americans ever experience; and Mark was traveling the world doing deals in places like Tanzania, Mozambique, Brunei, Nigeria, Malaysia, Italy, Russia, Australia, Brazil, Egypt, Thailand, China, Japan, Saudi Arabia and London.

Working transactions in such far flung locales often posed personal and professional risks attorneys rarely encounter—from needing a military escort to the airport in Lagos, as his motorcade snaked through snarled traffic in an apocalyptic rush hour, to surviving an enraged Thai taxi driver's 100 miles per hour sprint to the Bangkok airport, to forcing down frozen Yak carpaccio in a Beijing restaurant so as not to dishonor his Chinese hosts, to having his passport yanked for days without explanation at the Riyadh airport by the Saudi secret police. He found that the extraordinary often became ordinary in high stakes petroleum negotiations. His jet-lagged, sleep-deprived life turned out to be anything but predictable and buttoned-down; often, it seemed as risky and adventurous as panning for gold along the Yukon.

During his down time traveling the pro tennis circuit, Mark had begun reading faith-based books widely and deeply. He'd been raised in the Episcopal Church, but attended sporadically with his siblings and mother, Lorraine. As an adult, he was a self-described "average western church goer" with a mild curiosity in spiritual matters. But that began to change when he read C.S. Lewis's Christian apologetics—books like *Mere Christianity, Miracles* and *The Problem of Pain*, which present a historical, reasoned and evidence-based case for Christianity and a defense against its naysayers. His reading of Lewis led him to J.I. Packer and R.C. Sproul, famous theologians who had strongly influenced Lewis's towering intellect.

In his travels to the far reaches of Africa and Asia, he was amazed to see churches full and to see those Christ had called "the least of these" seemingly far more spiritually attuned. The contrast was stark to life in the West, where material accumulation was an all-consuming focus. He was further confounded to see Europe's magnificent cathedrals nearly empty on Sundays and even desecrated as skateboard parks. He began to wonder if the West finally had lost all sense of the sacred, the spiritual and the eternal. That paradox made him even more aware of the false gods of the West—wealth, power and sex—and their intractable hold on recent generations.

During his travels to exotic places, Mark had gradually acquired a good many beautifully carved wooden figurines, which he and Susan displayed throughout their home. His favorite was a sculpture of two exotic heads of African royalty; Susan's was a lovely carving of an affluent 18th-century Thai couple, which sat on the den mantel on Van Ouwenlaan Straat. A seemingly small incident involving these objects forced him to think much more deeply about his own life and his blindness to invisible realities the scriptures warn about.

One night in January 2007, his 15-year-old daughter, Holly, woke up after dreaming she was standing in the den surrounded by piercing orange eyes staring through pitch black. She was terrified and it took a long time to calm her. But her dream kept recurring, and Mark gradually came to realize that for a year or so the family had been on edge, that petty strife often erupted without warning, that relationships were fraying and harsh words increasingly disrupted the harmony he and Susan had always prized.

More than once Mark lay awake late at night worrying about the surrounding atmosphere of unease. Then one night, a blunt edict began to echo in his head: *I am the Lord thy God, thou shall not have any gods before me.* Could he have violated the very first Commandment? What did he truly know about the figurines? For him and Susan, they were simply *objets d'art*—mere ornaments for the mantel or a bookshelf. But perhaps they stood for something more in the faraway places they'd been acquired. Had previous owners seen one or more as gods? That was possible, he told to himself. And if that was true, it could mean that the figurines, like spiritual termites, had invaded their home and seriously disrupted its harmony and Holly's life.

Suddenly, for the first time in his life, Mark experienced an epiphany: No matter whose eyes Holly was seeing in the dark, he had to accept that there were things the Western mind, with its highly secularized view of reality, could not account for. Could he and Susan jettison their own cultural biases and accept that there might be no rational explanation for what was happening to their daughter? Could they trust, with child-like faith, in a God who knows the unseen world and could restore peace to their household? After much discussion, they agreed that they could and then resolved to burn all the figurines in their fireplace. Not long after that, Holly's terrible dreams stopped and peace returned to the house on Van Ouwenlaan Straat.

In that deeply troubling experience, Mark began to believe that many troubles, fears and anxieties are spiritual in nature; and that by addressing their cause, a path could be found to the freedom and peace that so often eludes us in the West. Something he'd learned at a couples' Bible study in 1993 had touched him deeply. The leader had emphasized that a "relationship"—not religion or performance—was required for closeness with God. That revelation opened a door and kindled a yearning to deepen his faith.

Mark and his family returned from The Hague to Houston in 2008. Soon thereafter, Mark established a weekend prayer ministry that examined the spiritual or physical symptoms that plague so many. He had no formal training as a counselor and no medical or theological credentials, but he did have a deep, Bible-based appreciation for the spiritual world so obvious in the less developed world and yet so alien in the West. Even more important, he was convinced that a spiritual and prayer-based approach could alleviate the source of many symptoms of physical and emotional distress.

Slowly, over the span of a few years, mostly by word-of-mouth, he found himself and the team he developed ministering for most waking weekend hours to the depressed, the rejected and the guilt-ridden, many of whom were suicidal. Overwhelmingly, their identity was defined by negativity that had controlled their lives for years, even decades. For many, identity as a child of God had been fundamentally marred by the main authority figures in their lives, some well-intentioned, some not. "Christian counseling on steroids" is how he describes his ministry to these suppliants.

"I came from a wonderful family," Mark told me. "Before I got into this, I just had no idea the lives that so many people live—the hurt they've endured, the pain they carry, and the emotionally desperate nature of their lives, where muddling through for a day can be a great victory. So many think they'll never amount to anything, never be of any use to God or man, and always be unlovable. These are the things that keep us bound to depression, despair, and misery—to the haunting lie that nothing will ever change for the better."

I told Mark I found it hard to believe that a corporate lawyer, who spent his professional life dotting the "i's" and crossing the "t's" of agreements defining projects costing billions could move so seamlessly into the abstract world of faith and the supernatural.

His reply was: "I suppose some do see me as an oddball, but that doesn't bother me at all. Christ said, if my word abides in you and you abide in me, ask whatever you wish and it will be done for you. If you think about that and who spoke it, you must decide, can that possibly be true? It sounds fantastic. Sense knowledge will tell you that is ridiculous; don't waste your time. But I take that to heart."

Understanding the limits of sense knowledge—which he describes as knowledge strictly derived from our rationalism and our physical senses, mainly hearing and seeing—is at the heart of his ministry. "It's very limited," he holds. "As with the issue of the figurines, it's not going to tell you all there is about reality. It's quite foolish to base your life on sense knowledge because we have very finite minds. Sense knowledge tells us nothing of the greater, eternal call of God on our lives and his magnificent purposes for us. Sense knowledge leaves most of us with nothing but an overwhelming fear and loneliness as we contemplate our place in the physical universe. We take as Gospel what the culture and others say to us and about us, and this unfortunately often leads to brutally negative emotions that can keep us in bondage the rest of our lives."

G.K. Chesterton once wrote: "There is a road from the eye to the heart that does not go through the intellect." Implicit in that thought is the idea of faith, a trust in that which is greater than ourselves. I have no doubt that Mark engenders deep trust in those who seek his help. About 80 percent are women (he says most men, unfortunately, are too proud to ask for help), but he never meets with a woman alone. Many are emotionally fragile and highly vulnerable, so one or two of his female assistants are present for all sessions, many of which can last up to four hours. Mark's process begins with making a detailed inventory of fears, scars and resentments that have a hold on his suppliants. Most already have seen a psychiatrist or a counselor and made no real progress or have seen a minister who urged being a better Christian or attending more Bible study. By the time they get to Mark, they are desperate and open to a new approach. Though he may spend thirty hours or more with those who come to him, his services cost nothing at all.

A somewhat typical encounter is that of Janet (whose name has been changed), a 52-year-old woman who came to Mark through a referral. A divorcee with two grown children, Janet had been alone for 10 years, and her former husband had remarried a younger woman. Her low-paying job and small alimony payment gave her barely enough to live on. Her children couldn't offer emotional or financial support because of their own difficulties. Janet conceded that by the time the children were teens she and her husband were exchanging sharp words. Their estrangement deepened, and he finally filed for divorce. His rejection left such deep emotional scars that Janet spiraled into depression and declining health. She tried counseling, but that led nowhere.

Her initial session with Mark focused on an intake questionnaire in which she identified a long list of hurts, traumas and resentments that mired her in bitterness and her unwillingness to forgive, especially her ex-husband. Mark explained that bitterness is like a pill taken to poison someone else but we get poisoned instead. Tears came to Janet's eyes and she began to sob as, one by one, she and Mark discussed her hurts. Once she composed herself, he led her through a prayer of repentance in which she disavowed her lack of forgiveness and the deep resentments she'd held onto for so long.

In subsequent sessions, Janet and Mark discussed articles he'd given her to read on his website (www.healingisgodsjustice.org). Mark stressed how much she needed to give faith a chance, to believe that, "You are no longer bound by negative emotions that are reinforced by thinking incorrectly about God and thinking incorrectly about yourself." He insisted that she let go of emotions that were telling her, "You will never amount to anything, no man will ever love you again and you will never be of any good to anyone."

In time, Janet's confidence began to return and a huge weight was lifted. Her eyes were clearer; she stood straighter and a smile replaced her once-perpetual frown. She told Mark she felt freer. It seemed clear that her sessions with Mark had convinced her that life is not so random, that she had reconnected with a trustworthy God who would stand by her in any crisis.

Mark retired at the end of 2017 and began devoting full-time to his ministry. In its eight years of existence, he has worked with approximately 150 suppliants. Many of them now help others with similar problems. His is indeed a Life in Full. I can think of no one who embodies more the sixth trait of the scholar-athlete, which is to give back writ large. He has shown faith in every area of his life: faith in his exceptional family, in his schools, in his team at Duke, in his own game, in me as his coach and in his ability to negotiate complex legal agreements under intense pressure. Most of all, Mark had faith in a power greater than himself—the God he searched hard to find and came to trust at the core of his being. In many ways, such faith is the most essential quality of the scholar-athlete: Without faith in a power greater than ourselves—however we, as individuals, choose to define that power—none of us could lead, nor could we fulfill, our birthright of potential.

Mark knew that the Book of Exodus told the people of Israel that: "[The] Lord went before them by day in a pillar of cloud, to lead them the way; and by night in a pillar of fire, to give them light." He answered that call deep within his heart—a call, I can imagine, not unlike what Moses heard when he struck a rock with a rod twice and waters came gushing forth to quench those thirsty in body and soul.

CHAPTER FOURTEEN

The Ripple Effect

A catastrophic earthquake struck Haiti, the poorest country in the Western Hemisphere, at 4:53 p.m. on Tuesday, January 12, 2010, causing the collapse of thousands of buildings, devastating loss of life and a knock-out blow to infrastructure essential for recovery, including the main airport and seaport, electrical networks, phone systems and hospitals. At the epicenter, 16 miles southwest of the capital of Port-au-Prince, the shock measured 7.0 on the Richter Scale, the worst in the quake-prone country's history; over the next two weeks, 52 high-magnitude aftershocks would cause even more death and destruction. An estimated three million people, a third of the country's population, suffered losses, a million of them left homeless. Because tens of thousands of victims could not be found or accounted for, a reliable death estimate was never established, though most parties engaged in recovery agreed that the disaster cost more than 100,000 and perhaps up to a quarter million lives.

By Thursday, January 14, twenty countries were rushing military personnel, emergency food rations, water containers and other aid to the scene, but chaos on the ground almost completely stymied distribution. U.S. military air traffic controllers had managed to get the one runway at Port-au-Prince airport back in operation, but severe air traffic congestion was causing long landing delays and diversion of flights to the Dominican Republic and elsewhere. It took nine days to get one pier at the main seaport operational for offloading humanitarian aid. Massive collections of impenetrable rubble blocked most main roads, and a lack of equipment to clear them meant that weeks, even months, would pass before many could reopen.

Most victims, both fatalities and survivors, had been crushed beneath buildings poorly built due, in part, to the lack of building codes; sadly, only a handful of people trapped beneath the rubble were saved. Because Port-au-Prince's hospitals and morgues were quickly overwhelmed, bodies were stacked in streets for collection by dump trucks and taken for burial in mass graves, mainly large trenches dug with heavy equipment. The stench of decaying corpses hung heavy in the air on Saturday, January 16, when an emergency medical team from Stanford University managed to reach the Hôpital d l'Universite d'Etat d'Haiti (Hospital of the State University of Haiti) in the center of Port-au-Prince, the largest referral center and teaching hospital in the country. Prior to the earthquake, it had been a poorly resourced and inadequately staffed facility. When the quake struck, the situation became desperate, because all but a very few of its doctors, nurses and staff had fled, mostly to take care of family and friends. Patients dying hourly were being added to the collection of corpses that had been deposited in one location at the hospital. It was a surreal and profoundly sad scene to the arriving physicians from Stanford, unlike anything they'd ever witnessed, except for a war or disaster zone. About a thousand surviving patients within the hospital compound were lying inside badly damaged buildings or outside on the ground on blankets, cots, boards, bare mattresses and a precious few bedframes recovered from the ruins. Though most were suffering from severe trauma, few of these victims had been seen by a physician or nurse.[1]

The arriving four-doctor, four-nurse team from Stanford included a physician who played on my first tennis team at Duke.[2] Paul Auerbach was not a star athlete, but he was a superstar student, a recipient of the prestigious Angier B. Duke Memorial Scholarship, which today has a four-year value of more than $250,000. After graduating magna cum laude with a B.A. degree in religion, he went to Duke Medical School, where he studied under superb professors like Dr. Robert Lefkowitz, who would share the Nobel Prize for biochemistry in 2012. One of Paul's classmates, Richard Schatz, co-invented the cardiac stent. Another of his professors, David Sabiston, Chairman of the Department of Surgery, inspired Paul to write a textbook on wilderness medicine, a rapidly evolving specialty about taking care of people in remote settings—typically medicine for adventurers, athletes, explorers, soldiers, scientists and others engaged in outdoor activities. Now in its seventh edition, Paul's textbook, *Wilderness Medicine,* is the bible of the field. He also wrote *Medicine for the Outdoors,* a bestseller for the general reader now in its sixth edition, and co-authored *Enviromedics: The Impact of Climate Change on Human Health,* which describes the catastrophic human consequences we can expect if environmental degradation and global warming continue. The idea for the textbook—and for wilderness medicine as a field of study—occurred for Paul in the summer of 1975 when he served an externship with the Indian Health Service at Fort Belknap Indian Reservation in Harlem, Montana. He'd gone west to explore practicing public health medicine on the Indian reservation, and in his free time explored places like Yellowstone and Glacier National Parks. He was struck by how the unique features and treatment of the cases he saw—drowning, snake bites, animal attacks, etc.—weren't well described in the medical literature. He teamed up with Duke Medical School classmate and lifelong friend Edward Geehr to create the first two editions of the textbook; when Geehr decided to focus on other pursuits, Paul continued expanding and updating the textbook on his own. His seminal writings, teaching and research on the subject made him one of the leading architects of an entirely new medical specialty—wilderness medicine, which continues to grow, as he puts it, "like crazy. We were in the right place at the right time."

Dr Luanne Freer, Medical Director at Yellowstone National Park, calls Paul's textbook the definitive work on the subject and says he "is widely recognized as the father of wilderness medicine. As a young physician, he recognized that healthcare education was focused on treatment delivered in an office or hospital on patients suffering from illnesses and injuries that occur near those facilities. He saw the need to learn and teach more about what happens in the wilderness and to develop a body of knowledge around how to improvise care in austere settings." In 1983, Paul co-founded the Wilderness Medical Society and later served as its third president; the society's top award is named for him. Today, the organization has approximately 75 medical school chapters.

Along the way, Paul became an expert scuba diver and world-renowned expert on the behaviors and medical afflictions associated with hazardous marine animals, such as sharks, stingrays, and jellyfish. In doing so, he volunteered to offer advice via the Divers Alert Network to doctors and patients in need of assistance. He's done research and written extensively on the topic, and is considered the "go-to" person for divers, doctors and organizations around the globe. For his contributions to diving, he was awarded a NOGI from the Academy of Underwater Arts and Sciences, Dan Diver of the Year from Rolex, and other honors. As news of the earthquake's devastation in Haiti began to spread, an urgent request for Stanford to send a team came from the Los Angeles-based International Medical Corps (IMC), global first responders to emergencies caused by war, natural disasters and other calamities. Stanford Emergency Medicine agreed without hesitation to IMC's request, selected its team and requested support from the hospital, which generously donated a large supply of medications and allowed the team time away to assist in another country.

Paul would apply nearly everything he'd learned in more than four decades of practicing emergency and wilderness medicine when he arrived on the fourth day of the crisis at the university hospital in Port-au-Prince. In his career, he'd faced many split-second, life/death decisions, but nothing of the magnitude of pain, suffering and death he'd encounter there. The prostrate city center looked like it'd been leveled by an artillery barrage. The hospital's main buildings—mostly one-story concrete structures—nearly all lay in ruins, leaving no operating rooms, no maternity ward and no testing labs. Many nurses had been trapped and killed in the building that housed the nursing school. Their loss was a reminder of the gravity of the situation and the fragile nature of life.

Electricity was unavailable. There were a few back-up generators, but power was intermittent, at best, during the team's entire ten-day stay. Potable water, too, was unavailable. That meant it initially had to be carried in from outside the compound in buckets, bottles, and other containers for drinking, hand-washing, wound-cleaning, and toileting. For surgeries and other procedures, chemicals were used to disinfect water. Making matters worse, the team and its patients sweltered without air conditioning in mid-day temperatures of 100 degrees on the ground, with no ventilation in buildings and scant breezes outside. Everyone was suffering.

"It was my first major disaster. Flying first to Miami and then the Dominican Republic, and then driving by bus into Haiti, I was frightened, but once I got busy, I was okay. It was the most challenging situation I'd ever encountered as a doctor," Paul now says. "I'd dealt with emergencies involving 20 or so victims, but nothing even close to this. We quickly ran out of pain medication and other supplies such as traction devices—which meant we had to improvise with whatever we could find for weights and pulleys to put tension on replaced or dislocated bones or joints. We asked permission from patients to treat them with little or no pain medication, and to a person, they graciously agreed. They were brave beyond belief."

From start to finish, Paul's team faced deeply troubling choices in deciding a rough order for treating victims based on who was likely to live or die. They used standard triage criteria to prioritize among a welter of afflictions: crushed limbs and spines, concussions, blood vessel occlusions, soft tissue lacerations, infections, tetanus, gangrene and severe dehydration. The dire prospects of so many forced a frantic pace to save lives, and yet, the team could not ignore the physical and emotional needs of those about to die. I asked Paul about that, and he told me about being filmed from behind while ministering to a dying patient. When Paul turned around, he admonished the cameraman, who crossed himself, and then pulled the tape cassette from his video recorder and handed it to Paul.

"I was contacted a few years ago by a journalist who came across a mention of my name in the book *Five Days at Memorial* by Sherry Fink," Paul recalls. "She had watched me save a patient in Haiti. The reporter asked me if I had ever written anything about triage or euthanasia during disasters. I wrote back that I hadn't written anything along these lines, because while I've been in the position of having to make these sorts of difficult decisions, I don't consider myself to be an authority on the topic. In Haiti, and in other situations where I faced decisions posed by multiple patients or limited resources, there were difficult decisions to make, which involved deciding who receives what treatments, deferring or withholding treatment from patients, and palliative care. One does the best that one can based upon the situation, resources, preferences of the patient and loved ones, experience and comfort level of the caregiver, and perceived ethics of the situation. It can be one of the most difficult experiences of a person's medical career, because regardless of decisions made, the outcome is usually not optimal. If it is an end-of-life versus suffering decision, it may be irrevocable and something that you carry with you for the rest of your days."

IMC had found a large room at a nearby hotel that sustained light damage for the mixed-gender team to share. Located on the first floor, it offered a quick exit outside if an aftershock occurred, and one did a few days after the team arrived. When they hurried to the hospital, the situation had become predictably worse. In addition to injuries were added heat stroke, tetanus, and a growing sense of despair.

Paul's daily rounds to check on patients could trigger huge emotional swings. He looked forward to seeing a young woman who was a professional dancer. "Her smile was infectious," he recalls. "One of her legs had been badly injured and had to be amputated. Despite that enormous loss, she was cheerful and had an uplifting spirit that gave us a much-needed boost during very somber and stressful times." After he got home, he helped arrange for her to receive a prosthesis, and she emailed to tell him that she could walk and hoped one day to teach dance.

Another case tugged hard at his heart. As he approached the pallet of a three-year-old boy with two amputated limbs, he could see that his small patient was taking immense pleasure from eating a cracker. As Paul neared his bed, the little boy held out the cracker to offer Paul a bite. Tears welled in Paul's eyes as he remembered his two sons and daughter when they were three—how safe and secure they'd been. In such moments, he and his teammates had to fight hard to keep their composure.

"We treated many patients who did not survive," Paul says. "We tried to help them with as much dignity as possible. They and their families were very brave. We all wished we could have done more to help them."

IMC contracted with the hospital to provide management services in the aftermath of the earthquake, and after a few days, Paul was put in administrative charge of the entire facility. On Wednesday after he arrived, the 82nd Airborne from Fort Bragg, North Carolina, and The Comfort, the U.S. Navy's Mercy-class hospital ship, reached the scene. With them came essential supplies, military medics and doctors and greatly augmented options for transporting patients with specialized needs via helicopter from the city center to shipboard sick bays. Meanwhile, a growing influx of physicians, nurses and technicians from around the globe was arriving daily, and many were being sent to the university hospital, causing an exponential increase in the need for coordination and Paul's administrative responsibilities.

In 12 days, much was accomplished. From a first day that was a combination of chaos and battlefield medicine, where everyone attempted to see as many victims as possible mostly to save lives and attend to the worst wounds, coordination with Partners in Health, Doctors without Borders, the Canadian and Norwegian Red Cross, Swiss Humanitarian Aid, teams of U.S. physicians and surgeons, the Clinton Foundation, and many others led to a functioning medical effort, albeit handicapped in many ways. Amidst a media barrage, tents were erected, patient care was organized, and rudimentary laboratories, dialysis, maternity services, blood transfusions, and surgeries were accomplished. A small tented emergency department was created, and soon managed 250 new patients each day. The quality of medical services soon exceeded what had existed on that site prior to the earthquake.

Paul and his colleagues slept on average three to four hours a night in Haiti. Food was most often military rations supplied by IMC or the U.S. military, an energy bar brought from home, or occasionally a meal prepared in a hotel kitchen. In addition to the emotional toll, working nonstop for days on end took a huge physical toll. On his 10th day in Port-au-Prince—the day prior to departure—exhaustion finally caught up with Paul. His grueling days and frantic pace caused him to collapse; it took an IV and more than eight liters of fluids to revive him. While he was unconscious, members of the team huddled around him, all smiles, to have a photo taken. In the midst of everything, they kept their sense of humor.

The team left Haiti emotionally subdued and in a deeply reflective mood. Any sense of accomplishment was overshadowed by worries of how Haiti's staggering medical needs could ever be met. "When I got home, it seemed wrong to be so privileged, to sleep in a bed—a clean one at that—to eat good food when tens of thousands of Haitians didn't know if they'd have a next meal. Haiti stripped me to the nubs physically and emotionally, and many of us eventually suffered some form of PTSD."

Five years after going to Haiti, Paul served on IMC's disaster response team in Nepal, where a 7.8 magnitude earthquake struck on April 25,

Paul Auerbach with an orphaned boy in Haiti. Chuck Liddy, *The News and Observer*

2015, causing 9,000 deaths and leaving 22,000 persons injured. Several years earlier, he'd become a founder and instructor for the Nepal Ambulance Service. Following the earthquake, Paul worked in Kathmandu and the Dhading district, once again treating injured and ill victims. He watched the young emergency medical technicians he had trained rise to the occasion and become pivotal to the earthquake response.

Paul's career impact is the best example I know of the enormous ripple effect a scholar-athlete can have over the course of his or her career. At Duke, his native intelligence and love of learning led to an enduring passion for medicine. His inquisitive mind enabled him to see an untapped area of medicine, a large potential practice area that was undiscovered and undefined. He recognized it as a close cousin to emergency medicine; while that may seem obvious today, it wasn't at the time. After getting his MD at Duke, he served an internship at Dartmouth and then did his residency in emergency medicine at UCLA. A series of university faculty appointments in emergency medicine followed at Temple, UC-San Francisco, Vanderbilt and Stanford. He took a year away from medicine in

1989 to earn a master's in management at the Stanford School of Business. Today, he holds an appointment as the Redlich Family Professor in Stanford's Department of Emergency Medicine.

As dramatic as his work was in Haiti and Nepal, it reflects a small part of his overall ripple effect. He has helped educate about 10,000 emergency (and other) physicians, each of whom treats about 5,000 patients in average a year, or a total of 150,000 in a typical 30-year career. In aggregate, those he has taught have treated or will treat approximately 1.5 million patients—an extraordinary impact by any measure. It's even more remarkable when his indirect impact, as the father of wilderness medicine and as an influential author, is added.

The bedrock of all his written work is a definitive 2,250-page textbook for medical professionals entitled *Wilderness Medicine.* It provides detailed "how to treat" chapters on hazards from avalanches to lightning strikes and wilderness survival, written by 157 contributors, each an authority in his or her field. Publishers call it an "evergreen book" because it's embedded in the curricula of so many medical schools and gets updated periodically in new editions (seven and counting...).

My knowledge of medicine and backcountry adventure is skimpy at best, but in nearly two hours of browsing through the textbook, I encountered many hair-raising topics, like what to do when charged by a grizzly bear. The answer: Don't even think about climbing a tree; instead, drop to the ground face down as fast as you can and clasp your hands behind your neck. Whatever you do, don't try to stare the beast down; you'll only cause confusion and invite attack. Though written for medical professionals, the first edition of *Wilderness Medicine* got an enthusiastic review from the outdoor writer for the *New York Times.* Its subject matter—snake bites, mountain medicine, wilderness dentistry (imagine having a tooth pulled in the wilds without anesthesia) and myriad other topics—can be quite riveting. It's a weighty tome in substance *and* size: My copy tipped our bathroom scales at 10.6 pounds—a library item for sure. Fortunately, for doctors who'd like to carry a book on a wilderness trek, there's a companion *Field Guide to Wilderness Medicine*—a paperback with all the important clinical advice from the "big book."

His aptitude for explaining highly complex subjects in an understandable way has enabled Paul to reach large non-technical audiences too. In *Medicine for the Outdoors,* he has made his textbook content available in a condensed and simplified form for the lay reader. A bestseller, it turns up in remote settings all over the globe because its compact size makes it an attractive backpack stuffer. As Nelson Bryant, a former outdoor columnist for the *New York Times* put it, "If a doctor isn't with you on your wilderness wanderings, this splendid book should be in your pack." Now in its sixth edition, it garners consistently strong reviews. Richard H. Carmona, the 17th U.S. Surgeon General, wrote *Medicine for the Outdoors* ". . . remains the most comprehensive and authoritative work in the field."

In 2017, Paul and Jay Lemery, head of Wilderness and Environmental Medicine at the University of Colorado, co-wrote *Enviromedics: The Impact of Climate Change on Human Health,* the first such analysis from a physician perspective. The authors reach one conclusion in *Enviromedics* that hit me especially hard: "If your chest was hurting, you couldn't breathe, and your pulse was undetectable, we wouldn't sit still and ponder the situation. We'd do everything possible to make an accurate diagnosis and try to save your life. We'd act fast, because we know that moments count. Should we be any less concerned about our planet? The current situation in Glacier National Park is instructive. In our children's lifetime, it may need to be renamed Glacierless National Park. Does that matter? We believe it does."

They go on to say that while they rely on the science of others to understand the macro effects of climate change, as doctors they see for themselves the micro effects on the patients they treat: "The composite patients suffering from post-flood diarrhea, wildfire-induced shortness of breath, and heatstroke-induced organ failure are the same cases seen every day in emergency departments and medical wards around the globe. Climate change will add to the burden of disease, and sooner or later it will affect people you know, and hundreds of millions you never have met."

Carefully avoiding any political agenda, Paul and his colleague emphasize, instead, "cultivating a shared sense of responsibility for our fellow humans." They conclude by asking if we will be the cursed generation of "Great Procrastination," or if we will leave our children "a legacy of creativity, peace, prosperity, and the best possible place to live."

In its review, *Publisher's Weekly* called the book "a no nonsense 'doctor's approach'" by physicians working on the front lines of climate change impact. Laurie Garrett, Pulitzer Prize–winning author of *I Heard the Si-*

rens Scream, warned, "Heed Lemery and Auerbach's message before it's too late."

Paul Auerbach has made a distinctive and admirable contribution in defining a new field of medicine, one practiced in the field far away from hospitals, clinics or a doctor's office. He pioneered a place for wilderness medicine as a new medical specialty in a very short time. As Americans spend more and more time pursuing outdoor adventures in our pristine wildernesses, that effort will continue to grow in importance.

I have no doubt that tennis had a profound impact on Paul's career, but far differently from others profiled in this section and elsewhere in the book. My predecessor as Duke tennis coach was an assistant football coach who coached varsity tennis on the side. It was a full-time job for me, because I was tasked to put the team on a par with Carolina and Clemson, perennial tennis powers of the Atlantic Coast Conference. Before I arrived, recruiting had not been emphasized, and I set out on day one to change that. But first I had to get a baseline evaluation of the players I inherited—Paul among them. I began by watching each one hit and play at least one match. After that, we privately discussed goals for the team and the player's aspirations; we also ranked each player in talent and determination.

I remember how startled I was by Paul's candor in assessing his chances of playing in team matches. As a freshman, the year before I took over, he'd played in only two—both when the overall match outcome was not in doubt. He'd had an injury-plagued year, marked by an operation just before fall tryouts and a serious shoulder injury a month before the season began. A slow recovery had put him at a distinct disadvantage, but he shrugged that off as no excuse and admitted, "I might not have played much anyway." We agreed, toward the end of our one-on-one conversation, that his prospects for playing in varsity matches—in singles or doubles—weren't very good.

Then he told me: "I'd like to be part of the team, even if I don't get to start. That'll be enough for me." Those words impressed me. He'd played No. 1 singles on his high school team in New Jersey as a junior and senior. I knew accepting a not-so-heady role had to be deflating. No one else I'd talked to had taken the position he took. All the others expected to be in the starting lineup, and many had rated themselves unrealistically high. I assured Paul that I'd welcome him as a member of the varsity and would see that he got to hit often with players in the starting lineup. I cautioned, however, that I expected him to participate fully in daily practice and conditioning drills.

"No shortcuts," I cautioned.

"No shortcuts," he came back with a big grin.

In the first month of fall practice, Paul made an indelible impression by opening my eyes to the importance of having players whose main asset was the energy they brought to the court, those who might not have a big serve or a knee-buckling crosscourt, but the sort who would fight, even in practice, with all the intensity they could muster. Paul was only five feet eight inches tall and barely weighed 160 pounds, but what he lacked in size, he more than made up for with heart. That made him a terrific practice partner because he forced better players to hustle hard and concentrate on each shot. And, true to his word, I never saw him shirk in hitting and conditioning drills, or in "suicides"—a much-dreaded, exhausting series of sprints forward to the net and backpedaling to the baseline. It was soon clear to me that the other players liked Paul, knew and respected why he was there and felt that he *was* an important member of the team, even though he might never play in a team match.

"That was huge for my self-esteem, friendships, outlook on life," he told me years later. "Looking back, it emphasizes how important coaches are—why they have to understand the complicated journeys of young athletes, particularly when they get to the next level and realize that being good in high school doesn't guarantee success in college. You could have just let me go, but you didn't."

I don't think I ever seriously thought about cutting him, but if I did, it was a fleeting thought, nothing more. While he never set out to do this, Paul greatly elevated, in my eyes, the value of players who'd never be stars and the important contribution they could make to overall team success.

One of Paul's bedrock values is collaboration, one he learned a lot about in tennis. He says, "There's very little that I've done alone. You do your best when you work with other people in teams." That's held true throughout his long and distinguished career—from his work in defining wilderness medicine as a new specialty, to the part he played on emergency response teams to earthquakes in Haiti and Nepal, to his many books and articles for technical and lay audiences.

Despite his demanding profession—one that often pulled him in more than one direction many times—he and his wife, Sherry, built a close-knit family. She was a student at UCLA when he did his emergency medicine residency there. She was a part-time ticket-taker at the rec center when he showed up to swim wearing a Duke T-shirt.

"I might go to school there," she told him with a warm smile, pointing at his shirt.

"You should," he replied. By then, he now wryly admits, he was already in love.

They have three successful adult children: Brian, 31, an intellectual property attorney in Philadelphia, volunteers for the Support Center for Child Advocates and is president of the board of directors for Singing City; Lauren, 29, who recently graduated from medical school, is headed for a career in emergency medicine; and Danny, 27, is getting a master's degree in environmental science and is an assistant rugby coach at Washington State University.

Through his teaching, writing and outreach in Haiti and Nepal, Paul Auerbach has had the greatest ripple effect of any player I coached. His textbook has become the bible of wilderness medicine, a field of medicine he helped coalesce. A vast number of people have benefited from his work. Recently, he told me: "Spare time makes me nervous; I have a hard time figuring out what to do with it." I wouldn't call him a workaholic because he makes time for outdoor adventures with his family. But rarely, if ever, a day goes by when he doesn't "dial in" to check on a patient, research a topic or to make sure that a major disaster hasn't struck. To suggest that Paul is "wired in" to seismic forces—and not just those that cause quakes—seems entirely plausible.

In *Moby Dick*, Herman Melville wrote of "the ever-rolling waves but made so by their restlessness." In many ways, Paul is a restless man. Otherwise, he'd never have turned so many ripples of frostbite and snakebite into a rolling curing tide.

Part III

How Scholar-Athletes Win

How scholar-athletes learn to win and have fun doing it. Narrated by John LeBar, Part III describes how he built winning teams comprised almost entirely by scholar-athletes.

CHAPTER FIFTEEN

A Road Trip Down South

As we loaded our gear into a big white crew van on March 5, 1982, it never occurred to me that its occupants—all members of the Duke University varsity tennis team—were "throwbacks" to a vanishing breed: the scholar-athlete so proudly hailed in a bygone era. As John LeBar wrote in Chapter One, from roughly 1890 to World War II, most Americans lauded collegiate sports heroes who had brawn *and* brains, athletes who ran with blazing speed and applied gray matter just as fast. The young men piling into the van were very much like that: fast-footed and quick-minded too. All but one would earn an advanced degree; they all went on to achieve high-level professional success; and they all would give something back for the greater good.

Their spirits could not have been higher as we headed south on spring break to play seven matches in seven days. Leaving the athletic parking lot, we drove past Duke Gardens, where redbuds, cherry trees and flower beds were about to burst into bloom. That morning we'd beaten nationally ranked Tennessee, winning six singles matches so decisively that the Volunteers had decided to forego playing the three standard doubles matches, a de facto forfeit. (Collegiate matches consist of six singles and three doubles matches, each worth one point.)

The Tennessee Coach, Mike DePalmer, had shrugged off that decision, telling me: "No real point in prolonging this."

We had just swept the singles matches 6–0, giving us a win over a ranked team with two All-Americans: the coach's son, Mike, Jr., and Paul Annacone, who was later inducted into the NCAA Tennis Hall of Fame. Annacone would go on to coach Pete Sampras and Roger Federer, two of the game's all-time greats. That win gave our confidence a huge lift: For the first time, we sensed that the '82 team could bring Duke the championship it long yearned for, its first ever in the Atlantic Coast Conference (ACC). Some merry soul climbing into the van had likened the win to "We're ridin' a rocket now."

In 1971, when I became tennis coach, Duke was the doormat of the ACC and had just gone 6 and 12. Despite having no scholarships, my first year we managed to eke out a winning record at 10 and 8, barely good enough for fifth place in the then seven-team Atlantic Coast Conference. The following year, we got our first scholarship, and I awarded it to Mark Meyers, who is profiled in Chapter Twelve. Before he finished at Duke, Mark established the highest winning percentage in school history, a record that still stands. He also turned out to be a magnet, as more and more top-ranked players came our way. By 1982, we were ready to compete with the University of North Carolina, who'd dominated ACC tennis for decades, and Clemson, a recent powerhouse; by then, we also had the maximum five scholarships.

On our 400-mile drive to Atlanta, I took the first turn at the wheel. Sitting in the bucket seat beside me was the first twenty-four-year-old freshman I'd ever heard of, let alone coached. His name was Chaim Arlosoroff and he was from Tel Aviv, Israel, where he'd just completed three-plus years of compulsory military service. While in the Army, he'd been a member of the Israeli Davis Cup team, which gave him match experience against many of the world's best players. One look at Chaim darting around the court at our first practice told me he'd be a great asset to Duke tennis.[1]

I'd given him a full, four-year scholarship on the recommendation of Harold Landesberg, who'd been a three-sport star at Duke. By the time I got to know him, Harold was a Philadelphia philanthropist and a founder of the Israel Tennis Centers. He'd seen Chaim play in Israel and talked him into coming to Duke.

From the first, I developed quite a liking for our elderly frosh. He had an infectious, outgoing personality and was not in the least pretentious about his prodigious athletic talent, or the academic aptitude that made him a pre-med whiz. Until arriving at Duke, he'd spent very little time in the United States—coming mainly for a few junior tournaments—yet his understanding of English was quite good. On occasion, he did utter bloopers that caused the team to howl with laughter. It was obvious that Chaim was well liked; as best I could tell, no one begrudged him playing at Number 1.

In the morning match against Tennessee, Chaim had defeated their Number 1, Mike DePalmer, Jr., who was later ranked 23rd on the pro circuit. Our Number 2, Marc Flur, had achieved an equally impressive win over their second All-American, Paul Annacone, who would later be ranked 12th in the world. Flur had come to Duke a year earlier and soon underscored for me the maxim, "Never rush to judgment on anyone." When I first saw him hitting balls, I wasn't sure he'd make the team. He was a gangly, six-foot-four walk-on from New England—hardly a hotbed of tennis—all arms and legs with strokes that, at times, seemed unorthodox, even a bit awkward. But when Marc took the court in competition, his powerful backhand and crosscourts were stunning to behold. By the time he graduated, Marc Flur had become an All-American and ACC Player of the Year. He went on to become a formidable opponent on the pro tour and one of Duke's all-time tennis greats. So much for first impressions.

In contrast to Chaim's outgoing exuberance, Marc was quiet and introspective. Even so, they became good friends and bonded in knowing that, as they went, so went the team. During fall practice, I had them play a challenge match to determine who'd be Number 1. Instead of first to win two of three sets—the collegiate standard—I had them use the pro format: first to win three of five. Mainly, I wanted to know how they'd play in pressure cooker points when tired to the bone.

With long rallies and explosive points, they more than met my expectations. Neither one took control, and dark fell with the score even. The next day, they came back and fought through a riveting fifth set that seemed to last forever. Finally, Chaim won 6–4, but they were both so exhausted they could barely move. Such a long, hard battle often engenders deep respect for an adversary; and it was that kind of match—burned into memory as a test of skill and endurance, fought point-by-point to the very end. Wrung out as they were, Chaim and Marc shared a golden moment they'd never forget and went on to become very good friends.

As we made our rounds down south, I likened our progress to bowling: We dispatched opponents like ten pins in bowling. We rolled a perfect game at Georgia Tech, winning 9–0 on their home courts; came close to another ten strike with a 6–1 win at Furman; then went 7–2 at Auburn; 8–1 at South Florida; 6–3 at Ole Miss; and closed with another 9–0 ten strike over Illinois (in Little Rock). After two early season setbacks on the West Coast, we'd come roaring back and were fully confident that we'd be a force to be reckoned with in the ACC.

All the lopsided wins made us relaxed and at ease with each other. The van was full of laughter; maybe the jokes weren't that great, but any one of us could be the butt of one. Late one day, as the van approached Little Rock, someone in back yelled,

"Hey Chaim, where are we staying tonight?"

From his upfront perch in the passenger seat, Chaim reached for the itinerary on the console, read that we were staying at a Ramada and yelled back an inconsequential malapropism. After all, English was his second language.

"The RAH-mah-dah," he shouted with certitude.

Howls of laughter filled the van. "RAH-mah-dah . . . RAH-mah-dah," his teammates gleefully chanted, as if he'd invented a new bon mot.

Chaim gave me a toothy grin and shrugged, as if to say, "What did I do? I must have made their day."

Somehow his slight miscue got etched into collective memory. At Duke reunions and other gatherings years later, he often got greeted with "RAH-mah-dah" and some inanity like: "Are you checked in at the RAH-mah-dah yet?" Somehow, he always managed to parry the jibes with nonchalance, and always was comfortable with laughing at himself.

Who could have known with spirits running so high that we were headed for a fall? In our last match of the road trip, we rolled a gutter ball—one so wobbly it forced us to ask ourselves: *What the hell? Maybe we're not that good after all.*

That night, as usual, I slept with one eye open but didn't bother with a bed check. I rarely did, because the players all knew I expected them to get a good night's rest, especially on the eve of a big match. And so, I was somewhat baffled when a late-night clatter arose a few doors from mine shortly after midnight. As my feet hit the floor, I wondered what the fuss was all about. Clearly, someone was pounding on a door in the outer corridor of our Little Rock motel. Then the noise stopped and a familiar, half-pleading, voice called out, "Come on guys, open up."

My cursory probe in pajamas revealed that our ace doubles player, Ross Dubins, was seeking entry at the door next to his and two from mine, while Chaim and his roommate, Russ Gache, played dead inside. It turned out that Russ had just returned to the room with two—yes, *two*—adventurous girls wearing cowboy boots and hats banded with rattlesnake skins. Russ had seen the girls earlier that evening sitting a few rows off at a University of Arkansas basketball game. They were pretty, self-assured and seemingly unfazed by his yell, "Let's get ready to party!" They gave him coquettish smiles, but when the game ended, they had disappeared in the swirling crowd.

En route back to the motel, Russ decided to stop for a beer at the White Water Tavern, well-known thereabouts for country rock music, and as a place where Bill Clinton, as state attorney general, and his staff often celebrated the end of the work week. Russ strolled in to a rowdy, packed saloon with a quartet playing some melancholy tune popularized, I'd guess, by a George Strait or J.J. Cale. Apparently, he was waving for the bartender's attention when the lovely gauchos he'd seen at the game sashayed in. Lest they slip the net again, Russ dispensed with a formal introduction and yelled, "Grab a table. I'll get the beer and glasses."

Later he told me—and I had no reason to doubt his word—that these were nice girls from Little Rock, roughly his same age, enjoying a night on the town. But the more I learned, the more his credibility began to slide. Russ said he was filling their glasses for the second time when the girls asked, "Where's the party?"

"What party?"

"The one you were pushing at the game."

"Oh, that party," Russ temporized. "We were thinking of a party in our room."

"*We?* Who's we?" one of the girls asked in mock surprise.

"My roommate. You'll never believe this but he's a sheikh. Very wealthy—has a boatload of oil wells. You should meet him."

A short time later—as best I could piece things together—the night owls woke the putative sheikh from a deep slumber. Things got noisy as Russ and the girls insisted that Chaim get up and give a personal report on his sheikhdom, a line of malarkey, if I ever heard one. A few moments later, Chaim gravely informed Russ:

"Excuse me, but the young ladies have got to go. It's after midnight and I've got a match in the morning."

By then, the noise next door had awakened Ross Dubins, who heard female voices and got up to check things out. When I investigated, he told me he was worried that Russ and Chaim weren't getting enough sleep. That struck me as a flimsy concoction, because I was pretty sure he wanted to join the powwow himself.

I was irritated, to say the least, that my guys were entertaining young women in their room at such an ungodly hour. I told Ross to stand aside and knocked firmly twice and said, "Okay guys! It's me—coach. I know you've got two girls in there. It's past everyone's bed time—yours and theirs. Now open up!"

A sudden rustling noise came from within. Moments later, the door cracked open, and a girl wearing a cowboy hat peeped out. I stood partially aside as the door opened wider.

"And a very goodnight to you all," one of the girls said cheerily as she and her companion edged past me and hurried down the outer passageway. When I looked inside, Russ was standing near the door with his hands in his pockets and a doleful look. Chaim was sitting on the bed in pajamas, his torso wrapped in a blanket.

"What the hell's been going on in here?" I asked with indignation.

"Nothing—nothing at all," Russ blurted. Chaim leaned forward, arms on knees, slowly shaking his head side to side.

"This does not look good at all for the team," I admonished.

"It's not what it seems, Coach," Chaim advised. "It may not look too good, but it was harmless."

"Well, I don't like it, no matter what you say," I replied. "I'll skip the inquisition, but I hope this isn't typical of how you conduct yourselves. I'm going back to bed now. By the time I get to my room, I expect you both to be in bed for the rest of the night." I didn't wait for a reply; they knew what I meant and were plenty embarrassed as it was.

Next morning, at the breakfast buffet, Russ and Chaim both looked sheepish and bleary-eyed. My only comment—"Hope you're bringing your A game today"—left the late-night incident otherwise unaddressed.

Unfortunately, their A games were nowhere to be found; they'd picked the worst possible time to roll an alley ball. In Arkansas, we faced the sixth-ranked team in the country, one with two All-Americans and loaded with talented players from Australia and New Zealand. Chaim was facing off with one of the All-Americans, an Aussie named Peter Doohan, who would defeat Boris Becker five years later as the top-ranking star sought a third consecutive Wimbledon title. With that victory, Doohan achieved enduring fame as the "Becker-wrecker."

From the very beginning of the match, I could tell that Chaim was not himself. He was half a step slow in getting to everything and not hitting deep at all. Shots that normally put his opponents on the defensive were coming back with unusual force and depth. Doohan won the match in straight sets. It was one of the few—very few—times Chaim got a drubbing. Doohan went on to a moderately successful pro career, but, sadly, died at 56 of Lou Gehrig's disease.

Their Number 2 was another Aussie All-American, Pat Serret. Somehow Marc Flur managed to win that match, but I was sure Marc, who was a bit strait-laced, got a full night's sleep. It's noteworthy that at the end of the '82 season Serret and Doohan would win the NCAA national doubles championship.

Russ lost badly playing at Number 6, and, overall, we lost the match 6–3.

There'd been a team-wide buzz about the late-night caper; that and the loss put everyone in a sour mood. Despite all our heady victories, everyone knew we were going home with our tails between our legs. It took nearly 13 hours, but we drove straight back to Durham. I was never much for recriminations; clearly, we were far from our best and could not afford to indulge that kind of behavior again. I'd always felt that any punishment should be swift and certain. But somehow, the stinging loss seemed punishment enough; I wanted to put the incident behind us as quickly as possible. To encourage that, I made one oblique reference to the ruckus as we left Little Rock—

"Guys, no need to rehash what happened last night or agonize over why we lost today. Let's just lick our wounds and recommit to doing a whole lot better next time."

No matter how high-minded my sentiments were, the team didn't buy them at all. Just moments later, a voice in the back of the van growled—

"Try the rascal. Put him on trial."

"Who?" a second voice asked.

"Russ. He should pay for what he did."

"Okay," the second voice retorted, "but what's the charge?"

"Treason. Sabotage. Call it whatever you want," came the blunt reply.

The tone of this exchange was caustic and biting with a wry hint of the comic. Clearly, it was a players-only matter, which told me to stay out of it.

After a lot of animated back and forth, Russ stood unanimously indicted, and Will White had been universally acclaimed as prosecutor. All the other players were to serve as a jury of peers. To outsiders, Will might have seemed like an over-stuffed teddy bear with a countenance to match. But to the team, his persona was completely different, and his nicknames—"The Enforcer" and "Big Cheese"—said it all. He had the physique of a middle linebacker, who'd flatten anything in his path. Whenever tempers flared on the court over close calls—and on the rare occasions when blows seemed imminent—Will would step in as a menacing, hulking and calming presence. The guys called him the Big Cheese because he was looked up to as a strong leader—someone they could call on in a pinch.

In contrast, Russ had a slender build, a mischievous, even boyish look, accented by a big cowlick over his forehead. He was well-known for innocent comments that often came off as abrasive. But if there were any lady-killers in the van, Russ was one of them.

As the trial proceeded, Prosecutor Will addressed the defendant in ornate speech that covered the obvious establishing questions.

"Mr. Gache, were you in fact present last night at a well-known Little Rock watering hole? I believe it's called the White Water Tavern?

"Did you, in fact, lure two innocent young ladies to your room with the spurious claim that your roommate, Chaim Arlosoroff, is a sheikh and the proprietor of lucrative oil wells?"

That question elicited unbecoming whoops and catcalls—"Cad!" . . . "Lowlife!" . . . "Gigolo!"—which raised the question of juror bias. It took Will several moments to restore order, whereupon, he delivered a spirited summation: "I submit that this jury can render one, and only one, verdict:

GUILTY . . . GUILTY AS CHARGED!" That set off a rousing cheer, which meant Russ's prospects for acquittal were somewhat less than nil.

Then, any pretense of neutrality was completely discarded as the jurors chanted in unison: "Guilty! . . . Guilty! . . . Guilty!" They soon switched to chanting the sentence to be carried out in punishment: "Rump drill! . . . Rump drill! . . . Rump drill!"

The sentence was not unfamiliar; most often it got applied it to laggards who came in dead last on our cross-country runs. The dawdler's punishment was to stand on the baseline, back to the net with his hands on his knees while his teammates struck a prescribed number of serves at his posterior. Any on-target blow would cause a painful sting. Russ's sentence called for each player to fire away at his backside five times—more than enough to make a lasting impression.

The remainder of the trip back was uneventful except for a turn Chaim took at the wheel of the van. On our last leg of the trip, a state trooper pulled him over and gave him a speeding ticket. His position was that his teammates should all chip in to pay the fine; that drew a tepid response at best. Five or six players were preoccupied with a penny ante poker game where cards were dealt on an upturned suitcase; they shrugged him off and continued with the betting. Those not playing had their heads buried in a textbook.

"Wait 'til we get back," I advised Chaim. "I don't want you to get stuck with the ticket."

Our ignominious return was hardly the occasion for a victory cigar, a custom I'd borrowed from Red Auerbach, the basketball coach who'd turned the Boston Celtics into a dynasty. I decided to light one of my favorite J.R.'s anyway. The team's lighthearted self-policing action was hardly punitive, but it had made a point: I doubted that midnight capers would occur again. In any event, the trial had cleared the air and seemed much more effective than any disciplinary action I might impose. The team had ganged up on Russ, but after the long ride home, the book had been closed on the midnight caper in Little Rock.

That suited me just fine. I had no use whatsoever for prescriptive approaches in which players were told how to behave. Sure, what Russ had done hardly fit profile of a scholar-athlete. But I had to keep in mind he was not yet 20 years old—also that girls and talk of girls can render males of that age somewhat senseless. Russ's adjustment to Duke academic life had not been easy, but, down deep, I knew he had the ability to become a high achiever—and he did!

I can well remember how defeated he seemed when he got put on academic suspension at the end of the spring semester in 1980. He had taken less than a full course load to free up time for tennis and make sure his grades didn't suffer. What Russ hadn't planned on was meeting a girl who'd take up a lot of his time too. He got a D in linear algebra, a very tough course, and got suspended for two semesters. Even though he hadn't failed the course, suspension was automatic because he hadn't taken a full load. I remember how distraught he was when he came to my office to tell me what had happened.

"Coach, I don't know what to do. Maybe I just can't hack it at Duke."

"You're being way too hard on yourself," I told him. "Accept the suspension and take classes for two semesters at a school near your home in Miami. You can come back to Duke then, and the suspension will all be forgotten." I also had stressed, "Stay involved in tennis. I have no doubt that this will all work out."

It was an agonizing choice, but Russ made the right one. He took classes in engineering at the University of Miami and worked out on a regular basis with the Miami tennis team. When he came back to Duke for fall semester in 1981, he was reinstated with no questions asked. Once he got back in school, he told me, "It's like I haven't been gone at all. You've welcomed me back and so have all the other players. No one's said a word about my suspension."

The experience taught Russ to appreciate what he had; he redoubled his efforts academically, working much harder than ever before. That set the stage for a marvelous season the next spring ('82) in which he won 27 matches while losing only seven at Number 6 singles. Russ ended up winning an ACC individual championship and an ACC doubles championship playing at Number 3 with Will White. I counseled Russ on the correct path to deal with his suspension, but the redoubling of effort could only come from him. He went on to earn a law degree and has become a very successful patent attorney in Birmingham, Alabama.

The above account provides the essence of how I dealt with behavior issues with the scholar-athletes who played such a prominent role in the Duke Tennis Program. Each of them proved that superb athletics and academics can co-exist. The incidents I've cited make it clear that scholar-athletes don't belong on a pedestal; they're human and make mistakes too. I tried to form a personal relationship with each player based on mutual trust. I wanted them to gain confidence from acting on their own judgments without a "do" or "don't" list. Confident players instinctively know what's right and wrong. Trusting and being true to one's instincts is a much-to-be-desired form of maturity. Being a scholar-athlete hones good instincts that will last a lifetime.

CHAPTER SIXTEEN

Nineteen in a Row

Our humiliating loss in Little Rock—humiliating not because we lost to the sixth-ranked team in the country but because we shot ourselves in the foot—had an immediate bracing effect. I sensed a new resolve, a no more monkey business mindset, when the team took the courts in Durham, four days after our grueling road trip down south, to play a very good team from Texas A&M. We won 6–3 to begin a 19-match winning streak in which we dominated nearly every opponent we faced. During that time, no win meant more than our 9–0 defeat on April 14 of the University of North Carolina. The shutout was Duke's first in the long history of Duke-Carolina tennis. I still find it hard to believe that we lost only two sets in the entire match; it was that decisive.[1]

To me, more than anything, the 9–0 score said Duke tennis had truly arrived. For the first time, we had outmatched Carolina in depth. Deep down I knew the scholarships I'd lobbied so hard for and our tenacious recruiting of top-ranked players were finally paying off. It was not, however, our first win over the Tar Heels: We'd beaten them for the first time in 24 years in an epic contest at Duke in 1978.

The team match was tied 4–4 when the last doubles match turned into a three-set razor's edge duel. With the score tied at five games apiece in the last set, our duo of Mike McMahon and Brad Van Winkle fell behind 15–40 on Brad's serve. The lanky six-foot, seven-inch Brad had a powerful serve and hadn't lost it all day. But our prospects had taken a dire turn in the gathering gloom of a cloudy day with dark falling fast. I knew the Duke fans sitting in the packed bleachers behind the court were fighting off the thought: *Oh, no, here we go again.* I remember thinking to myself: *Maybe we just can't beat these guys.*

But at 15–40, Brad reached deep and served a rocket of an ace to make the score 30–40. On the next point, one of the Carolina players tried to pass Mike down the line. Fortunately, he hadn't tried to poach and volleyed a crosscourt winner. That seemed to take something out of the Tar Heels who quickly lost the next two points to put us up six games to five. I'll never forget that last game: Our boys fell behind 30–40, but Mike hit a crosscourt backhand winner to make the score deuce. A long rally followed on the next point; finally, one of the Tar Heels netted a ball to give us match point. Carolina responded with a strong serve that Mike returned deep in the backhand court. A weak return came back; Brad cut it off at the net and volleyed for a winner. The mayhem that followed will be forever etched into the memory of anyone from Duke who was there. Players and students stormed the court to celebrate the dramatic and unexpected win. Mike and Brad had come back from the brink and we all knew it. That made their victory that much sweeter.[2]

Brad went on to become a teacher. Mike was a bright kid, but struggled a lot his first two years at Duke. His path clearly shows the achievements of a scholar-athlete aren't always reflected in a GPA. With French as his first language, he'd attended primary and secondary school at the Lycée Chateaubriand in Rome. He chose Duke because his mother was impressed with its academic reputation, and because Mike thought he'd like to play tennis there. His SAT score was borderline, mainly because his reading comprehension in English was low. For the first two years, he took class notes and wrote papers in French. I arranged for a tutor, who helped him translate his papers into English. It was not until his junior year that he began speaking English fluently. Once that happened, he did quite well academically and earned a double major in French and Management Sciences (a degree since discontinued). His overall GPA was 3.2, somewhat lower than that of most scholar-athletes. But I knew he was plenty smart, worked hard and got a very good education.

He experienced "burnout" after 20-plus years in real estate and decided to take a break from work by returning to Europe, where he lived several years, three of them in Sardinia. In Sardinia, he got exposed to the party boat business and began writing a business plan and, ultimately, decided to try his hand at hosting parties. He came back to the United States in 2007 as Captain Mike, skipper of the Chamonix II, a party boat on Lake Lewisville outside Dallas. The 70-foot long, 100-passenger Chamonix II was built in St. Croix and sailed to Galveston, Texas, then transported overland to the lake north of Dallas. That trek was a logistical feat of monumental proportions. But the risky move paid off; Mike gradually built a strong business catering to high school graduations, office parties, weddings and many other types of events. He decided to sell his business in late 2017 to investors in San Diego who plan to transport the Chamonix II overland back to Galveston, then sail it through the Panama Canal and on to its new home port near Coronado Beach, California.[3] To say that Mike has led an adventurous life is an understatement.

We beat UNC again the very next year by an identical 5–4 score. With an influx of top-ranked young players, it was clear that our '78 win was not a fluke. We'd been led that year by Ted Daniel of Tulsa, our No. 1 in '77 (when he went 22–1) and again in '78. Replacing Ted, the team captain, was not easy, but David Robinson, John Stauffer (see their profiles in Chapters Eight and Twelve, respectively) and Ruby Porges, a former member of the Israeli Davis Club team, had already proven that they could win consistently in the ACC. Mike McMahon had gone undefeated at No. 5 singles during the regular season and finished third in the conference tournament. All by way of saying that by '78–'79, Duke tennis was on a strong upswing.

I should note that we were far from alone in our frustration with Carolina's decades of dominance. They had risen to national prominence at the end of the 1920s; after that, beating them became an almost impossible task for everyone. Their remarkable surge began when John Kenfield of Chicago, then 35, answered an ad in a tennis magazine for a full-time coach at UNC. At the time, he was a part-time tennis instructor and vice president of the Curtis Candy Company, where he'd proposed the name "Baby Ruth" for a new candy bar. Named for the great Yankees' slugger, it became a smash hit and made Curtis millions.[4]

Kenfield took the reins at UNC in 1928 and remained there for the next

28 years, posting 434 wins, 30 losses and 2 ties for a winning percentage of .933. His incredible overall record included ten unbeaten seasons and 15 Southern Conference Championships.[5] (UNC, like Duke, left the Southern Conference to join the ACC when it was formed in 1954.) Kenfield groomed one of Carolina's all-time greats, the legendary Vic Seixas, who won a host of collegiate honors before becoming the number one ranked American pro. He won the Wimbledon singles championship in 1953 and the U.S. Open singles title in 1954, the year before Kenfield retired.

A second era of dominance began under my contemporary, Don Skakle, who coached the Tar Heels from 1959 until his untimely death in 1980. Don was a great gentleman and the most generous coach I've ever known. His teams dominated the ACC during his 22 seasons at the helm, winning 16 conference crowns, tying for two others and finishing in the top 20 in the nation nine times. His overall match record was 418–55.[6] Among his greatest protégés were George Sokol, who won three ACC titles from 1962–64 and was named an All-American his junior year; Freddie McNair, Carolina's only four-time All-American and the winner of three ACC singles and three ACC doubles titles; and Rich McKee, a three-time All-American and the winner of two ACC singles and two ACC doubles crowns.[7]

During my tenure as Duke tennis coach, I sought out Don on many occasions for advice on how to build a tennis program like his. On most occasions, I'd drive over to Chapel Hill after practice to get his advice. I never felt he held anything back, even though I was asking him to share strategies that would improve our chances against his team. When I first started out, I can remember Don stressing over and over "You've got to get the full complement of scholarships; you can't compete without good players." I knew he was right and made getting five full scholarships my number one priority.

I remember how stunned the entire ACC tennis community was on April 18, 1980, when we got word that Don had died suddenly in his sleep of a heart attack. It was the eve of the ACC tennis tournament. Trim, fit and the picture of health, Don was only 56. I attended his funeral in Chapel Hill with a standing room only crowd. Most of the great stars he'd coached were there and gave moving testimonials. Like his highly successful predecessor, John Kenfield, Don epitomized the spirit of Carolina tennis: play your best, win with grace and give opponents the respect they deserve. I felt the Carolina fans were imbued with that spirit; they appreciated the finer points of the game and always treated their opponents with the courtesy every guest deserves. That same decorum was by no means universal; on certain campuses, raucous yelling and even harsh invective often occurred.

Next to beating Carolina, our second biggest win in that 19-match winning streak came on April 4 against Clemson, another archrival. Ranked sixth in the country at the time (we were 14th), the Tigers had become a perennial power under their volatile coach, Chuck Kriese.[8] A strong recruiter, Kriese's '82 team featured All-Americans Mark Dickson at No. 1 and Jean Desdunes at No. 2. Dickson turned pro after the '82 season and was warmly praised by Arthur Ashe, then United States Davis Cup captain, for his "daring" game.[9]

Somewhat unexpectedly, the April 4 contest turned into a grudge match. The previous fall, Kriese had forfeited a match to us in Columbia, South Carolina, when six courts were not available simultaneously. "We play as a team," he said, "or we don't play." It was a thin reed to hide behind, because five courts were available at the tournament site and a sixth court was available a mile or so away. The real reason Kriese didn't want to play was his best player, Dickson, was in Europe.[10] The situation was further aggravated when Kriese wrote a letter to coaches on the national tennis poll panel saying Clemson—not Duke—was the ACC's best representative for an upcoming West Coast tournament.[11] He also wrote that if Duke went, we'd embarrass the ACC. That insult goaded us even more when our players overheard Kriese's pre-match pep talk admonishing his players: "Clemson has better players than Duke, Clemson has a better team than Duke and Clemson is a better school than Duke." It gave us more than enough motivation for the clash on April 4.[12]

The headline match of the day pitted Chaim Arlosoroff against Mark Dickson, who had a career record of 122–38 and was ranked sixth in the country.[13] Thirty-mile-an-hour wind gusts forced both players to alter shots, especially Chaim, who countered the six-foot, four-inch Dickson's constant rushing of the net—the "daring" Arthur Ashe spoke of—with topspin lobs. The first set featured several service breaks by both players with Chaim finally winning 7–5. In the second set, Chaim fell behind 3–0 and 4–1 before reeling off five straight games to win the set 6–4 and take the match. The topspin lob was one of Chaim's best shots, and he exploited it relentlessly. His straight set win was the only one among the singles matches. Overall we won 6–3, taking four matches in singles and two in doubles. But one of the steadiest players I ever had, No. 2 Marc Flur, had a rare off day, losing to 19th-ranked Jean Desdunes 4–6, 6–4, 5–7. His loss set the stage for a rematch in the ACC tournament that would prove to be the greatest match in Duke tennis history.

On the way home, we were told Kriese scolded the team for disgracing themselves and the school. We also heard that Kriese had the team van stop on the outskirts of Clemson and ordered his players to get out and walk the rest of the way back to campus. I don't want to be too critical of Kriese, because every coach has his own way of dealing with disappointments. There is no denying that Chuck Kriese was one of the most successful tennis coaches in the country. His teams won 11 ACC championships, and he was named national Coach of the Year three times. I'm sure one other factor stuck in his craw: Our win on April 4 snapped a 25-match Clemson winning streak.

After the Clemson win, we cruised through the rest of our schedule, handily defeating in order: West Virginia, NC State, Appalachian State, Maryland, South Carolina, Old Dominion and North Carolina. We ended the season with a 7–0 record in ACC play, which made us the favorite in the ACC tournament set for April 16–18. Our overall record for the year was 31–3, the best in Duke tennis history. Inexplicably, even after we beat Clemson, and their forfeit to us the previous fall, the Tigers were still ranked ahead of us in the national collegiate tennis poll.

During our heady '82 run, we never put tennis first and let academics slide. That was even reflected in news coverage of our championship season. In his account of action the first morning of the ACC tournament, Ron Morris of the *Durham Herald Sun* noted that Chaim had defeated Wake Forest's Jimmy Jenkins in "a mere 41 minutes, and Jenkins appeared elated to have won one game in the two-set match."

"After passing a chemistry test in the early afternoon," Morris continued, "Arlosoroff returned to the Duke courts and teamed with Mike Smith in a 6–2, 6–1 victory over Maryland's team of Blasé Keating-Denis Rende." Chaim had a 3.9 average that semester and was working hard to get into med school. I was sure he'd aced the test; peak performance on the court and in the classroom made him the classic scholar-athlete.

As I've mentioned, nearly every player on the '82 team was a scholar-athlete. All 65 players on the Duke teams I coached earned a degree and about 40 percent earned advanced degrees. That meant I often saw my players studying on campus—pouring over a textbook in the bleachers, reading next to a flower bed in Duke Gardens, studying in the cafeteria or on the green grass of the quad. They always took textbooks and studied hard on road trips. Even so, I never felt casual observation of their diligence was enough. When David Robinson (see his profile in Chapter Seven) fell behind in physics, I got him a tutor and he ended up passing with ease.

Dr. Jim Bonk, a tenured chemistry professor, was a volunteer assistant for my entire tenure as head coach. We became best friends, and I trusted his advice on academic counseling more than anyone's. When a player had a difficult time with a certain class, we always strategized on how to find him the right support. A few players, including Chaim, even stayed with Jim for a few months at a time. As a bachelor, he welcomed them and readily advised them on a host of topics. In 1978–79, Jim served as head of tutoring for the entire athletic department. Students had a great affection for Jim; deep down, most knew he was devoting his life to Duke chemistry and Duke tennis.

I made it a practice to monitor each player's grades every semester, a key step in tracking academic progress. After getting the grades from Harry Demick, the Assistant Registrar, I reviewed all the results with my contacts in the Admissions Office to inform them of how my players were performing. The Admissions Office always wanted to know how their decisions were working out. Our collaborative relationship enabled me to get prospects considered who had great tennis credentials but borderline grades and SATs. It's important to note that many of my players would have been admitted at Duke without citing tennis as a credential. At the time, Duke was admitting about 10 percent of applicants; that meant those scoring below the 10 percent had to have special credentials—stardom in sports, community service or something else—to get admitted. To get a star tennis player in, I had to provide strong evidence to an admissions officer that the player could do the academic work required by Duke.

From the outset of my tenure as tennis coach, player grades ranged from good to great. I stressed that a teamwide 3.0 GPA (before the era of grade inflation) was our minimum goal and all my teams scored that or higher. Players accepted that goal and expected others to do the same. Jim

Bonk and I frequently asked "How are your classes going?" and "Do you need any help?" To set proper expectations, we stressed, time and time again, that academics had to come first. Thus, Duke tennis players were expected to do well academically and did.

Never before or since has there been an ACC tournament like the one that began on Duke's home courts on the morning of April 16, 1982. At the time, tennis, itself, was peaking in popularity in the United States with American players like Jimmy Connors and John McEnroe engaging in on-court hijinks that thrilled and infuriated fans all over the world.[14] That year, the men's finals at the U.S. Open attracted the second highest television ratings in history.[15]

That same level of interest was reflected in media coverage in Durham and the Research Triangle area, and in attendance at the event itself. In contrast to the typical attendance of 100 or so for a dual match between Duke and an ACC foe, opening round matches for the '82 tournament attracted an attendance in the range of 500 to 1,000. In anticipation of a big turnout, I'd arranged with the campus Maintenance Department to set up 10 sections of bleachers, about 1,000 seats in all, behind the courts on the north end of our tennis complex. To accommodate as many fans as possible, we even borrowed bleachers from Durham's City Recreation Department.

The tournament featured three rounds over three days (Friday through Sunday) with six flights of singles and three flights of doubles on the opening day. It was a single elimination event, which meant a player had to win three matches to win his flight and an individual ACC championship. A point system was used to determine the overall conference champion.

From the very first match, the ambience was unlike anything I'd ever seen in collegiate tennis: packed stands, a gaggle of newsmen interviewing players on the courts before and after matches, the drama of the umpire calling out the score from his high chair at mid-court and a fraternity dispensing beer from kegs behind the stands. The coaches and players of all seven teams were awestruck by the bubbling excitement as play got underway.

Duke got off to a good start by winning all six singles matches and all three doubles matches on Friday. That gave us a 45–40 lead over Clemson and a 45–30 lead over Carolina, an outcome that broadcast outlets all featured prominently on the evening news and in newspapers on Satur-

The 1982 ACC Tournament

day morning. That helped the tournament draw an even larger crowd—a thousand or more, the Duke Athletic Department estimated—on Saturday. Because the players were well-known and quite popular on campus, their friends turned out en masse. The beer flowing freely from kegs behind the stands was an added enticement and helped make for a highly convivial atmosphere. Once again, Duke fared well, winning four singles and two doubles matches to get to the finals.

It all came down to Duke, Clemson and UNC for the championship on Sunday with a crowd estimated at 4,000, the largest ever to see a tennis match at Duke before or since. People were lying on the ground, even peering under the fence at the action; others were standing on top of the groundskeeper's tool shed. In the Number 1 flight, Chaim, once again, was matched with Clemson's Mark Dickson, who won the first set 5–7. But that didn't rattle Chaim at all; in the second set, his precision shots—especially his topspin lob—were decisive. That set lasted only 23 minutes, and Chaim only lost seven points, winning the set 6–0. In the third set, Dickson managed to knot the score at 3–3, but Chaim reeled off the next three games to win 6–3. When Dickson volleyed the last point into the net, the crowd roared its approval.

After the match Clemson coach Kriese told a reporter: "I just think Mark must have lost his concentration." But as one of our players put it after the match, "Chaim just destroyed Dickson."

The contest of the day was a revenge match between two All-Americans: Marc Flur and Jean Desdunes, who had narrowly defeated Marc in three sets in our dual match with Clemson on April 4. It was easily the best match of the tournament, and many have called it the greatest match in all the years of Duke tennis. Marc got off to a terrible start, dropping the first set 1–6; it was only the second time all year he'd lost a set by such a margin. But the second set became a battle of survival and sheer will for Flur when he fell behind 5–4. Desdunes had built his lead staying on the baseline, patiently waiting for Marc to make mistakes. Then, slowly the momentum began to shift; Marc stopped making errors and started to play the best tennis of his life. With his two-handed, Bjorn Borg-type backhand, he started hitting powerful crosscourt winners over and over. It occurred to me: *All those tight challenge matches he's played against Chaim are really paying off.* Marc was hitting as hard as he could on every point—what one reporter called "Russian roulette-style." It was a good metaphor, except Marc would need all six shots in the chamber.

Not all his go-for-broke shots were winners; somehow, Desdunes managed a down-the-line winner that earned him match point at 6–5 in the second set. A long rally followed, full of blistering shots on both sides; finally, Marc made a brilliant passing shot to get back to deuce. That left only five shots in the chamber.

On the opposite baseline, calmly yet with cat-like quickness, Desdunes hit another winner for match point two. I began to wonder if Desdunes's incredible quickness might be too much for our lanky, power-hitting No. 2. But once again, Marc reached deep and fired another winner. At that point a dream-like trance seemed to envelop us all—players, coaches and fans alike—as we watched the unfolding of that never-to-be-forgotten drama. With 4,000 voices roaring on every point, Flur and Desdunes were engaged in a titanic struggle that, rightfully, neither should have had to lose. In that moment, Desdunes reached a third . . . then a fourth . . . then a fifth . . . and, finally, a sixth match point—a feat I'd never seen before and doubt anyone else had either. On his side of the net, Marc kept staving off defeat, reaching deep for power and precision when there was no margin of error whatsoever. On the sixth match point, Marc charged in and sent a shoulder-high volley crosscourt for a winner. At deuce, a long baseline rally led to one of Desdunes's few unforced errors. Marc won the final point of the second set with an unreturnable serve. The score of the emotionally draining tiebreaker: Flur 7–3. At that point, the crowd seemed emotionally wrung out.

In the third set, the momentum was all on Marc's side. He played like a man who just escaped the hangman's noose, while Desdunes became tentative and a half a step

Marc Flur's epic win

slower. Marc won going away to win the match by the final score of 1–6, 7–6, 6–3—once again, one of the greatest wins in the history of Duke tennis. One of the reporters who covered the match said Flur "pulled an escape act that would have made Harry Houdini blush." After he won, Marc held both fists in the air and bowed to the crowd, which was going berserk. I've never seen another wave of euphoria and sheer joy like the one that swept those who saw our first ACC championship. It was a moment that made us all proud to be a part of Duke University and Duke tennis.

Afterward, I sought out Desdunes to offer consolation and to congratulate him for playing such a superb match. As it turned out, the final round of the ACC tournament looked a lot like the lineup for a Duke dual match. In addition to the Chaim and Marc who won at No. 1 and No. 2 singles, Todd Ryska won at No. 5 and Russell Gache won at No. 6. Our doubles teams of Marc Flur–Ross Dubins and Will White–Russell Gache also won championships. In the final round consisting of six singles and three doubles matches, we won six of the nine to win the tournament decisively. Thus, it irritated me no end that the post-tournament coaches' poll ranked Clemson at No. 8 and Duke at No. 12. No wonder, I told my-

The 1982 ACC Tournament Champions

self, there were only six coaches on the polling panel and Chuck Kriese was one of them.

A few weeks later I drove the team in the van to the NCAA tournament in Athens, Georgia, on the campus of the University of Georgia. The facilities there were among the best in the nation. In retrospect, I feel that the ACC tournament was so exhilarating and so emotional that we had a letdown in Athens. There were two tournaments there: one for teams and a second for individuals. We lost our first team match 6–3 to Texas Christian University, the fifth-ranked team in the country. We were very evenly matched with TCU but did not play our best. In the individual rounds, Chaim and Marc both won first round matches but lost in the second round. Chaim was named an All-American, and the team finished 12th in the country.

It would be a mistake to think the players on the '82 team alone carried Duke to its first ACC championship. Many from prior teams—beginning with Mark Meyers, who won three ACC championships and still has Duke's highest winning percentage—set the stage for that accomplishment. Mark was the first player I offered a scholarship. As I've said, it was one of the best decisions I ever made: Mark was the big barracuda who attracted a whole school of fish.

Without him, we'd never have gotten Teddy Daniel, another of Duke's all-time best. Teddy came from Tulsa with great tennis genes. His mother was a former Oklahoma state champion. Teddy began playing at age 10 and was such a prodigy that Arthur Ashe came to see him play at 14. When he first came to Duke, he was a bit temperamental, but he gradually outgrew that. He won the ACC tournament at No. 4 singles in 1975 and won in doubles with Chip Davis to become the first Duke player to claim two crowns. Two years later, he won the ACC championship at No. 2. His forte was finesse—steady, well-rounded, error-free tennis.

Teddy graduated from Duke in 1978 with a degree in management sciences and went to law school at Southern Methodist University. For many years, he's been a partner/litigator in the Dallas office of Norton Rose Fulbright, one of the world's largest law firms.

Other players who paved the way for our '82 championship were Chip Davis, David Robinson and John Stauffer, each of whom is profiled in Part II of the book. Reuven "Ruby" Porges, the first player to come from Israel, helped pave the way too. Like Chaim, he'd played on the Israeli Davis Cup team and was an outstanding student. After getting an undergraduate degree, he went to med school at Duke and established a highly successful OBGYN practice in Miami. Several others helped set the stage for our '82 championship, among them: Mike McMahon (who is referenced earlier in this chapter): Ross Dubins and Joe Meir (whose profiles appear in Chapter Seventeen); Neils Rathlev from Denmark, who is a physician in Boston; and Tim O'Reilly, who transferred to Duke from the University of Southern California. After his first semester at Duke, Tim told me "I've decided that Duke really does expect me to do good academic work."

I'm not sure I could coach today's players. Being a player isn't an avocation; it's become a job, one that often leaves little time for academics. Top players sometimes come to Duke with their own support system: a personal coach, a nutritionist, a sports psychologist and a hovering family. Everyone seems so tightly wound, so methodical and so predictable. Sometimes I ask myself if anybody's having fun? Then, I think of our guys in the back of the van playing poker on top a suitcase, arguing hard over penny ante stakes. I can still see their astonished looks when my wife,

Carole, once nonchalantly lit up a victory cigar. Or how stunned they were by my infamous "takedown" of Teddy Daniel.

One day Teddy came to the court for a match moping because he thought I'd placed him too low in the singles lineup. When I saw his body language, I growled: "Teddy, you know I can't stand pouting."

Something incoherent came back, so I grabbed him in a headlock and wrestled him to the ground.

The opposing coach rushed over and asked with concern: "Is everything okay?"

"Yeah, we're okay," I replied as Teddy squirmed beneath me. "We're having what I call an attitude adjustment."

"Oh, I thought he might be choking," the relieved coach observed.

As the two of us got up and dusted ourselves off, one wag deadpanned, "Well, John, if tennis doesn't work out, you can always coach wrestling."

Throughout my tennis coaching career, I told my players to never telegraph their emotions in the heat of a match. An opponent who sees sulking or an outburst of temper knows you are half whipped already. If, instead, I'd said, "Teddy, please don't do that again," what effect would that have had? Such a milquetoast admonition would have gotten what it deserved—a bored shrug and ho-hum *I might, and I might not*. But Teddy got my point; I don't think he ever sulked or moped again. He was a terrific kid who went on to become a great player and team captain in '78. His temperament improved significantly at Duke; and he would display sterling character in a long and successful legal career.

While the players laughed many times about my wrestling match with Teddy, I'll confess it was an unorthodox way to make a point. But being predictable, so methodical everyone always knows the drill—that was not how I liked to operate. Today, wrestling a player to the ground might well get a coach fired. Do it by the numbers, or else—that's the modus operandi too often expected.

After beating the Tar Heels for the first time in 24 years, I called Duke's Athletic Director Tom Butters at home in the early evening to let him know that we'd ended one epoch and started another. The conversation went something like this—

"Tom, Duke tennis turned a big corner today."

"How so?"

"We beat Carolina 5–4."

"That's nice. Thanks for letting me know."

And that was it. He hung up, puncturing my balloon completely. There were only two people I could tell what a blow Butters had dealt me: my best friend and volunteer assistant, Jim Bonk, and my wife, Carole, an ardent fan of Duke tennis and my coaching.

The Butters brushoff was hard to swallow after a long, hard, eight-year climb. For the first time, I began to wonder what the future of Duke tennis might hold for me.

CHAPTER SEVENTEEN

Unexpected Endings

Little did we know that Chuck Kriese, Clemson's fiery coach, couldn't let well enough alone. Members of my '82 team felt that losing three times to Duke in the '82 season—two on the court and one by forfeit—led to his vengeful attack on our star, Chaim Arlosoroff. Only eight days after the ACC tournament, Chuck began pushing to get Chaim declared ineligible by the NCAA. He stoutly denied to his own athletic department that sour grapes were involved, but it was clear that Chaim's decisive wins over Mark Dickson, the sixth-ranked collegian and one of the greatest stars Kriese ever produced, were too hard to swallow. Dickson was a three-time All-American and had a successful pro career. Ironically, in the final college poll for the '82 tennis season, Dickson would be ranked No. 13, four spots ahead of Chaim. In that same poll, Mike DePalmer of Tennessee was ranked No. 2 and David Pate of UCLA was ranked No. 4; yet Chaim had beaten both that season. It was baffling, too, that Clemson was ranked 9th, three notches ahead of Duke in the final poll. Was that decision influenced unduly by Chuck, who had a seat on the polling committee of eight? I certainly felt it might have been. One small consolation: I was named runner-up for the NCAA's National Tennis Coach of the Year.

Chuck's effort to keep Chaim from playing began with an

April 26 memorandum to Clemson's Associate Athletic Director, R.W. Robinson, entitled, "Eligibility Status of Chaim Arlosoroff, Duke University." It complained that: "It is very disheartening to devote totally for 4 years, to the development of 18 year olds we have coming into our program, only to have to compete with a player 6 years older than they are."[1] He urged Robinson to complain to the NCAA that Chaim was ineligible but gave no reason why Chaim should get the boot other than age. The memo to Robinson never mentioned that, as an Israeli citizen, Chaim had three years of mandatory military service after high school; nor did it mention that Chaim was a scholar-athlete with a high A average.

Within a matter of weeks, the NCAA notified Duke that Chaim was ineligible, citing a rule adopted at its January 1980 convention. It penalized any athlete who participated in organized competition after his or her 20th birthday and prior to enrolling at an NCAA member college or university. The penalty was loss of one year of eligibility for any 12-month period of pre-enrollment competition.[2] After high school, Arlosoroff had played occasionally for the Israeli Davis Cup Team while performing his military service; after he was discharged, he played for two and a half years more in amateur tournaments. The NCAA further told Duke if Chaim continued playing on its team, sanctions would be applied.[3] It also served notification that his freshman year at Duke was his final year of eligibility.[4] While the Over Twenty rule was adopted the year before Chaim enrolled at Duke, the NCAA applied it to him retroactively, even though he'd never heard of it until he finished his first year at Duke.

In many respects, the Over Twenty rule was a complete farce: It was aimed at East African distance runners in their late twenties or older, who got recruited by "rent-a-runner" programs that put little or no emphasis on academics. Chaim was a solid A student, but that made no difference at all to the NCAA. Whether his scholarship was guaranteed didn't either. Chaim would go on to graduate magna cum laude with a 3.8 GPA, but the Over Twenty rule would force him out of tennis for good. In effect, the ruling forced the de facto resignation of a quintessential scholar-athlete: not only an A student, but one of the best players in the country.

It was a terrible decision that threatened to unravel Chaim's future completely. His long-time Israeli girlfriend, Yael, had spent the spring semester with Chaim at Duke. After exams, they'd gone home for the summer, but she soon told him she wouldn't go back to Durham without a wedding ring. He wanted to hold onto Yael, but badly wanted to become a doctor. That meant eight more years of study with very little income. Even though I'd assured him from the outset his scholarship was guaranteed for four years, it wasn't nearly enough for a couple to live on. That meant someone would have to work. Could Yael find a job in Durham? If not, he'd have to work and couldn't continue with tennis. As these head-scratching questions swirled about, a small bomb dropped: Word came that Clemson had challenged his eligibility.

Formal notification came in a letter dated July 16 from Bill Bradford, faculty representative to the Duke Athletic Department.[5] It emphasized that while the NCAA had ruled against him, Duke would honor its four-year scholarship commitment, even though he'd be barred from playing varsity tennis. A letter dated August 2, 1982, from Athletic Director Tom Butters further confirmed that Duke would stand behind its commitment to provide six more semesters (three years) of full scholarship. Butters called the NCAA's decision "an unfortunate circumstance and one that will be Duke University's loss."

Shortly after that, Duke appealed to the NCAA to reverse its decision, holding that it was "patently and harshly discriminatory" because of its retroactive application to Chaim "who could have had no knowledge of a rule not yet in existence when he competed in tennis tournaments after his 20th birthday and before his discharge from the Israeli army."[6] When the NCAA refused to budge, the issue went to court, where it dragged on for over two years before a landmark ruling was reached.[7] A North Carolina district court first granted a preliminary injunction blocking NCAA enforcement of its decision to rule Chaim ineligible. When the NCAA appealed, the case was moved to federal court, where the U.S. Court of Appeals for the Fourth Circuit reversed the state court on October 25, 1984.[8] Chaim's case alleged denial of due process and equal protection under the Fourteenth Amendment of the U.S. Constitution. The state district court had upheld that claim, but the federal court denied it, holding that the NCAA rule was private conduct and not state action. That meant the due process clause of the Fourteenth Amendment—"nor shall any *state* deprive any person of life, liberty, or property, without due process of law"—did not apply.[9] At least one major law review article called the implications of that decision "very disturbing. The decision allows the NCAA to promulgate virtually whatever rules it desires, because most of the Constitution's guarantees of individual rights shield individuals only from government action.... A finding of state action, then, would be a 'safer' approach because it would allow the judiciary to monitor the NCAA."[10]

The practical effect of the NCAA ruling and subsequent litigation was to force Chaim out of collegiate tennis. While the state court deliberated on issuing an injunction, he was in limbo: He could practice with the team but not play. Playing at No. 1 requires constant fine-tuning that can only be achieved through competition with peers. Denied that access, his conditioning also began to slip. Once the injunction was granted, he played sporadically for the team in the spring of '83 and the spring of '84—mostly at No. 2—but I don't think his heart was ever in it. When the Fourth Circuit Court of Appeals denied a petition for rehearing on January 28, 1985, the decision was final.[11] That forced a de facto resignation on a superb scholar-athlete, a type of player the Over Twenty rule had never been intended for. It's noteworthy that the Over Twenty rule was long ago rescinded.

In time, this type of picayune NCAA rulemaking only got worse. "Why Does the NCAA Exist?" the *Huffington Post* asked in an article on August 6, 2013. "After all, [it] denied the University of Iowa's request to wear jerseys honoring the death of a teammate, while at the same time, [it] was unable to conduct a non-corrupt investigation into allegations that a rich booster had bought University of Miami football and basketball players jewelry, prostitutes and had even paid for an abortion."[12]

Chuck Kriese's role as instigator of Chaim's misfortune drew a sharp rebuke from Harold Landesberger, the prominent patron of Duke athletics who first recommended Chaim to me. In a letter he wrote to Chuck on October 13, 1982, Harold called Chuck's actions "despicable, unreasonable and done with malice of forethought."[13] At the time, Clemson was facing severe sanctions for recruiting violations in its football program that resulted in a two-year ban on television and postseason bowl appearances by the school, as well as the loss of 20 scholarships.[14] In light of that action imposed by the NCAA, Harold wrote that the complaint against Chaim "is beyond my comprehension." He further demanded that Chuck "withdraw your objections to Duke and this young man." He sent a copy of the letter to Clemson Athletic Director William McLellan demanding that Clemson withdraw its complaint.

At the time, Chaim was convinced that Chuck Kriese was out to destroy him. "I can't imagine that he even considered how that decision could destroy my life and any professional career I might seek." In retro-spect, I'd have to say that judgment was somewhat harsh. What Chuck did was an example of the "win-at-all-cost" mentality that can cloud a coach's thinking. I doubt that Chuck knew much, if anything, about Chaim's financial circumstances—that he couldn't continue at Duke without the scholarship; even though his father was a prominent water expert, the family couldn't afford the cost of a Duke education. I'm sure Chuck had no idea that Duke had guaranteed Chaim a four-year schol-arship whether he played tennis or not. Chuck saw Chaim as an impos-ing roadblock to Clemson championships for the next three years. I'm relatively certain Chuck never considered how much damage his actions could cause; Chaim's future was not a factor in Chuck's calculations—a type of thinking that has become even more pervasive today in collegiate athletics.

It's important to note that Chuck was one of the most successful tennis coaches the ACC ever had. When he retired at Clemson in 2008, he was the winningest coach in ACC history, having led the Tigers to 10 ACC titles and seven berths in the "Elite Eight." He coached 38 All-Americans and won four national Coach of the Year awards.

Chaim would go on to graduate magna cum laude with a 3.8 GPA and became a prominent orthopedic surgeon. He recently told me: "Going there (to Duke) was hands down the best decision I ever made. It led to everything that came afterwards for me."[15] Although he did not have leg-acy status for purposes of admissions, Chaim's family background made him especially attractive to admissions officers at Duke: He came from one of the most famous families in the Middle East. As noted in Chapter Fifteen,

He bore the same name as an iconic grandfather, who might well have been Israel's first prime minister, if not for his tragic death in 1933. The cir-cumstances surrounding why radical rightwing Jews assassinated Chaim's grandfather while walking on the beach near Tel Aviv cast a lingering shadow over the struggle for Jewish independence and even over Israel after its birth in 1947. I learned from Chaim's father, Shaul, that a haunt-ing sense of missed potential, not unlike the assassination of President Kennedy, surrounded his father's death. Streets in nearly every Israeli town—even neighborhoods and kibbutzim—were named for the first Chaim. That made young Chaim a curiosity wherever he went: People wanted to see and even touch him, to know if one of their country's iconic founders lived on through his grandson.[16]

On June 14, 1933, Chaim's grandfather took a stroll with his wife, Simi, on the beach in Tel Aviv. Two members of a rightwing Jewish party with fascist tendencies shot him dead as his distraught wife watched. They gave as their reason his efforts to foster Jewish-Arab cooperation. His funeral attracted an estimated 100,000 mourners, the largest such assemblage in the history of the British Mandate. Many believed that had he lived, he would have been the first Prime Minister of Israel. His death led to deep fissures within the Zionist Movement.

Chaim's father, Shaul, became a prominent water engineer, who assisted the World Bank with projects in about a hundred countries. He recalls his son as a lad of eight being shy and keeping mostly to himself. "I finally dragged him to the tennis court to bring out the fighting spirit that is hidden inside his character." At the time, Shaul never could have imagined how far those competitive fires would take his young son.

¤ ¤ ¤

By 1982, my coaching duties had mushroomed. In 1971, when I became head coach at Duke, we played a 17-match season; a decade or so later, we were playing 34 matches with postseason tournaments on top of that. Tennis at Duke had become a year-round sport with a lengthy fall practice, followed by a spring season that began in mid-February. As we added scholarships, I spent more and more time recruiting; and the logistics of a greatly expanded travel schedule all fell to me to arrange. In 1979, Tom Butters had made me Director of Tennis; that meant I kept my duties as head coach of the men's team, while managing the women's program, all without a bump in pay. On top of all that, I was still teaching four PE classes in tennis. The widened scope of my duties left hardly a moment to call my own or to devote to my family.

As the '82 season wound down—and after many long discussions with Carole and my closest friend and volunteer assistant, Jim Bonk—I decided that the situation had become untenable, that something had to give. The obvious solution was to hire an assistant to relieve my administrative overload. The head coaches at Carolina and Clemson both had assistant coaches, but no coach of a non-revenue sport at Duke had one. I knew it'd be tough to sell Butters on hiring one, but I felt my only option was to try.

By 1982, Butters had been Duke's Athletic Director for five years and was on track to become one of the most successful athletic directors the school ever had. A former pitcher for the Pittsburg Pirates, he had coached baseball briefly at Duke and later organized the Iron Dukes, the fundraising arm of university athletics. In 1980, he hired Mike Krzyzewski as basketball coach and stuck with him through a rocky start when many fans loudly called for his dismissal. In 1984, after two 17-loss seasons, Butters gave Krzyzewski a contract extension—an astute, if unpopular, decision, because Coach K went on to become the winningest coach in NCAA history. With his Caesar-like thatch of silvery hair, his leathery face and solid frame, Butters carried himself with the air of command. I never disliked him but always felt uneasy with his gruff manner.

I arranged to see him on April 5, the day after our decisive win over Clemson. By then, it was clear Duke had the best team in the ACC; I felt that gave added weight to an already strong case for hiring an assistant. As I walked to his office near the entrance of Cameron Indoor Stadium, a repressed memory resurfaced: How Tom had barely reacted at all when I told him we'd beaten the Tar Heels in tennis for the first time in 24 years. By the time I sat down across the desk from Tom, I had doubts that I could persuade him.

His opening comment—"Well, what's this all about?"—did nothing to boost my resolve.

I began by describing the details of my ever-increasing work load, but before I could finish, he interrupted,

"So what are you saying?"

"I'm saying that the tennis program needs an assistant."

"You've already got Jim Bonk," Tom replied. "Why do you need someone else?"

"Jim's a volunteer who helps coordinate our practices and conditioning drills. He has a full teaching load and doesn't handle anything on the administrative side. That's where I need help. We're playing twice as many matches as we were when I started."

Tom thought for a moment and shrugged, "I just can't see it. If you get one, I'll have to give one to everyone else coaching a non-revenue sport. That'd break the bank."

"Then what am I supposed to do about my increasing work load?"

"You'll have to do the best you can."

"So, no change for the foreseeable future—maybe not ever?"

"John, the bottom line is: We've never had an assistant tennis coach at Duke and never will."

"And that's final?"

"Yes, it is."

I was angry when I left, mainly because I hadn't quit on the spot. I'd have been irate had I known that in a couple of years, my successor would get an assistant. Conversations later that day, first with Jim and then with Carole, settled me down. I told them Tom had given me no choice but to resign. Jim, a mild-mannered soul, urged me to reconsider; in time, he predicted, Butters would have to give in on the issue. But Carole felt enough was enough: she was tired of the grind, tired of having a husband who was rarely around.

"Trust your instincts," she counseled. "You need to do what's in your heart of heart." I knew her advice was sound, that it was based on her many years as a psychiatric nurse. I had great confidence in her judgment on all potentially life-changing issues. It made our decision much easier that since 1970 I'd been a tenured professor in the Department of Physical Education—that gave me other good options within the university.

The next morning, I addressed a one-sentence letter to Butters: "Dear Tom, I hereby resign as head tennis coach of Duke University effective July 1, 1982." I delivered it in person, but, again, few words were exchanged.

"After thinking more about our conversation yesterday, I've decided to resign effective July 1."

"You're sure?" he asked with apparent concern.

"Yes—I'm sure."

"I had a feeling you might decide to step down. This is not good news, because you've done an outstanding job. Can I assume that you'll stick around for the tournament? It looks like you guys are going to win it."

"Yes, I'm planning to stick around until July 1. I've called a team meeting to let the guys know. I don't want them finding out from someone else."

With that, he wished me luck and said goodbye. The team met that afternoon in a classroom at Card Gym. My news came as a total shock. The players' first reaction was to try to change my mind; next they vowed to go to Butters and change his. The more we talked, the clearer it became that our unexpected ending was final. Deep down, they knew my reasons for resigning were valid and wanted what was best for me. As reality sunk in, we talked of all the good times we had together, leavened with laughs like the old standby: "Hey coach, if you ever need a hotel, Chaim can get you in at the RAH-ma-da (Ramada)." There was one recurring theme: how much we'd improved and how far we could go. Finally, someone said, "Hey coach, with the entire team coming back next year, Duke ought to win the national championship." That made me flinch, to entertain a fleeting doubt about my decision.

Even so, I urged the guys: "Let's keep our focus on winning Duke's first ACC championship ten days from now."

Russell Gache, who'd recovered a few months earlier from academic difficulties to become a star on the court and in the classroom, brought us to closure: "Coach, you can bet your last chip"—an allusion to my over-hyped losses in our back-of-the-van poker games—"that *this year* we're going to win the ACC for you. They might as well hand over that trophy right now." I'd always urged my guys to play for the team, for the school and for themselves, but, I'm sure that playing harder for me was a factor in winning the ACC tournament.

Several friends tried to get Tom to bring me back, all to no avail. David Robinson, a star on Duke teams between '76 and '79 then in med school, urged Tom to patch things up. Marc Flur, our No. 2 in '82, did the same. They went on their own without me knowing, but got nowhere. My resignation was final, once and for all. But it wasn't as if I had nothing to do. I went back to teaching and developed a demanding and popular course on Sports Management. Later, I was asked to take over the Faculty Club; its membership doubled in my decade there. I also had my tennis camp, which brought 75 to 80 kids to campus every summer. The basketball camp had been the first such camp at Duke and mine was second; it grew steadily over the seven years I ran it.

As it sunk in that my coaching days were ending, it occurred to me that in 20-plus years of coaching fencing and tennis, my superiors on the athletic side had never commented on—let alone encouraged—my efforts to develop scholar-athletes. I had made clear to every player on every team I coached that academics came first. Counseling players on courses to take, finding tutors when academic difficulties arose, adjusting for afternoon science and language labs and tracking each player's academic performance on a semester-to-semester basis—I'd always felt these tasks were essential to develop scholar-athletes to their full potential. I'm sorry to say that since I left coaching, the fundamental disconnect that permits the scholar side of the scholar-athlete equation to be grossly undervalued has only gotten worse.

Every member of Duke's '82 ACC championship team, except for Ross Dubins, returned for the '82–'83 season. By the time spring matches began, the state court had issued its preliminary injunction permitting Chaim to play. But somehow, the team's chemistry dissipated, and it soon became mediocre. Many players, including Chaim, found it almost impossible to get along with my successor, Steve Strome. He was tennis coach at LSU when Tom hired him. A couple of years later, Tom relented and gave him an assistant. Tom had been forewarned by no less than Mark Meyers, my first scholarship recipient, that Strome would not be a good fit at Duke. Mark was in law school at LSU and serving as assistant tennis coach when he voiced that opinion. He told Butters he felt Strome would not relate well to the players at Duke. At one point, the players called a team meeting at which Strome sat in the middle of a circle fielding tough questions and many complaints about petty rules, especially his ban on small stakes poker in the back of the van. I heard plenty of complaints about Strome but had a standard response: "Just give the guy a chance. Once he gets his feet wet, he'll probably be okay." But when I heard about his stance on poker, I had my doubts.

That fall after I resigned, I bumped into Chancellor Ken Pye one day on the quad. He'd taken tennis lessons from me, sent his son to my sports camp and over the years we'd become good friends.

"Why didn't you tell me you and Butters were at loggerheads?" he asked. "I'd have called Tom and tried to work something out."

"I just didn't think that was a good idea."

Ken gave me a knowing grin and said, "Can't undermine the chain of command, can we?"

"I guess not," I replied.

In retrospect, I already regretted my decision: I missed the guys, the comradery, the competition and that always-elusive quest for a national championship. In many ways, it was the best job I ever had—one in which I made great friendships and established bonds that would last a lifetime. I winced at Ken Pye's reference to the chain of command. I didn't need to undercut it; deep down, I knew I should have soldiered on. Unexpected endings often are like that: They can cause an acute sense of loss.

CHAPTER EIGHTEEN

Unbreakable Bonds

Unbreakable bonds to an alma mater must be based on something deeper than the stirring sounds of its marching band. The bedrock value of the greatest academic institutions is an unwavering commitment to truth and the freedom to express truth no matter what, even when harsh reactions echo in the public square. In 1903, Duke (then Trinity College) faced just such a test when John Spenser Bassett, a talented young history professor, published an article in *South Atlantic Quarterly*, a scholarly journal he founded, entitled, "Stirring Up the Fires of Race Antipathy." One sentence near the end of that article—"Booker T. Washington [is] the greatest man, save General Lee, born in the South in a hundred years"—provoked a storm of outrage and widespread calls for Bassett's resignation.

A partisan political press led by Josephus Daniels, Publisher of the Raleigh *News and Observer*, and leaders of the then-dominant Democratic Party demanded that Bassett be fired; parents were even urged to withdraw offspring from the school. The pressure got so intense that Bassett offered to resign for the good of the university. A climactic resolution occurred on the evening of December 2, 1902, when the Trinity Board of Trustees debated Bassett's future until 3 a.m.

with anxious students listening through a skylight and heating vents. A final vote of 18 to 7 against his resignation touched off the bonfires of a jubilant student celebration that lasted until dawn. Few knew that Trinity President John C. Kilgo and leading faculty were prepared to resign if the vote went against Bassett. The school's patron, Benjamin N. Duke, voted in Bassett's favor, refusing to "pander to widely held prejudice." After the vote, Trinity basked in a national outpouring of praise for its courageous stand. A year later, when President Theodore Roosevelt spoke in Durham, he strongly commended the school for its commitment to academic freedom.[1]

Despite humble beginnings in rural North Carolina, Bassett became an intellectual star at Trinity. He taught what was called "new history," which moved away from feel-good themes, self-serving memoir and ancestor worship that often characterized history taught in the postbellum South. In contrast, Bassett emphasized original research based on diaries, court records, newspaper accounts and interviews. He was among the first scholars to write about the importance of the schism between Booker T. Washington and W.E.B. DuBois, the two greatest proponents of African American progress.[2] The former advocated incremental progress through vocational education, the latter called for primary emphasis on the intellectual development of a favored few. Bassett came down in the middle, holding that white southerners should support both types of improvement simultaneously.[3] Bassett went on to write about national themes in U.S. history as a much-admired professor at Smith College in Massachusetts.

By my time, the years had dimmed the prominence of the Bassett affair, but it remains undeniably at the heart of Duke values. Even so, few of my players and students knew who Bassett was, but they all knew Duke had a strong moral compass, that Duke stood for more than athletic exploits, fraternity parties or just getting a degree. Values that encourage a deep attachment to an alma mater are hard to define because most are acquired by osmosis: by being exposed to the tenets of a liberal arts education, which Duke has always embraced, to great professors, to world-changing ideas and, more recently, a culture of collaboration. Duke's new President, Vincent Price, calls that culture a "special mix of collaboration and compassion. And more so than any other place I've worked, Duke feels to me like a community and family. We celebrate, we compete, we argue sometimes. But at the end of the day, everyone here wants Duke to be the best it can be."[4]

Its faculty has always included professors, like Bassett, who make the university years a life-changing experience for countless students. In my 40-plus years at Duke, no one inspired students more than my best friend, Jim Bonk, a much-beloved chemistry professor, who taught an estimated 30,000 students in his 42-year career.[5] He was already a volunteer assistant tennis coach when I became head coach in 1971, and we quickly bonded. A dyed-in-the-wool bachelor, he lived alone in a modest white stucco house near the West Campus. Having no immediate family, Jim became a fixture at our house for Thanksgiving and Christmas dinner. His keen sense of humor always sparkled at these gatherings.

"John and I are going to find you a woman," Carole would threaten from time to time.

"Where would I put her?" Jim would ask.

"In your home, of course."

"No, I'd need a new house with two wings—one for her and one for me."

Carole often teased that he'd never find a woman to measure up to his mother, who was nothing short of a saint to Jim. She might have had a point.

It's not an overstatement to say that Jim was extraordinarily popular at Duke. A third of Duke freshmen took his "Introduction to Chemistry," most fondly referring to it as "Bonkistry." He spent up to six hours preparing for each lecture and wrote his own lab manual. To make it fully accessible, he had the manual printed and sold it for the cost of printing—about $1.50 a copy, or thereabouts. He kept long office hours with a large plastic banner—"The Bonk Is Here"—hanging above his door.[6]

When Jim retired, Dean Robert Thompson asked, "How do you replace an institution? Jim Bonk has single-handedly taken care of the freshman aspect of our curriculum. It will be a great challenge for us to put together a course with the same impact that he has had."[7]

Never one to seek the limelight, Jim got trapped in it unexpectedly on March 31, 1975, when a prankster tried to "pie" him during a lecture. The hit man was hired by a shady enterprise—Pie-Die Ltd.—offering $30 to a student with the "dexterity and cunning not to mention a dash of insanity" to hit a Duke professor in the face with a pie. The scofflaw dashed in,

Dr. Jim Bonk

lemon merengue projectile in hand, but Jim nimbly dodged, and the pie bounced off his shoulder. The rascal ran with Jim in hot pursuit and his 200 students chanting, "Go, Bonk, go!" I'm sure the pie thrower had no idea that Jim was an avid runner and quite capable of chasing him down; that happened in a patch of woods near the lecture hall. In collaring his assailant, Jim advised, "Didn't count on me being a pretty good runner, did you?" The incident made national news and prompted a treasure trove of headlined puns—none better than the one in Duke's own *Chronicle*: "Bonk Gets Bonked."[8] While Jim laughed the whole thing off, I recall that news coverage of the incident prompted more than a thousand calls and letters from incensed alumni and the public in general.

Jim's wry sense of humor—which often took a devilish twist—became a part of campus lore. Four students once came back from a weekend of heavy partying, so the story goes, unprepared for a chemistry exam. They asked Jim for an extension, claiming a flat tire caused their late return to campus. Jim agreed to the make-up, but when the time came he put the four students in separate rooms and wished them luck. The first question on the exam, worth five points, was easy. The second question, worth 95 points, simply asked: "Which tire?"[9] Jim, however, took exception to this account, holding that he'd never have given the tire question that much weight.

Jim always advised anyone planning to teach chemistry that "one of the most valuable things you can do is tutor. When you go into tutoring, it is a one-on-one kind of situation and it has the tremendous advantage of immediate feedback . . . It's much better to get it there than it is when you start lecturing to 200 or 300 people. You don't want to confuse 300 people."[10] He'd tutored extensively while earning his PhD in chemistry at Ohio State. He later became an assistant professor, volunteer assistant coach for tennis and a tutor to Ohio State athletes. When Ohio State's legendary coach, Woody Hayes, heard that Jim was leaving, he phoned Jim in a booming voice to ask, "What the hell do you mean you are leaving?" He then invited Jim to his office for what turned out to be a two-hour visit that ended with a blanket offer from Hayes to recommend Jim wherever he might want to go.[11]

I couldn't have hoped for a more dedicated assistant or loyal friend. He never missed practice, always went on our weekend cross-country runs and must have hit a million tennis balls to our aspiring stars. Because of his extensive tutoring experience, he was asked to set up the tutoring program for the entire Duke Athletic Department. That meant he could find a tutor in any subject one of our players might need. The door to his home was always open to players or ordinary students for an overnight stay or for a semester or more. Chaim Arlosoroff lived there twice for the equivalent of a full academic year; several other players stayed for extended periods. Jim ate most nights at the Piccadilly Cafeteria (now long gone) and often picked up the tab for house guests or others who joined him. It's sad to say that NCAA rules today prohibit such generosity, no matter how badly the assistance might be needed.

Jim died on March 15, 2013, at 82, as simply and privately as he lived. The cause of death was colon cancer, which he fought bravely in his final years. He chose not to have a service and had his cremated remains buried in a faculty plot at Duke Gardens. Only four persons were present: two close colleagues from the Chemistry Department; the longtime attorney, who made his final arrangements; and me. His three great loves had been the Chemistry Department, the tennis team and classical music. His house had a sound system that replicated the feel of a concert hall. His frugality enabled him to save prodigiously: He left $2 million to the Chemistry Department and $1 million to the tennis program.

To call Jim's a life well lived would be an understatement. He won three major teaching awards and helped change the lives of countless students. Many students called him Mr. Chips, after the teaching hero in the popular film *Goodbye Mr. Chips*. When Jim died, it left a huge hole in the hearts of all who knew him. Years after his passing, hardly a day goes by that I don't think of Jim; I'll never stop missing the understated persona that belied his prodigious accomplishments.

To become a front-rank university would be impossible without deeply committed, generous alumni. Duke has a strong national—and even international—alumni network that assists the school in a myriad of ways. One example will illustrate its strength and reach. In mid-January 1982, or thereabouts, I got a call from Herb Kohler, Jr., Chairman, President and CEO of Kohler Company, one of the largest manufacturers of bathroom and plumbing fixtures in the United States. He asked if the Duke tennis team would come to Kohler, Wisconsin, where the company is based, to play a "round-robin" with three Big Ten schools. The event, he explained, would inaugurate a state-of-the-art tennis complex the company had built for its personnel. I told Mr. Kohler we'd love to come but couldn't cover the travel costs. No problem, he responded, he'd send an eight-passenger company jet to Durham to pick us up. His daughter, Laura, a student at Duke, would fly up with us. He mentioned that she knew Will White, our No. 3 in singles.

At the time, I had no idea Kohler was one of America's oldest and largest privately held companies. John Michael Kohler, an Austrian immigrant, had co-founded the company at age 29 in 1873. A gifted innovator, he found a way to apply enamel to a cast iron horse watering trough, which became the first Kohler bathtub. Many innovations followed, including a cutting-edge factory with an immigrant work force that today numbers 36,000 plus. The company was widely praised for its generous pay scale and employee benefits that include a resort with a five-star hotel, four golf courses, a spa and a fitness center and six-court indoor tennis. We helped dedicate the courts on our trip, and well enough in the round robin to defeat Wisconsin 7–2, Northwestern 9–0 and Minnesota 5–4.

On the flight up, I learned that the company founder was Laura's great grandfather. She played volleyball at Duke freshman year and was majoring in political science. She went on to become a scholar-athlete exemplifying values Duke wants to instill in all its graduates. As an undergrad, she volunteered for Meals on Wheels and a soup kitchen in Durham. It was "an eye-opening experience ... [to see] that kind of poverty right in Duke's backyard," she says today.[12] That experience has informed who Laura is as a fourth-generation Kohler at the company. Her younger brother, David, went to Duke and is CEO and President; he and Laura both serve on the company board of directors. As Kohler's Senior Vice President for Human Resources, Stewardship & Sustainability, Laura manages ambitious programs to reduce or offset all greenhouse gas emissions, to send zero waste to landfills and to develop energy and water-saving products. She also oversees Kohler's Arts/Industry Program Center, which includes a residency program for artists from around the world. They create artwork in the pottery and iron foundry, alongside Kohler employees (called "associates" within the company). Laura's daughter. Rachel Kohler Proudman, entered the freshman class at Duke in the fall of 2019. Kohler ties to the school will continue far into the future.[13]

No tie to a great university means more than lasting friendships. My former players often get together for golf outings and ski trips; they come back to Durham for tennis and other reunions; and many married Duke women, which has made their ties even stronger. With one of the most diverse student bodies in the country, Duke offers a melting pot experience, especially in the undergraduate years. Duke, fortunately, has not succumbed to the trend in bigtime athletics toward "athlete-only" dorms, which badly undercut the student experience described above.

The deepest bond of all may be the strong sense of place a great university can engender. It owns a spot in the mind's eye, and for Duke the image often is a campus in the woods, a chapel rising within. President Price has described that image especially well: "I can't imagine anything more inspiring than traveling up Chapel Drive in the morning and seeing the Chapel towering over the trees. It's wonderful." To the west, the university is bounded by a 7,000-acre preserve with many champion trees covering parts of three counties—Duke Forest. The campus, itself, has the feel of a lush forest.

The cornerstone of the iconic chapel was laid in 1930 based on architectural plans drawn by Julian Francis Abele, who couldn't have attended Duke until 1961 (had he lived that long) because he was black. Abele came from a prominent Philadelphia family and distinguished himself as an excellent student at an early age. He was the first African American to graduate from the University of Pennsylvania's School of Architecture and, in his senior year, was elected President of the Architectural Society. Later, he joined a prominent Philadelphia firm founded by Horace Trumbauer,

Duke Architect Julian Francis Abele

who greatly valued Abele's services. His designs would include hundreds of stately public buildings, Gilded Age mansions and prominent university buildings, such as Widener Memorial Library at Harvard. Abele based his design of Duke Chapel on Canterbury Cathedral, and went on to produce many other designs in collegiate gothic at Duke, among them Cameron Indoor Stadium, the football stadium, Perkins Library, Duke Hospital, the medical school, faculty houses and many other structures. No one more profoundly influenced the ambience of the West Campus, and yet Abele's contribution went largely unacknowledged until the mid-1980s.[14] His portrait is prominently displayed today near the entrance to the Administration Building.

Abele died in 1950. In the years that followed, Duke hued closely to the principles he established to preserve the iconic ambience and architectural integrity of the campus he helped create. Many innovative architects have provided designs as the campus expanded, among them Ted Van Dyk, a scholar-athlete who'd been a varsity wrestler at Duke. In 1996, he founded the New City Design Group in Raleigh, a boutique studio specializing in urban infill.[15]

His first design for Duke was the Devil's Bistro, a pub near the center of campus that's still popular. "Duke has been very successful in creating a culture that maximizes interaction, providing a hub where food service, the bookstore, student groups and culture events can all intersect," says Ted. "The school really wants to push students to interact, thus there's a student activities quad where everybody goes to eat, where you're much more likely to have interactions. One huge benefit is this approach leads to an on-campus culture in contrast to an off-campus party culture." This becomes doubly important with a drinking age of 21.

I've always felt lucky to be a part of Duke, always harbored in my mind's eye the image of a campus in the woods, the chapel on the hill. In 1937, Aldous Huxley made a visit to Duke and was amazed to find, "a whole city of grey stone . . . this huge and fantastic structure which houses a large university . . . is the most successful essay in neo-Gothic that I know." All in the pine forests of North Carolina, as he put it, "where one would never expect anything in particular to happen." And yet, so much happens there—most of it building alternatives to the dystopian future Huxley warned of in his groundbreaking novel *Brave New World*.

Part IV
Renewal of American Ideals

Acting with integrity is the only path to meaningful reform. We must recommit to time-tested American ideals. Part IV is narrated jointly by the authors.

CHAPTER NINETEEN

Club Sports Point the Way

Halfway through the second period of the 2004 Atlantic Coast Collegiate Hockey League Championship in Charlottesville, Virginia, Duke and Georgetown were tied 2–2 when Dave Bradley, a third-line defensive grinder, felt the puck at his feet in a wild melee in front the Duke goal.[1] Instinctively, the powerfully built Duke center kicked the puck forward and controlled it on the toe of his stick. He then skated, as fast as he could, into the neutral zone. When he looked up, he was astonished to see only one defender—the same player whose bad pass had triggered the melee—between him and the Georgetown goalie. As the duo crossed the centerline, the backward skating Georgetown defender was 10 feet or so in front of Dave with a "can't-make-another-mistake" look on his face; he even seemed reluctant to poke at the puck or close the gap. In just seconds, four years of incredible passion and dedication to hockey as a club sport compressed into a life-changing moment for the Duke senior. As freshmen in 2000, he and his best friend, Jesse Swanko, had opted to forego fraternity life; instead, they became the "go-to guys" of Duke's then-struggling club hockey team. Dave and Jesse were both grinders on the ice, which meant they were the best back-checkers on the team and played a physical game around the boards—"grinding" opposing players to wear them down. They were also grinders off the ice in pursuit of an improved team. After meeting at an orientation for sports clubs, they bonded during drives to hockey practice at a rink 12 miles from campus. Soon, they were recruiting players, raising money to underwrite their expensive sport, scheduling midnight practices when ice time's cheap, lining up clunky vans for road trips, and even designing the team website and writing game recaps. Eventually, Jesse became President and Dave Vice President of the hockey club.

No one could confuse their sport with intramurals or pickup games where novices—so-called ankle benders, who can't skate—showed up at the local rink in mismatched uniforms to kill time before some afterparty. Instead, club hockey is a dead serious sport for experienced players, who practice several times a week, play as many as 40 games a season, including many on the road, and compete in playoffs and league and national championships.[2]

The team record was 10–10 in Dave and Jesse's first year (2000–01) and improved to 13–9 the next. They even captured the 2002 Canes Cup, a competition between four North Carolina universities—Duke, North Carolina, NC State and Wake Forest—on the home ice of the Carolina Hurricanes of the National Hockey League (NHL).

All their deep digging led to a gold strike in year three when Kevin Compton, a Silicon Valley venture capitalist who co-owned the San Jose Sharks of the NHL, decided to support the club financially after seeing the website Dave and Jesse had built. Compton's ties to Duke were through his daughter, a student there at the time, but he was quite taken with Brent Selman, the charismatic young coach who'd been named to the job in 2001. Compton could tell Selman lived and breathed hockey and wrote the first of many checks to support the club after meeting with him. Near the end of their first encounter, he'd asked Selman to "give me a figure" (to contribute). Selman remembered hemming and hawing as he mustered the courage to ask for $25,000, what he considered an astronomical amount. "Okay," Compton had replied, "but let's double that."[3] His generosity had instantly changed the fortunes of Blue Devil hockey.

"In no time at all," Dave recalled years later, "we had the best hockey coach I'd ever had (and could keep him paid). We were traveling in sleeper buses instead of old vans." As Jesse put it: "We were no longer staying eight to a room at the EconoLodge, and we could afford to schedule practices before midnight." Moreover, their new uniforms were as good as any Division I varsity in the country.

At that fateful moment, as he crossed the center line with the puck on his blade, all the years of hard work meshed with Selman's high-level coaching to give Dave what researchers call the "quiet eye": a moment of calm amid gut-wrenching stress, a flashpoint in which he saw exactly what he had to do. Absent the fanfare, it was a moment not unlike Serena Williams staving off match point at Wimbledon in 2014, or Bobby Thompson's dramatic walk off homer in 1951 to win the pennant for the Giants, or Christian Laettner hitting a buzzer-beater in 1992 against Kentucky to put Duke in the Final Four of college basketball. In such moments, the quiet eye can be the difference between winning and choking. Without it, the lesser player caves—goes for broke with a high-risk shot, or rushes to get the tension over and done with.

Instead, Dave coolly chose the best tactical option: to use the hulking Georgetown defenseman as a screen. He was only 10 feet away. Which meant the goalie could barely see Dave and might react a split-second too late once Dave made his move. The game turned when Dave, a lefthander, deked, or faked, right. The defenseman lurched to block his path. Dave then turned back sharply to his strong side and skated open in the attacking zone. An expanse of empty ice was all that separated him from the squatting goalie, some 50 feet away. In a glance, he saw the goalie had reacted to the deke and was scrambling to reposition himself at net center.

From the face-off circle 30 feet out, Dave fired the shot hockey players dream of: a snap shot with all the force he could muster. It zipped across the ice like a bolt of current and disappeared into the five-hole, the 12-inch aperture between the goalie's knees. He'd guessed the goalie would be a split-second late and he was. Dave stared, almost in disbelief, at the puck in the back of the net. Momentarily forgetting himself, he crashed on his left shoulder into the sideboards. As he righted himself, teammates were pummeling him in elation. He pumped his fist and grinned ear-to-ear at the bench, where Jesse was catching a breather between shifts. Jesse recalls, "We were pounding our sticks against the boards as hard as we could and yelling Davey's name."

The celebration was short-lived. With lots of hockey still to be played, the refs were signaling for a face-off to resume play. The game became a grinding defensive slugfest in which neither team scored again. Dave's

Dave Bradley and Jesse Swanko after the big win

goal proved decisive in Duke's 3–2 win, its first ACCHL championship since 1998 and a victory he, Jesse and their teammates would never forget.

Afterward, all 25 Duke players stood on the blue line as the conference commissioner draped championship medals around their necks. Dave and Jesse posed for a photo at center ice with the trophy, a large and impressive silver cup. Jesse is sporting shoulder-length hair and an undernourished muttonchop beard he grew just for the playoffs; a clean-shaven Dave, at 6′4″, is a few inches taller and has a wry, the-world-is-my-oyster look. The pure joy of that moment was all the reward they expected or would get.

It hardly mattered that a crowd of less than two hundred watched, that no crazed fans stormed the ice, that there were no post-game television interviews, that no scholarships got renewed because there aren't any in club sports, or that no one would get a big fat pro contract. Instead, the game epitomized what uncommercialized sports look like. The real rewards were psychic, internal to the players, who knew what they'd accomplished, how much they'd learned, all the obstacles they'd overcome, on and off the ice, to lead Duke Hockey to its second-ever ACCHL championship. Standing on the center line afterward, in their spiffy Prussian blue and white uniforms, the Duke players were as proud as any varsity that ever won an NCAA national championship. And rightfully so. Their season record was 17–3–1.

"That puck had eyes," Coach Selman would say of Dave's shot years later. "It was very difficult, but what made it so special was that Dave made it. He was one of our best defensive players but not offensively gifted. He'd done so much for the club he really deserved that moment of stardom."

From the very start, the players had all looked up to their coach. They stood in awe of his life in hockey: how he'd grown up in Mooretown, Canada, a town of two hundred halfway between Toronto and Detroit; how he'd played as a kid, like so many Canadians, on frozen village and farm ponds; how he'd starred at Wilfrid Laurier University, one of Canada's elite schools; and how he'd played as a pro in a tough South Florida start-up league, where he had to battle to survive in every game. After that, he'd moved up in competition, playing for a year on a team north of London that competed all over Europe. By then, he'd given up on playing in the NHL, but a shoulder injury, near the end of the season, had ended his playing career. After that, he came home to pursue a career on the sidelines.

Selman was soon hired to coach club hockey at the University of Western Washington in Bellingham. Later, he collaborated with another coach and a psychologist to develop an anger management and self-esteem program for troubled youth called "Stick It to Violence." After the program won recognition from the NHL, the Carolina Hurricanes hired Selman to implement it in Raleigh. While making weekly trips there from Seattle, he thought, "This would be a great place to set up shop and move to." When he learned that Duke was looking for a coach for its club hockey team, he applied and was hired in September 2001.

Selman had two distinct qualities that enabled him to bond quickly with his players. First, he knew the game inside out from years of playing at a high level and had a gift for explaining its many finer points. Second, he knew how to make the game fun.

"Somehow," Jesse recalls, "he had a million sayings that cracked us all up. After we won big, he'd say, 'Those guys folded like a cheap tent.' He'd call somebody who made a dumb mistake 'about as sharp as a bowling ball.' A good time was a 'Hee-Haw.' When it was time to go onto the ice, he'd say, 'Get your buckets (helmets) and twigs (sticks) and get out there.'

But the greatest of all, to me, was, 'That guy has more moves than a shopping cart with a busted wheel.'"

Selman would go on to coach a second Duke ACCHL championship team in 2006 with several players from the '04 team. He's the longest-serving coach among Duke's 37 club sport teams. Throughout that time, he has worked closely with Mike Forbes, who became Duke's Director of Club Sports two years after Selman was hired. During their tenure, participation in club sports has increased dramatically. For the five-year period ending in 2017, club sports participation increased 50 percent at Duke to 1,270 players. That increase is part of a nationwide trend: more than two million college students now play club sports—four times the number playing varsity sports.[4] The NCAA does not regulate club sports, and teams are fielded in just about any activity students want. For example, there are club teams for polo, trap and skeet shooting and even parachuting. The Hockey Club membership fee has risen to $600, three times what it was when Jesse and Dave played, but still modest compared to many other schools.

While many schools adopt a hands-off attitude toward club sports, "Duke is more parental," says Forbes.[5] "For us, the challenge is to provide a leadership learning lab. We have juniors and seniors who are managing sports club budgets in the $200,000 range. They get elected by their peers and handle logistics for forty or fifty players that involve out-of-state travel. Nearly all our teams have paid coaches, because we've found teams perform better with coaches. Many of our coaches are grad students, who may have played varsity and get a modest stipend. Getting a guy with the experience of a Brent Selman is rare; naturally, we pay him a lot more, but when all is said and done, you can't really put a price on his value."

On a practical level, Forbes wants to stimulate more interaction among students and less dependence on digital media. "You can't play a sport and check your phone," he says. "You have to put it down. I'm just a believer that facetime is not on a phone; it's face-to-face interaction with another human being."

In recent years, club sports have become an attractive alternative to over-hyped, over-commercialized, win-at-all-cost varsity sports. Forbes says participants love representing their school in high-level competition and put great value on developing relationships that may last a lifetime. The chance to build those bonds is enhanced considerably at Duke by the

Gorter Foundation, which funds "Dream Trips"—often to international destinations—and travel to regional and national championships. Gorter funds also are used for need-based travel. The Foundation is named for Kevin Gorter, a former president of the club hockey team, who died in a car accident in Australia the summer after he graduated from Duke. The team played a memorial game for him in 1988, a 9–2 dismantling of NC State. His father, James P. Gorter, was part of the senior management team at the investment banking firm Goldman Sachs; he funded the foundation that pays for the dream trips club teams at Duke take.

Gorter-funded dream trips have taken the Duke field hockey club team to Amsterdam, the water polo team to Greece and the taekwondo team to South Korea. In January 2019, 41 ski club members took a dream trip to Banff in the Canadian Rockies. The club treasurer, Adrian Rivas, who grew up in Waterville, Maine, helped organize flights, accommodations and other trip logistics. He says skiing all day for several days amid Banff's spectacular mountain peaks was "truly fantastic."[6] Adrian takes special pride in having introduced freestyle skiing, a Winter Olympic event, to the ski club. It's an alternative to traditional alpine skiing that can involve spectacular feats: aerial flips and spins and sliding rails and boxes.

During the 2018 season, Duke had its first Southeastern Conference freestyle champion, Kelsey O'Donnell. "It was a terrific accomplishment," Rivas says, "because freestyle has been so male dominated and has always been on the fringes of the sport. The fact that we even have a female free-style skier is pretty big, but for her to have won was really momentous." O'Donnell was among the freestyle skiers that made it to nationals in 2018 and part of the women's alpine teams that made it there too. The Duke men's alpine team just missed when one of their best skiers slid out on the course and failed to finish.

Club sports tend to be egalitarian, especially when it comes to gender equity. Despite hockey's rough reputation, Selman has had several female players. He says, "They all played hockey growing up. They were good enough to play with the boys. Several came from small towns that didn't have separate teams for boys and girls, so they just played together. Having girls as members of the club didn't seem unusual at all."

He cited Emily Sherman as an example. A recent graduate, whose parents both played varsity sports at Duke, she played hockey at a demanding level growing up. "Emily could very well have played Division I women's varsity at most schools," Selman says. "She was a very talented hockey player, who had a love for competition that was just outstanding."

Sarah Putney, who's in her second year as President of Duke's Club Swim, says gender issues rarely come up in her sport.[7] The club has about 45 members, about half of whom take part in eight hours of practice weekly. Membership is divided evenly between women and men. Sarah's predecessor as president was a male, but the executive board for the 2018–19 season is all female; no men ran in the election. While they all swim in the same pool, men and women don't swim against each other, which helps keep egos under control. Sarah says members root hard for each other, and the club has a family-like feel.

Swimmers tend to be a brainy sort. She estimates that 75 percent of her members are scholar-athletes with GPAs of 3.3 or better. Sarah, herself, was valedictorian of her high school class in Dallas, Texas. She's majoring in biomedical engineering and expects to graduate with honors in the class of 2020. After that, she'll study for a masters of engineering degree and pursue a career in medical device development. She'd like to stay in the Raleigh–Durham area.

Adrian Rivas is an excellent student. He says, "For me, coming to Duke and school in general is about learning. I think that gets lost a lot of the time . . . [students] focus on their grades and they'll cram for a test and they'll do great, but then they'll forget everything they learned . . . school isn't only about the academic learning; it's also about learning how to socialize and learning how the world works."

Jesse Swanko and Dave Bradley, too, were outstanding students at Duke. Both graduated magna cum laude. Jesse majored in biology and now lives in Narragansett, Rhode Island, with his wife, and their twin three-year-old boys. Jesse and his wife both play in adult hockey leagues, and both boys are already skating. He has a security clearance but can't talk much about his work in environmental chemistry for a large defense contractor. Dave finished with a degree in sociology and a minor in political science. As an undergrad, Dave worked in the men's basketball office for three years. After that he was hired full-time to help with recruiting, using many of the creative skills he learned as an undergrad to promote Duke Hockey. Additionally, he has been the Duke team's social media manager since social media first became popular. In 2018, he was promoted to Creative Director overseeing Duke basketball's social media strategy, messaging and branding. In early 2019, the basketball team's social media following exceeded four million, leading all of college athletics. Dave's wife, Gina, is Assistant Director of Athletics for Business Operations at Duke. They live in Durham with their daughter, Quinn, son, Owen, and dog, Piper.

It's not an exaggeration to say that club sports can profoundly influence the trajectory of players' lives. Dave's and Jesse's would be good examples. The huge investments they made to upgrade the hockey club contributed mightily to a glittering, high-profile success—the ACCHL championship in 2004. But even more impressive is the way they went about it: their unwavering four-year commitment to the thankless tasks that got little or no recognition. As the saying goes, they made the trains run on time. As a rising junior, Jesse gave up the chance to study for a semester at Duke's prestigious Marine Lab on the North Carolina coast because he didn't want to miss the start of the hockey season. At another point, he and Dave redecorated the team's locker room at Triangle Sportsplex, a large facility west of Durham, where the team practiced and played. They got permission from the manager to repaint it with Duke's colors and to put a giant school logo on the wall. Jesse recalls how proud he was when small kids checking in at the Sportsplex would ask, "Can we dress in the Duke hockey locker room?"

While seemingly small, such efforts symbolized their efforts to raise Duke hockey's profile, to attract more and better players, to make it—in the vernacular of the times—a cool place to be. After the team's 2004 championship, they expected to get coverage in *The Chronicle*, the Duke campus newspaper. But they were told the paper's policy of not covering club sports included championships. So, with Selman's approval, they took out a full-page ad in the paper costing $500 to draw attention to their victory.[8] "Everybody was coming up to us after that ad appeared," Jesse recalls, "saying how great it was that we won. Even varsity basketball players stopped us to say how proud it made them feel. We felt we represented the highest level of Duke Hockey and wanted everyone to share in that win."

Throughout their years on the team, Jesse and Dave were absorbing lessons that boded well for their future: the importance of managing time, of a shared passion, of communication in building strong relationships and how working together brings the impossible within reach. Both say these lessons stuck with them, still guide them fifteen or more years later.

While the funding from Kevin Compton made life easier, as president and vice president, Jesse and Dave, still had to work closely with their coach to make sure it was spent wisely. They also had to work hard to motivate players—especially getting them to show up for late night practices and go on long road trips during exam periods when they weren't required to.

Dave and Jesse both feel strongly that the real turning point for Duke hockey was Brent Selman's arrival as coach. "He changed everything," says Dave. "He had a vision for the program and guys wanted to be part of it. Because of him, I got in the best shape I'd ever been in. Coach's commitment inspired me to show up earlier and skate harder. We'd practice after midnight and he'd be there with that contagious enthusiasm for our team and the sport of hockey. He was doing it for the love of the game and for our group. I can't tell you how much that meant to all of us as players."

The relationship between Brent Selman and his former players has endured. They stay in touch via text messaging, especially during the National Hockey League playoffs when there's often a text chain that Selman and several players are part of. Selman has organized many hockey reunions, the most memorable of which took place on November 7, 2010. About 50 alums from teams in the mid-1990s to 2010 came. Through his connections with the Carolina Hurricanes, Selman secured a suite, or sky box, at the RBC Center (now the PNC Center) for his former players, who saw the Hurricanes beat the Florida Panthers 3–2 the night before the reunion game. At 7 a.m. the next morning, the Duke grads returned to the RBC Center to play their reunion game, the first such game in team history on the ice of an NHL franchise. Jesse recalls seeing, "a few—maybe more than a few—bloodshot eyes that morning."

Did anyone remind Selman of a guy with as many moves as a shopping cart with a busted wheel? Probably not. But he'd structured the event to have fun and accomplished that aim. On a deeper level, he and Mike Forbes are preserving the spirit of amateurism by emphasizing a much more collegial experience than big-time varsity sports can ever hope to offer. Their brand is a growing, viable alternative to the over-hyped, over-commercialized nightly offerings on ESPN. Along the way, their participants get indispensable lessons for life while playing for fun—for the pure joy of it all. In many ways, club sports point the way to a more balanced and beneficial sporting future.

CHAPTER TWENTY

Barriers to Reform

Although it first reared its ugly head more than a century ago, never has the ruthless rule of "win at all cost" so dominated big-time college sports in America. Win or be gone can be seen today in the bloated pay of coaches; in stadium upgrades costing tens of millions to provide luxury suites for fat cat alumni and big corporations; in rising athletic fees paid by students who now graduate with an average $30,000-plus in college loans; and in scandal after scandal—from the fake classes and academic fraud condoned by the University of North Carolina to keep athletes in school between 1993 and 2011, to strippers and prostitutes used to entice recruits at the University of Louisville between 2010 and 2014.

On the surface, it's a cut-throat zero sum competition with an equal number of winners and losers. In reality, only a few thrive: the 65 members of the Power Five Conferences—those with real athletic riches—grossed $6 billion in 2015, or $4 billion more than all the other NCAA Division I's 346 members.[1] Moreover, turnover among the favored few is remarkably small: 60 of the top spending schools today were among the top 100 in 1920.[2] But no matter how much money they get, only a handful of the big-time athletic departments turn a profit—somewhere between 15 and 25 annually, according to a study by the *Washington Post.*[3] No wonder: In 2015, Auburn University installed the largest video board in college sports—one as tall as a five story building that cost $13.9 million. The outlay came one year after the athletic department ran up a $17 million deficit, one of its largest ever.[4] To augment recruiting, the school also had two Cessna jets, a six-seater and a seven-seater, costing $14.2 million.[5]

"College sports is big business, and it's a very poorly run big business," says David Ridpath, a professor at Ohio University and a member of the Drake Group board, an organization advocating reform of the big revenue sports, football and basketball. "The current model does not work," he adds. "Someday it will implode."[6]

Despite recent attendance declines in football, an implosion is nowhere in sight. Critics of big-time college sports often cite wrongs and abuses while ascribing few, if any, benefits. No one has written a more balanced book on the subject than Duke economics and law professor Charlie Clotfelter. In *Big-Time Sports in American Universities*, Charlie describes both sides of the equation: how needed reforms are overshadowed by the lure of real and imagined benefits. Because many of the benefits of big-time college sports are intangible, they can't be quantified on a profit and loss statement. That explains, in part, why the revenue sports have never been run like a business—and won't be unless fundamental reforms are adopted.

The holy grail of these intangible benefits is enhanced institutional prestige. On the surface, nothing burnishes a university's image more than a national football or basketball championship. Duke has won five in basketball (tied for fourth all-time with Indiana behind North Carolina, Kentucky and UCLA). Co-author LeBar was on campus for four of the five championships (1991, 1992, 2001 and 2010). He can attest to the intensity of the shared experience, how it brought the entire campus together, from the guys tending flower beds in Duke Gardens, to the women in cafeteria serving lines, to the provost, president and trustees—they all experienced the unalloyed joy of winning. "I can't remember any other time when everyone at Duke felt so united in a sense of common purpose or felt a part of something much bigger than our individual selves," LeBar recalls.

Enhanced institutional prestige is made up of several lesser but still potent benefits: a boost in campus spirit and cohesion; a wellspring of pride among students, alumni and friends; enhanced student experience and widespread favorable news coverage. The role of minority players in winning reinforces the importance of diversity, enhances racial solidarity and underscores that championship teams are true meritocracies. In addition, a consistent winner gives the president, chancellor and other high-level university officials an important perk: premium seats at games to give legislators and other notables they want to influence.[7]

As enticing as these intangible benefits are, nothing gladdens the heart of a university president (or his bursar) like the jingle of cash—the financial windfall that comes with a national championship or big bowl win. Technically, the national championship winner in football gets no direct reward; the prize money goes to conferences, which distribute winning shares. In 2017, the four conferences with teams qualifying for the playoff got $6 million each. But the big payoff comes in the form of a surge in alumni contributions to athletic departments and a boost in ticket, apparel and other sales that can last two years or more. Between 2005 and 2012, *Forbes* found that the national championship winner in football got an 11 percent bump in football revenue in its championship year and more thereafter.[8] While the year-to-year take can vary widely, *Forbes* estimated that the average for recent winners is $20 million or more.[9] One other big win impact is the so-called Flutie Effect. On November 23, 1984, Boston College quarterback Doug Flutie, who later won the Heisman Trophy, heaved a desperation pass with time running out that a wide receiver caught it in the end zone to beat Miami. The dramatic win led to a 12 percent spike in admission applications to Boston College.[10] Dramatic wins have had a similar effect at other schools, a phenomenon that leads to greater tuition revenue and, potentially, more applicants to choose from.

But for all the multiple national championships winners like Alabama in football or Duke in basketball, there are dozens upon dozens who play their games in near-empty stadiums or arenas, who have no chance of recruiting top-tier athletes, who'll never attract a big-time coach and who will never experience the Flutie Effect. These schools struggle on, year after year, in the shadow of the glitz and glamor of the so-called branded programs that have dominated college football for a century or more.

With adoring fans and fawning media as tacit allies, the branded programs have long operated as autonomous fiefdoms within the university—sacrosanct and virtually untouchable. That status is indefensible to many in the academic realm who cite a host of reasons for reining in the high-flying big spenders, including: poor academic performance and other irregularities among varsity athletes; the isolation of athletes in an on-campus bubble that often includes a luxurious "player-only" dorm; excessive practice time directly undercutting the educational mission; bloated spending on salaries for coaches and their assistants; posh practice facilities; exploitation of athletes who play the revenue sports; unfairness to have-not athletic programs; and unsustainable economics in general.[11]

From the Carnegie Foundation's blistering report on athletic abuses in 1929 to the Rice Commission on basketball infractions in 2018, college sports have been in near-constant crisis. Much like the blind men in the ancient parable, who touch parts of an elephant and guess what it is, soothsayers have found it much easier to identify symptoms than causes of wrongs. Today, three underlying causes threaten college sport with the greatest crisis it has faced since the widespread cheating scandals of the late forties and early fifties.

Shambolic Identity

The first of these is a shambolic identity epitomized by the highly misleading and totally bankrupt term "student-athlete." Who are these gladiators we shower with such lavish attention and expensive benefits? Is winning all we should demand of them? In a sense, the term student-athlete was a sham from the start. In his autobiography, *Unsportsmanlike Conduct,* the NCAA's first executive director, Walter Byers, wrote that the NCAA coined the term student-athlete to counter "the dreaded notion that NCAA athletes could be identified as *employees* by state industrial commissions and the courts."[12] That designation, Byers and his colleagues feared, would lead to disability and wrongful death claims from sports-related injuries.

Byers also noted in his book that the term soon "was embedded in all NCAA rules and interpretations as a mandated substitute for such words as players and athletes. We told college publicists to speak of 'college teams,' not football or basketball 'clubs,' a word common to the pros."[13] One result has been that for many years the term has been repeated ad nauseum on NCAA-sponsored broadcasts, where it falls, like the rain, on academic achievers and non-achievers alike.

New York Times columnist David Brooks has written, "Over the decades, the word amateur changed its meaning. It used to convey a moral sensibility, but now it conveys an economic one: not getting paid. As many universities have lost confidence in their ability to instill character, the moral mission has withered." Nevertheless, Brooks concluded, "The lingering vestiges of the amateur ideal are worth preserving."[14]

That part of the once-proud identity of college sports and its players is deeply undercut by the twisted values of a system now taking in roughly $1.6 billion a year from NCAA-sponsored telecasts of national football and basketball championships, while dispensing most of those funds to schools that operate, athletically, like professional farm teams.

Despite the largess, the NCAA still does not mandate that member schools insure their players against injury or provide them with workers' compensation benefits. Get injured and you're largely on your own; you may even lose your athletic scholarship. In Chapter One (A Brief History of College Sports), the authors described the formation of the NCAA as an organization to make college football safer. In a landmark case settled in June 2018, the NCAA was sued by the widow of Greg Ploetz, who played on a University of Texas national championship football team in 1969. After he died in 2015, neurologists at Boston University examined his brain and concluded that he had the most severe—and fatal—form of chronic traumatic encephalopathy (CTE).[15] His dementia had been diagnosed in 2009; thereafter, he had gradually withered into a vegetative state.[16] The NCAA took a hard-nosed position in opposing his widow's claim: Ploetz knew how dangerous it was to play football; thus, the NCAA was not liable for his death. Its position had not changed much since the first landmark case two years earlier—that of Derek Sheely (see Chapter Six)—when the NCAA held it had no legal duty to protect student-athletes. NCAA President Mark Emmert later told Congress that was a "terrible choice of words."[17]

This Darwinian nature of the system is nothing new. Between 1973 and 2012, the NCAA required that athletic scholarships be renewed on an annual basis. Coaches had authority to cancel scholarships for poor performance and many other reasons, including injury. The ruling made athletes peons, whose tenure was subject to the momentary whims of coaches. The ruling was modified in 2012 to permit multiyear scholarship awards, but many of the branded programs continue to operate the old way.[18] Permanent player peonage is further reinforced by the NCAA's sham requirement limiting practices to 20 hours per week and four hours a day. It leaves coaches free to schedule voluntary practices in addition and most do—which means players often practice 40 hours a week or more. After-dinner sessions watching game film are common—which, in effect, means athletes playing big-time sports have a full-time job. As a practical matter, there is no time left in their day to study. No wonder most take so-called crip courses and make lower grades than the rest of the student body.

One further huge time commitment is team travel. Orin Starn, a cultural anthropologist at Duke, writes that: "Every year, Duke athletes collectively miss classes by the thousands . . . they don't have time to do much more than pass." They don't have time for a semester abroad, for joining the school paper's staff or for joining student government. "We give our athletes an impoverished imitation of a real college experience. . . ." Starn concludes.[19] But for many big-time recruits, the college experience is even more sterile than that. In *Billion Dollar Ball*, Gilbert Gaul observes that: "A surprising number read at grade-school levels." Gaul gives a close-up account of the "phalanx of tutors, advisers and learning specialists" employed to help recruits based on site visits he made to academic support centers at the Universities of Kansas and Oregon.[20]

To a certain extent, the excessive practicing and catch-up learning reflect the determination of highly competitive coaches to control every facet of their young charges' lives. Most of us remember the famous warning of the British statesman and writer Lord Acton: "Power tends to corrupt and absolute power corrupts absolutely." Often forgotten is what came next: "Great men are almost always bad men." That may be too harsh, but many big-time coaches do wield their authority in a heavy-handed way. Do they care at all about the scholar-athlete ideal? The question begs the answer.

These vastly overpaid autocrats—and the autonomous, free-spending departments they run—have an iron grip on a system in which money nearly always has the last word. Alabama pays its football coach, Nick Saban, $11.1 million a year; Texas A&M gave Jimbo Fisher a guaranteed 10-year $75 million contract in 2017 that includes $300,000 annually for personal use of jet aircraft; Clemson pays Coach Dabo Swinney $8.5 million a year; and Mike Krzysewski at Duke is the highest paid college basketball coach at nearly $9 million a year. These stratospheric salaries are especially hard to justify when athletes—many of whom come from economically disadvantaged backgrounds—get no pay at all. Thus, the hue and cry to pay college players gets louder and louder.

The identity of big-time college sports already is deeply confused and in great flux. Do we truly want to take that final, irrevocable step to change it from amateur to professional status? With only a handful of schools currently operating in the black, where would the money come from to pay the players? Would fans accept games in which unpaid players compete against paid ones? How much would players get paid? Would linebackers, quarterbacks and point guards get compensated the same? These are difficult questions that no one has answered with hard data based on thorough research. It would be much easier to change the present system to increase the value of scholarships awarded to athletes playing big-time sports. Reducing practice time and team travel would be a good start by making more time available for study and getting a real education.

These questions all speak to the central issue of identity. Will we continue down the present path toward a shambolic identity in which the games and the final score must always come first? Or will we turn back toward the quintessential American ideal of the scholar-athlete once held in high esteem? Despite the current morass, experience shows that high-level academics and high-level sports can coexist at the collegiate level. For decades, the public will to pursue that ideal has been undercut by powerful forces of commercialization and professionalization. Only by redefining the basic identity of collegiate sport can we reject the shambolic and embrace an approach that makes learning and playing not just possible but, once again, entirely compatible.

Irresponsible Spending

Lavish, out-of-control and unsustainable spending is the second underlying cause of today's college sports crisis. Its effect is insidious: free-spending ways encourage the false and widespread notion that athletic departments can't operate in the black. Nearly all of them don't, but the cause, mainly, is competitive jealousies that perpetuate a "keeping up with the Joneses" mindset. In 1903, Harvard built a new stadium on the edge of the Charles River with a spectacular horseshoe design crowned with Roman columns.

The country's first to be built with reinforced concrete, Harvard Stadium could seat more than 30,000 spectators and inspired a host of imitators. School after school increased spending to stay competitive; thus, by 1930, there were 30 concrete stadiums in America.[21] And, yes, the rush to keep up has never stopped except during wartime. Alabama will install a state-of-the-art video board after the 2019 football season, following the lead of its archrival, Auburn, which installed a budget-busting video board in 2015. Auburn completed more high-dollar improvements to its football stadium prior to the 2018 season;[22] and Alabama will renovate its stadium at a cost of $75 million after the 2019 season.[23]

In an article distributed in October 2018, the Associated Press declared that big-time college football was engaged a in "never-ending facility arms race" that showed no signs of slowing down. It reported that Clemson's $55 million team headquarters, which opened in 2018, included a minia-ture golf course, a pool with slide, a basketball court and a nap room.[24] Why a slumber parlor? Unrestricted spending, perhaps, demands nothing less. "Where is it [the arms race] going?" Duke football coach David Cut-liffe asked. "We should be investing in student-athletes."[25]

He's right, of course, but the big-time schools keep spending aggres-sively on non-essentials like private jets, five-star hotel stays, on-campus barber shops and bowling alleys. They've also hired an array of special-ists—a museum curator and horticulturalist, for example—and pay them six-figure incomes.[26] Outside the Lines, an ESPN news show, estimates that net revenues increased by 50 percent at Power Five Conference schools and ten other schools that play big-time sports for the 10-year period ending in 2018.[27] Most of them still lost money because of the reck-less spending cited above.

Among the branded programs (Division I, or the Football Bowl Sub-division of the NCAA), only 24 of 128 teams (19 percent) operated in the black. The median deficit for FBS schools was nearly $13 million for the 2014–15 year. Even worse, this figure does not include capital expense for facilities, which were estimated in a 2005 NCAA study at $20 million annually. Moreover, the deficits did not include an allocation for athletic programs' pro rata share of indirect expense of top administrators outside the athletic department.[28]

In *Unsportsmanlike Conduct,* Walter Byers predicted that the big-time football powers would never have enough money. Ironically, he entitled

Chapter 13 of his memoir "Not Enough Money." In it he asked, "Do any major sports programs make money for their universities? Sure, but the trick is to overspend and feed the myth that even the industry's pluto-crats teeter on insolvency."[29] Byers describes at length the sleight of hand branded programs use to bury or hide major expenditures: covering tui-tion and fee expenses with state appropriations; using urban development funds to pay for stadium construction; and shifting subsidies for players meeting poverty guidelines from the athletic department to the Pell grant program.[30]

One other questionable practice to support the athletic depart-ment is the charging of student fees, which keep going up and often aren't even listed on the bills students pay each semester. At the richest schools—members of the Power Five awash in TV money—subsidies from state and local governments and student fees account for just 5 per-cent of the budget. But it's a different story at poorer schools, where half the athletic budget may come from such subsidies.[31] Students often have no idea what they're paying. Richard Vedder, director of the Center for College Affordability and Productivity, says, "They are aghast, 'My God, I only went to two football games when I was in college. They cost me $500 apiece.'"[32]

A joint examination by the *Chronical of Higher Education* and *Huffing-ton Post* found, "A river of cash is flowing into college sports, financing a spending spree among elite universities that has sent coaches' salaries soaring and spurred new discussions about whether athletes should be paid. But most of that revenue is going to a handful of elite sports pro-grams, leaving [most colleges] to rely heavily on students to finance their athletic ambitions."[33]

There are ominous signs that the days of lavish, out-of-control spend-ing may be numbered. In 2017, college football experienced its second-largest attendance decline in history at 3 percent. For the nine-year pe-riod ending in 2017, attendance dropped by 10.1 percent. Even figures for the Southeastern Conference—a perennial hotbed of fan interest—de-clined.[34] It's not clear why the drop occurred. Some say improved qual-ity of televised games prompts more fans to watch at home or at local sports bars; others hold that many of today's students and millennials find the long delays for commercial breaks, when players stand around with nothing to do, boring—an uncool way to spend time. Perhaps even more ominous, youth football is also declining: participation among kids ages 6 through 12 was down by 8 percent for the decade ending in 2008. Kids from low-income households are half as likely to play.[35]

A Crisis of Integrity

A caveat is in order here: widespread sex scandals involving major college athletes—a major cause of the crisis of integrity—are beyond the scope of this book. As Mike McIntire points out in *Champions Way*, many such scandals are ignored and covered up by athletic departments, college administrators and counselors and even police departments. McIntire describes in considerable detail the Tallahassee Police Department's refusal to investigate compelling evidence of rape committed by one star player at Florida State University. But FSU is far from alone; the problem of sexual abuse by college athletes is pervasive enough that Congress should appoint a national commission to study its causes and potential remedies.

The third underlying cause threatening the future of big-time college sports is a crisis of integrity. Despite the storm signals already cited, business as usual prevails: There is little or no real constituency for reform at either end of the spectrum—among the big-time schools that continue to take in two-thirds of the proceeds from the so-called revenue sports, or among the also-rans who continue to struggle with near-empty stadiums, no TV revenue and barren prospects for winning seasons. The leadership of the Power Five Conferences continues to operate as if the gravy train will last forever, but there are rumblings of discontent that can't be lightly dismissed.

Late in 2017, the highly respected Knight Commission on Intercollegiate Athletics questioned the NCAA's ability "to prevent abuses, protect the rights of athletes and clean up corruption."[36] Six months later, the Commission called on the NCAA to restructure its governance to provide for independent decision-making. As currently structured, 21 of 24 members of the NCAA Division I Board of Directors are college presidents or chancellors. They have conflicts on many issues they vote on. The Knight Commission has recommended that the NCAA board be comprised of truly independent decision-makers. (Note: Possible structural reforms are included in Chapter Twenty-Two.) Former Secretary of State Condoleezza Rice, who heads an NCAA Commission on College

Basketball tasked with reforming the sport, has warned that this issue must be addressed: unless university presidents, trustees, coaches, athletic directors and other stakeholders take far-reaching action, including structural reforms, "the cynicism and skepticism that is so prevalent now will be rewarded with the sport's collapse."[37]

Causes of cynicism abound. Amid the loud and ongoing chorus over paying the players, the Big Ten Conference awarded its commissioner, Jim Delaney a $20 million bonus. He was making $3.1 million at the time and said, "The optics are what the writers make of them." He conceded the conference had a legal duty to disclose the bonus.[38]

Not long before he got fired, North Carolina football coach Larry Fedora said, "I feel that the game (football) will be pushed so far to one extreme that you won't recognize the game 10 years from now. And I do believe that if it gets to that point, then our country goes down too." He also questioned whether the link between chronic traumatic encephalopathy has been proven.[39] The authors cite Fedora's comments because they may reflect the silo thinking that exists in many athletic departments. It harkens back to a central theme in the film *Knute Rockne: All-American* that football is an indispensable teacher of American values. That the country's future depends on football is a huge stretch—one that strains credulity and breeds cynicism.

There is a longstanding myth that the revenue sports of football and basketball fund tennis, lacrosse, golf and many non-revenue sports, thereby increasing opportunities for more students to play. Charlie Clotfelter has researched this issue and found little evidence that the revenue sports are funding non-revenue sports. The CFO of the University of Texas Athletic Department once told a reporter probing excessive spending: "We eat what we kill."[40] More than likely, any spare change that might have been spent on the water polo team, gets spent, instead, on jet fuel or a five-star hotel stay.

And then there's the all-time cynic of college sports: Walt Byers, who ran the NCAA for 37 years and then turned against it. As the NCAA's first executive director, Byers negotiated football and basketball TV contracts that would later run into the billions and turned the organization into a powerhouse. Though he was diminutive in stature, he was a gruff but colorful character, who wore cowboy boots, drank scotch and had free-wheeling ways.[41] In 1951, he opened an office with five employees in his hometown, Kansas City, Missouri. When he stepped down in 1987, the NCAA membership had nearly tripled—from 381 schools to 1,003; the full-time staff stood at 150.[42] As mentioned earlier in this chapter, by his own admission, Byers coined the phrase "student-athlete" to help member institutions avoid workers' comp claims for sports-related injuries. Despite the runaway commercialization during his tenure and the free-flow of huge subsidies into the revenue sports, Byers stoutly defended big-time athletes as amateurs.

After defending the NCAA for so many years in high-profile battles, Byers had a change of heart in the mid-1980s when the NCAA lost its monopoly for "Game of the Week" football telecasts. The Supreme Court ruled in 1984 that the big schools should be free to make their own TV deals independent of the NCAA. The authors happen to agree with Byers's position on this issue because the decision ended revenue sharing and greatly exacerbated the rich-poor divide by handing the Power Five schools a near-monopoly grip on television revenue. What we fault him for is the NCAA's deeply ingrained obsession with petty rulemaking. The Chaim Arlosoroff case is a prime example. A straight A student, Chaim, in effect, was hounded out of tennis by an "Over Twenty Rule," which was never aimed at him but got applied to him arbitrarily by the NCAA. In his 1995 memoir, Byers called for "a bill of rights" to protect college athletes to include repeal of the requirement that athletes had to sit out for a year before playing for another school. Like much of Byers's postretirement agenda, it was too little too late. With a hard push, Byers probably could have gotten the transfer rule changed while he was still in charge.

All by way of saying it's hard not to be cynical about big-time sports in America. But the games aren't frozen in time. From the era of the Flying Wedge to that of "I" backs and deep pocket passers, it's constantly in flux. Who knows, one day that giant video board at Auburn might flash, "Open for Business—a New Way of Doing Things."

CHAPTER TWENTY-ONE

The Folly of Pay for Play

For decades, American society has sent false signals to youth in economically disadvantaged neighborhoods: *You, too, can be the next Michael Jordan . . . the next LeBron James . . . the next Zion Williamson.* Mind-numbing repetition of that message inspired hope in millions of young basketball and football players that they, too, could play in the NBA or the NFL—that they, too, could bask in the limelight and claim great wealth as their own. Along the way, harsh reality got shoved aside: players with one-word names—ergo Michael, LeBron and Zion—are once-in-a-generation stars, so special that even great talent, herculean effort and phenomenal luck won't guarantee replication of their success. Another message—far more important than the first—never got through or embraced: that educational attainment is much more likely than athletics to lead to economic success and a fulfilling life.

In his ground-breaking 1997 book, *Darwin's Athletes: How Sport Has Damaged Black America and Preserved the Myth of Race,* John Hoberman wrote, "Black athleticism has complicated the identity problems of black Americans by making athletes the most prominent symbols of African American achievement."[1] He concluded, "black identity is athleticized through ubiquitous role models who stimulate wildly unrealistic ambitions in black children . . . an improbable number of black boys expect to become professional athletes. . . ."[2]

Twenty-two years later, Hoberman confirmed that not much had changed. "The media serves up encouraging stories for black kids to consume," he told *The Atlantic's* Alana Semuels in an article entitled, "The White Flight from Football." "Parents know that football comes with the risk of brain damage. But many black families feel the sport is the best option for their kids."[3]

Unfortunately, that option offers a very steep hill to climb. In 2019, the NCAA reported that of 16,346 draft-eligible NCAA football players, only 255 (0.016 percent) were drafted by the NFL. The prospects in men's basketball were even worse: of 4,181 players, only 52 were drafted by the NBA. A male high school player had a 0.03 percent chance of making it to the NBA.[4] These numbers do not include a few college football and basketball players who join teams in Canada, Europe or farm teams in the United States.

For those who do get drafted, or make teams as so-called "walk-on" players, rewards are modest at best, and crippling injury is a constant threat. A few basic facts explain why:

¤ The average career of a player in the NFL is two-and-a-half years—down from six a decade ago.
¤ Many are forced out by concussion, tendon, ligament and other injuries.
¤ The average NFL player earned $2.7 million a year in 2018, but that number is badly skewed by the high-end earners. The median salary was $860,000. The minimum for a starting first-year player was $435,000. Clearly players compensated in the bottom half do not make windfalls that set up them up for life.
¤ About 80 percent of NFL players go bankrupt or suffer financial hardship two years after leaving the game.[5]

Average pay and career length in the NBA are somewhat better, but not by much. In contrast, a career in high tech at a firm like Google or

Facebook can lead to career earnings of $10.5 million—far more than the typical professional athlete earns.[6]

These somewhat dismal prospects for aspiring professional athletes are one dimension of the folly of pay for play. A second is the notion that college basketball and football players should be paid. In recent years, a loud and insistent chorus has decried the anomaly of huge sums being generated in these sports, especially in the postseason, while the players, who are mostly black, get nothing. Meanwhile, coaches patrolling the sidelines make millions, while assistant coaches, athletic directors and others, who are mostly white, reap handsome rewards. The injustice of that sight is glaring and indefensible—stark enough to engender guilt among many who follow the games.

The list of those who advocate paying the players keeps growing and includes many who are prominent and thoughtful, among them three presidential candidates, two U.S. senators, a U.S. District court judge who has ruled in favor of pay for play, the eminent historian Taylor Branch, a leading authority on civil rights and an early advocate of pay for play and several of the leading sportswriters and commentators in the country. Even a a late night comedian has weighed in, likening those who oppose pay for play to "people who run illegal sweat shops out of their basements."

One wag has cited a solution advanced decades ago by much-beloved humorist, Will Rogers: "There is only one fair way to ever arrange amateur athletics in any line in the country, and that's let the athletes work on commission of what they draw at the gate then make them pay their own schooling expenses."[7]

Humor aside, it would be a mistake to dismiss the views of such an all-star cast out of hand. Public opinion still leans against pay for play, but it's gradually shifting toward the pro-pay side. Those advancing counter arguments have received a fraction of the same media attention, but there are compelling arguments against pay for play that must be considered before such a sweeping change gets put into effect. The authors have identified 21 reasons why pay for play is a bad idea (see list below). There may be arguments we missed, but the 21 cited are enough to wreck the games millions enjoy for the fun and excitement they provide.

21 Reasons Why Paying College Players Is a Bad Idea

1. Paying the players is an upside-down solution to deal with the moral dilemma that too many players—especially those from disadvantaged backgrounds—are exploited and not educated. The real solution is to achieve a proper balance between academics and athletics.

2. If the players are paid, the priority to educate them will diminish even further or disappear. Athletes won't be paid enough to offset the lack of a college degree and the benefits it offers.

3. Universities will be mired deeper than ever in running mega entertainment businesses—a type of enterprise that few, if any, are competent to manage.

4. The practice of permitting players to turn pro after one year of college must be stopped. A "one and done" policy is antithetical to the fundamental mission of colleges and universities. It also undercuts the ideals of amateurism by undermining the development of trust, integrity, teamwork and other worthy character traits.

5. If a free market *is used* to set salaries, colleges and universities will engage in bidding wars that lead to even greater scandal and abuse.

6. If a free market *is not used* to set salaries, who will determine who gets what? Will quarterbacks, linebackers and point guards all make the same? No one has answered this difficult question.

7. If men and women aren't treated the same, litigation under Title IX gender equity requirements is bound to occur

8. College athletic departments are likely to lose federal tax-exempt status. They qualify now because sports revenues help fund athletic scholarships deemed a charitable activity by the IRS. An IRS ruling that salaries are charity is high unlikely.

9. If federal tax-exempt status is lost, other complications will arise, among them an obligation for athletic departments to pay income and property taxes.

10. Changing the status of athletes from students to employees means schools will incur costs for Social Security, Medicare and possibly fringe benefits.

11. Pell grants of $5,000 per year will be lost when scholarships are replaced by salaries.

12. Athletic scholarships are likely to go away if players are paid. The shift from funding scholarships to paying players will profoundly change the current environment.

13. Where will funds come from to pay players? In any given year, only 20 or so NCAA Division I athletic departments operate in the black. Adding great expense without offsetting income is impractical and may prove impossible.

14. Paying athletes for the use of their name, image and likeness (NIL) has been widely advocated and is likely to be adopted by most states. The State of California enacted legislation in 2019 to implement NIL on January 1, 2023. NIL is the middle ground between paying an athlete a salary and paying them nothing at all (the status quo). Adoption of NIL follows by a year NCAA adoption of rules that make it much easier for athletes to transfer from one school to another without losing eligibility. In combination, these two decisions could lead to a bidding war on which colleges and universities use NIL enticements to encourage transfers.

15. Pay for play would dramatically increase the oversight responsibilities of the NCAA, an organization that has lost considerable public trust in recent years. Giving the NCAA even more authority will be widely opposed.

16. Fans may be turned off by college games played by professionals. Pro games are often criticized for lacking fun and excitement. Fan support may quickly wane if that happens to college basketball and football.

17. Further concentration of the athletic talent pool is bound to occur and will perpetuate the "rich get richer" syndrome. Who wants schools like Alabama and Clemson to win every year? The hyper-commercialized NFL can't come close matching the fervor of Friday night lights in Texas and in other states where passion for high school football is white hot. *The Economist* magazine has called top-flight high school football "a relentless quest for excellence . . . [and] sport at its best."

18. Today's shoe and under-the-table payment scandals will likely be dwarfed by those of a pay for play era; cheating may increase exponentially.

19. Paying the players may cause more cuts for non-revenue sports. Club sports are likely to get cut too, despite their growing popularity. In any event, payment by shoe and apparel companies to schools and coaches should be disclosed.

20. An omnipresent financial dimension for big-time college sports could turn off many fans.

21. An even more omnipresent financial dimension for big-time college sports—including high profile negotiations between players, agents and even the schools themselves—could turn off many fans. Athletic departments are unlikely to change priorities and operate transparently. More excesses and corruption can be expected from booster clubs, who already spend extravagantly on big-time coaches and even college presidents.

Several of the arguments above have been cited by John Thelin, a former scholar-athlete and an expert on public policy in higher education at the University of Kentucky. Thelin has punctured several illusions about pay for play, most remarkably the notion that salaried players would come out far ahead of those on scholarship. He calculates that after taxes and other deductions, a player receiving a $100,000 salary would come out only $100 ahead of a player with a full scholarship of $65,000 to schools like Duke, Stanford and Northwestern. The salaried player would net more at schools that cost less, but the difference is not what many might think.[8]

Thelin also has pointed out that college football is not the gravy train the media often portrays. Attendance and TV viewership are going down, and most bowl games have thousands of empty seats. Paltry payouts mean teams in bowl games often lose money—results that get overshadowed by the popularity and payouts of national playoff and championship games.[9]

The ultimate folly of pay for play is that major college sports are on shaky economic grounds that could be imploding. Too many schools have lost sight of their mission to educate all students, including their athletes. They will never be able to pay athletes enough to offset the loss of the education colleges and universities are bound by duty to provide.

CHAPTER TWENTY-TWO

The Road to Reform

When he was asked, "What is jazz?" Louis Armstrong replied: "Man, if you gotta ask, you'll never know."[1] That would be an apt reply as well to the contemporaneous "What's wrong with college sports?"—if not the much more perplexing, "What can we do to reform the games?"

The imperative first step toward answering the latter requires breaking an endless cycle of decrying egregious wrongs, empowering expert panels and dithering over recommended reforms—a cycle that has led to one impasse after another for ninety years. Throughout that time, the American sports establishment has dallied with worsening problems while spurning needed reforms. The closest brushes with real change were led by the Carnegie Foundation in 1929 and the Knight Commission 60 years later, with lesser efforts by the NCAA in between. Starting in 1925, Carnegie sent investigators to 112 colleges and universities and found that three-fourths of them were violating the NCAA amateur code.[2] A follow-up report by the *New York Times* in 1931 found that none of the violators had reformed the rampant commercialization practices cited in the original report.[3] That same year, an Associated Press survey found that influential members of the sports establishment—mainly athletic directors, faculty advisers and publicity directors at southern colleges and universities—overwhelmingly believed the Carnegie report had no impact in their region.[4] Abuses Carnegie cited in 1929, to name only a few, were under-the-table payments to athletes, runaway spending by a mega-entertainment complex and bloated salaries for coaches; they were strikingly similar to those cited by the Knight Commission in 1989, when it was formed, and its recent investigation of college basketball led by former Secretary of State Condoleezza Rice.

Throughout that cycle, there has been an underlying but rarely questioned assumption that big-time college sports in America can be reformed when experience tells us maybe not. Does anyone truly believe perennial football powers like Alabama will stop playing so-called cupcake games against teams like Mercer in the interest of a more balanced schedule? Alabama won 56–0 in 2017. The real reasons they played: Alabama could rest its starters the week before playing archrival Auburn, and Mercer got $600,000 just to show up.[5] What about the tailgaters and other die-hard fans at such games? Despite the lopsided scores, they still get to revel in commercialized hijinks—fighter jet fly-overs, firework strobe and brocade effects and the sight of up to 120 players running through machine-made smoke just before kickoff. For the denizens of sports bars (and couch potatoes at home), the networks air games from noon to midnight. Does anybody think we'd ever go back to a fifties-type Game of the Week between, say, Mercer and the Citadel? Or that March Madness with its Cinderella upsets and wildly popular "Pick 'Em" office pools will give way to sports clubs or intramural games on the quad?

The ritualized kickoff and other such "happenings" are deeply woven into the fabric of American society; collectively they give definition to who we are: our exuberant, fun-loving side, the big wins that bring us together, our passion for athletic excellence and our deep allegiance to colleges and universities whose teams we adore—schools that engage in a form of competition that rarely exists in other cultures and countries. If all the fun and spectacle were suddenly to stop, we would feel—and *be*—less American. But the "all-in-good-fun" benefits come at a steep price: far too many disadvantaged youths see big-time college sports as their only path to success, and their lives are thus stunted; billions of dollars pouring into the games have led to many types of unethical behavior, and a system that richly rewards coaches and many others while failing to compensate *or* educate those who make the games so exciting. Such failings may be ignored, but they can't be justified. The clash between feel-good fun and toxic fallout complicates reform enormously.

Beginning with the 1929 Carnegie recommendations, reform agendas have focused primarily on symptoms of an out-of-control system—overpaid coaches, under-the-table payments to athletes and runaway spending. Proposals to reform these wrongs often were dead on arrival because they antagonized powerful athletic departments and wealthy alumni backers. Only by focusing on the underlying causes of symptoms—the dysfunctional and unworkable governing structure of collegiate sports and a systemic failure to put academic achievement first—will workable and lasting reform be possible.

For more than a century, the NCAA has attempted to provide an overarching regulatory structure for college sports; time and time again results—especially for the so-called revenue sports of football and basketball—have been disappointing. Today, the NCAA's main policy-making body is a 24-member Board of Governors that includes 19 college presidents and chancellors, three athletic directors and a president/CEO.[6] The overrepresentation of presidents and chancellors has been criticized as a façade that allows the NCAA to operate as a trade association for coaches and athletic directors, whose interests often conflict with other important stakeholders.[7]

It's no surprise that coaches and athletic directors have dominated the NCAA from the start. In 1905, President Teddy Roosevelt invited six of them, alone, to the White House to discuss a spate of fatalities and maiming injuries that threatened college football with abolishment. An outgrowth of that meeting was a new organization to help reform the game, though it did not take the NCAA name until 1910.

In recent years, many critics have called for the NCAA, itself, to be abolished. The Drake Group, whose board includes several of the country's leading thinkers on college sports, has advocated replacing the NCAA with a federally chartered organization like the U.S. Olympic Committee.[8] Nearly a hundred such organizations have been formed under Title 36 of the U.S. Code. They operate on a non-profit and non-partisan basis and get no government funding at all. The American Legion, the Boy Scouts, Boys and Girls Clubs and Little League Baseball all are Congressionally Chartered Organizations (CCOs).[9] That structure adds prestige and credibility because it carries the imprimatur of Congress without congressional intrusion into how the organization is run. Since 1989, a moratorium on granting new charters has been in effect, but exceptions have been made.[10] A forceful appeal by the Drake Group and the Knight Commission would likely prompt Congress to consider chartering a new CCO with a name like Collegiate Sports USA. Drake and Knight also could recommend members of a founding board structured like the U.S. Olympic Committee (USOC), whose 15-person board includes several former scholar-athletes who've become prominent academic and corporate leaders.[11]

Whether a new organization is established or the NCAA is reformed, a more representative governing board should include one or more members from the following categories:

College Presidents—To reflect the best interests of the 1,117 colleges and universities who are members of the NCAA currently.

Athletic Directors—To represent the operation of athletic programs that are fiscally sound, that emphasize fully educating varsity athletes and that protect athlete health and safety.

Athletic Councils—To represent existing faculty councils at most NCAA member institutions who grapple on a continuing basis with the thorniest issues in intercollegiate athletics. (*Note*: Duke's Athletic Council is developing a plan to assist "one-and-done" basketball players in getting a degree once they stop playing professionally.)

Faculty—To help define policies that put academics first, and to advise on the impact athletic programs have on campus culture.

Athletes—To add the perspective of those directly affected by coaching decisions, playing conditions and performance-related matters.

Scholar-Athlete Alumni—To represent those who excelled in the academic and athletic spheres and who understand the profound importance of scholar-athletes to national wellbeing.

Students—Principally to provide an undergraduate perspective on the use of student fees for athletic purposes and student support of athletic programs in general.

Public Representative—One or more public official, former public official or persons who have made outstanding contributions to collegiate sports to assist in educating the public on the value of putting academics first.

A governing board of approximately 15 members could represent the major stakeholders and still be cohesive. Members must be elected who understand gender equity issues and a rapidly changing media landscape where commercialization practices threaten to make games unwatchable. The board won't be legitimate if elections are tainted by cronyism or attempts to perpetuate the status quo. In 2019, independent members will be nominated to the NCAA Board of Governors by its executive committee, a subset of the full board; incumbents will be permitted to self-nominate.[12]

These symptoms of a self-perpetuating structure strongly suggest the need for an independent nominating committee that will recommend candidates who are not beholden to any faction. After all, college presidents are not immune from conflict of interest. As Pulitzer Prize–winning author Mike McIntire of the *New York Times* points out in his exposé, *Champion's Way*, athletic program boosters "whose single-minded goal is increasing sports victories" even pay part of the president's salary at Florida State. That type of abuse is less likely to occur with a CCO whose founding board would have a mandate from the U.S. House of Representatives.

Whether a CCO becomes successor to the NCAA, or the NCAA undergoes comprehensive reform, the crises of identity, income and integrity described in Chapter Twenty must be addressed.

Clarifying the Student-Athlete Identity

For decades, the term student-athlete has been a sham, a caricature of a much-diminished ideal and the source of countless platitudes and misleading statements in NCAA-sponsored telecasts. The term, itself, cries out for reinvention. Suffice it to say that today's student-athletes—at least those on the 128 football and 347 basketball teams in NCAA Division I (D-I)—are not *students* in any real sense of the word; they are gladiators groomed to serve a mega sports complex. Even the term *nominal student* barely applies: In D-I sports, athletics come before everything else, except maintaining the bare minimum for academic eligibility. What is required of D-I athletes leaves no doubt about that: most practice as many as 40 hours a week, play an ever-increasing schedule of games, travel extensively, miss class after class and have no time for the life of the normal student—joining the debating society, playing in the band, acting in a play, joining the engineering club or studying a semester abroad.

The NCAA rule limiting practices for D-I players to 20 hours a week is another sham because voluntary practice in addition is allowed. That leaves coaches free to schedule additional hours of practice at their option. Players are loath to skip voluntary sessions because coaches can often cancel an athletic scholarship in any given year for almost any reason. Player tenure thus becomes a form of peonage subject to the whim of the coach. Moreover, the sheer number of games played is exhausting and keeps going up. Michigan played seven football games in 1920; it plays 12 today with a conference championship and a bowl game often in addition; in 2019, for the first time, the national championship added a 15th game for two teams, Alabama and Clemson. For the 2018–19 season, Duke scheduled 31 basketball games and would have to play six more to win a national championship. A 70-game baseball schedule is common. When John LeBar began coaching, Duke played a 16-match tennis season with the ACC tournament in addition; Duke plays twice as many matches today. Travel requirements have gone up too, especially in big conferences like the ACC whose 14 teams are scattered between Boston and Miami. Holiday trips to Hawaii and the Bahamas are now common for D-I basketball teams. It's even tougher for smaller schools that can't afford private jets and five-star hotels.

"You can spend an entire day trying to get where you need to go," says Mitch Strohman, the voice of Northern Arizona University basketball. "People don't understand how much energy that sucks out of you. You're exhausted. That's a lot to ask the body to do, no matter how young you are."[13]

When practice, game days and travel are combined, playing a big-time sport is more than a full-time job. No wonder players are too tired to study; no wonder the educational value of a D-I football or basketball scholarship is worth so little. Devaluation is evident in the hundreds of classes D-I athletes miss annually. The problem is so serious many branded programs employ a cadre of watchdogs to track who goes to class and who doesn't. In *Billion Dollar Ball*, Gilbert Gaul writes of hanging out with checkers at the University of Kansas—he calls them walkers—who cover "from one end of the thousand-acre campus to the other, taking up their stations outside designated classrooms, and waiting for football and basketball players to show up." Gaul also notes that KU employs more than a hundred tutors to keep athletes eligible.[14]

Big-time programs are engaged in what is often called an "arms race" in which there is always some state-of-the-art facility or improvement that "must" be acquired. Athletic directors aren't accountable to stockholders and don't worry about turning a profit; winning and losing are the only measures that truly matter. In recent years, the win-at-all-cost mentality has begun to infect the non-revenue sports, where coaches often get fired after one or two losing seasons. Clearly, putting academics first will require a sea change for the branded programs whose backers will bitterly resist cutting exorbitant pay for coaches, lavish stadium upgrades or the entertaining spectacle of games. The worst excesses can't be scaled back unless changes in the national governing structure are integrated with structural reforms at the university level that address the identity problem in a comprehensive way. Reforms at the university level should be spearheaded by a new governing structure to include:

Athletic Oversight Committee that the president of each Division I school would appoint to include its athletic director, one representative from its Faculty Athletic Council and one scholar-athlete alumnus. This committee would have authority to determine:

¤ A reasonable reduction in the number of football and basketball games to be played in any given season. A reduced schedule would make games more important and could help reverse declining attendance, especially in Division I football which experienced a 10 percent decline for the nine-year period ending in 2017. Loss of income from playing fewer games can also be addressed by improved financial stewardship.

¤ A reasonable limit on hours of team practice with the goal being 20 hours Monday through Friday (with games but not practice on weekends) and five to ten hours weekly of film sessions. Weight room workouts would be at the player's option.

¤ A reasonable limit—seven would be workable—on classes a varsity player can miss each semester.

¤ Shifting of academic support programs from athletic to academic control; and reorienting such programs from a primary focus on maintaining eligibility to an enriched academic experience with more demanding course work in major fields of study.

¤ A minimum GPA to be achieved progressively in each year of a student's matriculation; appropriate terms that designate academic status, such as Stage 1, 2, 3 or 4 Student-Athlete; and a minimum GPA of 3.2 to be become a "Scholar-Athlete." The goal would be to define levels of academic achievement that athletes would reach each year.

¤ Establish as needed remedial programs for varsity athletes that would permit them to play while catching up. Permit a reduced course load for juniors and seniors and extend scholarships, as necessary, from four to six years to encourage more players to graduate.

¤ Publicize the academic achievements of scholar-athletes by all possible means: on NCAA telecasts, in national and local media and in school publications. Task athletic departments to collect data on the "ripple effect" scholar-athlete alumni have in their communities and at the state and national level. Require broadcast contracts for the College Football Playoff and March Madness to highlight accomplishments of scholar-athletes.

Addressing the Income Crisis

As noted in Chapter Eighteen, only about twenty Division I athletic programs operate in the black. That means the branded programs are on an unsustainable path, especially in the face of declining football attendance. The following proposals would foster a rapid return to solvency:

¤ Require the Athletic Oversight Committee at each Division I school to submit annually a profit and loss statement that includes debt service for its athletics department operations; and further require that schools operate on a financially sound basis (i.e., no deficits) to be eligible for a financial payout from the College Football Playoff or March Madness. Such sanctions would be suspended when force majeure events (e.g., weather-related) occur. Because schools do not now use a standard accounting methodology, the NCAA or its successor should mandate one for universal use.[15]

¤ Standardize public reporting of athletic department financial performance for public *and* private universities.

¤ Limit the use of student fees to an equitable share based on student participation in athletic activities, such as sports clubs and intramural sports and related activities.

¤ Put a new or successor governing board in charge of the College Football Playoff and March Madness; and further, charge the board with establishing a fair formula for distributing net proceeds from both events to all 346 Division I member schools.

Providing for Greater Accountability

Donna A. Lopiano, who serves on the Drake Group Board and is a former Director of Women's Athletics at the University of Texas, holds that the NCAA and its member schools are not keeping faith with their mission to protect the health, safety and welfare of varsity athletes. She says any new governing body should devote "every rule in its book, and every dime of its revenue . . . to the players on the field, not to the barnacles who cling to and sponge off them." Revenues from television contracts, bowl games and licensing, Lopiano contends, "should cover injury insurance for athletes and the full cost of their scholarships through graduation." That would involve a profound shift in priorities based on the following reform proposals:

¤ Currently, the NCAA requires that varsity athletes be insured but does not insure them itself. Many schools only provide "bare bones" coverage. Instead, the NCAA or its successor should provide full coverage for injuries and sports-related health complications. Premiums for policies should be paid in full before any distributions of postseason events, such as the College Football Playoff or March Madness, are made.

¤ System integrity could be further enhanced by having the Drake Group and the Knight Commission—both of whom are widely respected for seminal and unbiased research on difficult issues in college sports—develop recommendations to Congress for establishing a CCO. Their recommendations should include the names of founding board members to include prominent athletic, academic, business and political leaders.

¤ The Drake Group and the Knight Commission also should recommend a list of topics for study on a high priority basis by the proposed CCO to include: replacement of athletic scholarships with need-based grants in aid to be administered by financial aid offices instead of athletic departments; an in-depth study on how scholar-athletes benefit the country and policies to develop more such high-achievers; and a study of how grassroots constituencies—alumni and non-alumni fans alike—can be cultivated and involved in a new and more representative system of governance for intercollegiate sports.

In a superb article in *The Antitrust Bulletin*, Jayma Meyer, a visiting professor at the University of Indiana, and Andrew Zimbalist, an economics professor at Smith College, wrote in 2017: "Litigation involving antitrust laws has been a particular thorn in the NCAA's side."[16] They point out that the NCAA filed more than a million pages of documents in litigation over the use of athletes' images and likenesses (the O'Bannon case), and that the judge ordered the NCAA to pay opposing attorneys $40 million. More cost was incurred in an appeal to the Ninth Circuit Court of Appeals, which affirmed, in part, and reversed, in part, the lower court ruling.[17]

On the thorniest issue of all—whether college players should be paid—Chief Judge Sydney R. Thomas of the Ninth Circuit noted, "The national debate about amateurism in college sports is important. But our task as appellate judges is not to resolve it. Nor could we."[18] Meyer and Zimbalist argue that, ultimately, Congress should grant a limited antitrust exemption that would enable the NCAA (or its successor) to clearly delineate the line between college and professional sports. As a practical matter, the exemption would allow the collegiate regulating body to control costs, prevent varsity sports from compromising the academic performance of players, insure competitive balance between schools and conferences and protect the physical wellbeing of athletes—all without risk of legal liability or the threat of violating the Sherman Antitrust Act.[19]

In return for the antitrust exemption, the governing body and its member institutions would enact reforms that put academics first and insure that athletes aren't exploited. On the most basic level, limits could be imposed on the pay of coaches, on spending for new facilities and on the size of football teams. Most vitally, restrictions on paying athletes could be imposed in the spirit of true amateurism.[20]

Advocates of paying players have offered no hard evidence on the budget impact such a decision would have. Nor do they specify whether all would be paid, or only the stars. This point complicates the issue enormously because a star-only approach could lead to messy litigation, even though few players contribute more than the value of their scholarship. Moreover, many of the branded programs already are running multimillion-dollar deficits, which are covered, in the main, by general funds. If players are paid, the cost of Social Security, workers' compensation, unemployment insurance and other benefits must be added to any salaries they are paid. Big-time programs already are on an unsustainable economic footing; it's highly unlikely they could absorb these added costs.[21]

Meyer and Zimbalist also call for reforms that are close akin to an athlete bill of rights. These reforms include requiring that schools pay for comprehensive injury insurance, guarantee of a full four-year scholarship, restrictions on required practice and travel and moving academic support programs from athletic to academic controls.[22]

Resistance to these recommendations among athletic departments and their wealthy patrons may be an absolute "never." But it's important to remember that opposition will be confined to a few schools—those with so-called branded programs. They are the same schools that bear primary responsibility for building the mega entertainment sports complex that disregards the basic educational value of putting academics first. That powerful minority—coaches, athletic directors, school presidents, trustees, broadcast executives and others—has prevailed in decision-making mainly because the governing structure is so skewed and unrepresentative. The public interest gets throttled time and time again because there is no organized constituency for reform. That makes it doubly important for the proposed CCO to define and cultivate broad-based support.

Years ago, Notre Dame Athletic Director Moose Krause told Murray Sperber, author of *Beer and Circus: How Big-Time College Sports Is Crippling Undergraduate Education*, "If you want to change college sports instantly, forget about athletic scholarships and bring in 'need-based only grants,' like the Ivies. . . ."[23] Sperber added that such action "would eliminate the athletic department's current employer/employee relationship with an athlete, as well as the coach's power to renew or cancel the scholarship every July."

Published in 2000, Sperber's *Beer and Circus* described a harsh truth: that the decline in undergraduate education has been caused to an alarming degree by our obsession with big-time collegiate sports. Nearly two decades after he wrote it, everything still stops for the big game.

For years, many American universities have based their reputations on pioneering research churned out by top-flight graduate programs. Athletic department deficits rarely come at their expense; undergraduate programs get whacked instead. As Sperber notes, teaching budgets for undergrads have been cut drastically by increasing class sizes, by employing adjunct faculty with no job benefits and by relying, more and more, on grad students. Soaring deficits in the athletic departments often drive such cuts. Sperber's fundamental conclusion is that it's impossible to square the circle of athletic and academic excellence.

Between 2013 and 2015, overspending by Washington State University's Athletic Department caused a $50 million drain on the school's reserves. That triggered elimination of the performing arts program and a hiring freeze for nearly all other university departments.[24] Winning football and basketball championships can't make up for qualitative cuts like that. University presidents may deny it, but they do pursue sports championships, in part, to compensate for the devaluation of undergraduate education. Like many of his counterparts at big public universities, WSU's President Kirk Schulz calls athletics the "front door of the university,"[24] implying that big-time sports is the last place to make budget cuts.

Rep. David Price, who represents North Carolina's Research Triangle, has pointed out that analyzing athletic budgets at schools with big-time athletic programs is hampered greatly by the lack of a standard methodology for reporting income and costs. Price and several of his colleagues are sponsoring the SCORE Act (Standardization of Collegiate Oversight of Revenues and Expenses) to deal with this problem.

A former political science professor at Duke, Price says the bill will "provide policymakers and university leaders with reliable and consistent data as they consider further-reaching reforms." He sees the legislation as an essential step toward understanding the full impact of sports entertainment complex at U.S. colleges and universities—one that could lead to other sensible and much-needed reforms.

"I sense a growing awareness among my House colleagues that problems with big-time college sports aren't going away, that sooner or later we'll have to address them. Thus far the responsible parties have been unable to check runaway spending but even worse the continuing erosion of academic integrity and a widespread unwillingness to put academics first. As it becomes more and more evident that the system cannot bring about needed reforms from within, congressional oversight is likely to increase. If the system can't reform itself, the congress won't have much choice but to step in. After all, academic excellence is a core source of national strength and competitiveness; it can't be sacrificed for fun and games."

The authors both live in Price's district and have observed his work for many years. As a senior member of the House Appropriations Committee, he is considered one of its least partisan members. His attitude toward reform will carry considerable weight with other House members.

At the heart of the challenge we face on the road to reform is reasserting America's most cherished educational values. For years, these values have been sacrificed on the altar of greater and greater athletic glories. But game-winning touchdown runs and three-point shots at the buzzer can never justify a sacrifice of that magnitude. Not to face that challenge means athletic departments will rule universities with absolute authority—all in the interest of a narrow few. A painful truth would then be all too plain: that we allowed our colleges and universities to put entertainment before academics once and for all. Then, the cry "On to the coliseum!" will ring louder than ever as we shuffle off toward the decadence of Rome, when qualities that made the empire great became dim memories at best.

CHAPTER TWENTY-THREE

Renewal of American Ideals

Mere mortals know all too well how fleeting time can be: the young grow old before they know it, and fate mocks all claims to great and near-great accomplishments with the grim reminder, "ashes to ashes and dust to dust." The Russians have long said the poet outlives the czar. After all, it was a poet, Percy Bysshe Shelley, who saw in a shattered stone pharaoh a stark and sobering image of infinity—

> And on the pedestal, these words appear:
> My name is Ozymandias, King of Kings;
> Look on my Works, ye Mighty, and despair!
> Nothing beside remains. Round the decay
> Of that colossal Wreck, boundless and bare
> The lone and level sands stretch far away.[1]

Even epitaphs carved in stone have finitude. The greatest performance records in sports all get shattered in time. Only values and character endure: achieving excellence through hard work and the integrity to put academics first.

At the end of his or her career, being remembered for having put academics first should be reward enough for a college coach. The profession has done far too little to stop the onslaught of sports commercialization that has tarnished so many otherwise great American universities. Today's coaches are bequeathing to their successors a system with amply charted ills, including fake courses, stand-in test-takers, lax and fraudulent admissions, too many athletes focused only on playing professionally, an arms race in facility-building and bloated athletic budgets that nearly all bleed red ink. Even under-the-table payments are still a problem. Coaches and athletic directors often are vastly overpaid, despite making wrong calls on the issues that truly matter.

In 1782, Benjamin Franklin identified a list of scoundrels from his days as a Founding Father. Among them were a shill who had borrowed money on false pretenses, an outright swindler and at least two who betrayed the cause of independence.[2] A list of scoundrels in sports today could easily populate a Dickens novel. We badly need authentic heroes to lead us in righting a slew of wrongs but mainly to find the integrity to put time-tested American ideals first in our universities.

One coach who has done that is Tony Bennett, who led the University of Virginia to its first national championship in 2019 and turned down a raise for his accomplishments, the *News and Observer* in Raleigh, North Carolina, reported. According to the report, Bennett also gave $500,000 to a career training program for his current and former players.

Looking back to a time before sports went big-time, Cornell Coach Carl Snavely epitomized what it once meant to be a hero. In the aftermath of an epic game against Dartmouth in 1940, he made a fateful decision that few, if any, coaches would make today. Snavely's opponent was Earl "Red" Blaik, who later led Army to three consecutive national championships. The game was played on Saturday, November 16, in Hanover, New Hampshire, and is believed to be the only game in collegiate football history decided by an off-the-field decision reversing an on-the-field result.

Cornell entered the game at number two in the AP national rankings and had spent four weeks earlier that season ranked number one. A year earlier, the Big Red had gone undefeated and finished number four in the final AP poll. Arriving in Hanover with an 18-game winning streak, Cornell was a heavy favorite over 3–4 Dartmouth and banking on a second consecutive undefeated season.

Strong defenses on both sides dominated the game. Dartmouth led 3–0 with less than two minutes to play when a pass gave Cornell a first down on the Big Green six-yard line. Three plunges into the line moved the ball to the one. With no timeouts left, Cornell's desperation fourth down pass was batted down in the end zone. It was Dartmouth's ball with three seconds left: game over . . . or was it? The referee, Red Friesell, got confused and gave Cornell a fifth down, despite vehement protests by the Dartmouth players. On the extra down, Cornell scored on a touchdown pass; the final score was Cornell 7, Dartmouth 3.[3] By Monday, the game films had made clear to Coach Snavely that the referee had made a glaring error. Coach Snavely promptly agreed to send Dartmouth a telegram relinquishing Cornell's victory and congratulating Dartmouth on winning. It's hard to imagine any coach doing that today.

Snavely went on to coach highly ranked teams at the University of North Carolina. Over the next half century, his sterling character became a faint memory as a win-at-all-cost mentality came to dominate in college sports. In 1990, referees awarded the University of Colorado a fifth down in a game in which the Buffaloes were contending for a national title. As Murray Sperber writes in *Incredible Victory*, "This time, the school did not forfeit the win, proudly counting it instead as part of a national championship season." Ironically, the Football Writers Association of America awarded Colorado the annual Grantland Rice Trophy as the nation's best team that year. Both decisions made a mockery of Rice's famous poem: "When the one Great Scorer comes to write against your name, He marks not that you won or lost, but how you played the game."

Both the authors have persons on their list of heroes who always put education first. In John's case, it was his parents, George and Dorothy, who battled through the Depression Era and never got to go to college. Their struggles convinced them that getting a college education was essential. All four of their sons—John, Tom, Jim and Jerry—got undergraduate degrees and three earned advanced degrees—a rarity for any family in the late forties and fifties.

Allen's mother, Elaine, dreamed of going to college, but the Depression had made that impossible. In 1960, the Ford Foundation awarded her a full four-year scholarship for her many years of community service in rural Eastern North Carolina. Even though she still had four young children to raise, she earned an undergraduate degree in three years, then earned her MA and got a PhD degree in her fifties. After that, she became a popular college history professor and retired in her mid-seventies.

¤ ¤ ¤

In 2011, on a beautiful fall Saturday just before a football game, about 50 of John LeBar's former players and friends attended a ceremony on campus to endow a Duke tennis scholarship in his name. During the ceremony, John kept thinking how much his players had accomplished in their lives. David Robinson had become one of the most successful eye surgeons in the country; John Stauffer, one of the best scramblers and most tenacious players he'd ever had, had become a tenured professor at Harvard and a leading authority on the Antislavery Movement; as a volunteer, Chip Davis had cured hundreds of poor adolescents in Guatemala of curvature of the spine; and Paul Auerbach had trained several thousand emergency room physicians at Stanford, established wilderness medicine as a popular field of study in med schools and led earthquake relief teams to Haiti and Nepal. The ripple effect of all four men, and that of other of John's players, had been enormous, due in large measure to their integrity.

Their impact reminded John of one of Assistant Coach Jim Bonk's favorite sayings, "It's not about us, it's always about the players." At that same endowment ceremony, a tennis court was dedicated to Jim, whose three loves in life were Duke, chemistry and tennis. He, too, was imbued with integrity.

A blown-out shoe sent the sports world into yet another convulsion over what's best for the players on February 20, 2019. Just 33 seconds into a Duke–North Carolina basketball game, the nation's top-ranked college star, Zion Williamson, fell to the floor when his shoe ripped apart, suffering a mild sprain of the right knee. His injury reignited the ongoing controversy over whether talented players like Williamson are being exploited by their coaches, schools with big-time sports programs and the NCAA. *Washington Post* Columnist Sally Jenkins wrote, "This is what happens when everyone gets paid but the guy who's really earning the money . . . the NCAA has managed to turn a Duke education into a risk that a talented kid can't afford to take."[4]

No one has made the exploitation argument more pointedly than Kylia Carter, the mother of Wendell Carter, yet another Duke star. On May 7, 2018, she told the Knight Commission that the system of not paying players was a form of slavery: "The only two systems where I've known that to be in place is slavery and the prison system, and now I see the NCAA as overseers of a system that is identical to that."[5] Two weeks later her son became the seventh pick in the NBA draft after only one year at Duke; a lucrative contract followed.[6]

Mrs. Carter's argument was not new. In a cover article in *The Atlantic* in 2011, Pulitzer Prize–winning historian Taylor Branch cautioned, "Slavery analogies should be used carefully. College athletes are not slaves. Yet to survey the scene—corporations and universities enriching themselves on the backs of uncompensated young men, whose status as 'student-athletes' deprives them of the right to due process guaranteed by the Constitution—is to catch an unmistakable whiff of the plantation."[7]

Outrage that the system is unjust is much more prevalent today. Many see paying the players as the best way to ensure integrity. But few critics, including Branch, have offered specifics on how to make this change. Patrick Hruby, an online sports columnist and adjunct professor at Georgetown University, has acknowledged that too few details have been forthcoming. In 2018, he wrote that the best plan is, "No plan at all. . . . A sane system would allow everyone—schools and athletes and sponsors alike—to bargain for the best possible deals, sign on the dotted lines, and go from there in accordance with existing tax, labor, and contract laws." He dismissed partial steps toward ending amateurism for denying athletes "the same basic economic rights and protections the rest of us take for granted."[8]

But a pure market-based solution would require schools to take a final and fateful step toward complete commercialism. True, many of the hypocrites—what Sally Jenkins calls pocket-liners "who skim the sweat straight off [the player's back]"[9]—would go away. But in its place, we'd get new problems: rich schools skimming off more talent than ever, and widespread litigation under Title IX. If the men get paid, courts may hold that women should be paid too.

Also troubling is the fundamental change paying players would have on how fans perceive major collegiate sports. The near universal popularity of games could sharply decline once college players become professionals. College teams already serve as "farm teams" for the NFL and the NBA. Paying the players could make these ties even more objectional to the average fan. Playing for the love of the game brings an atmosphere of excitement to college games that pro games often can't match. Much of that excitement could be lost if the players are paid, because the fundamental nature of games would change. Cinderella upsets might disappear because smaller schools like Stephen F. Austin, which upset Number 1 Duke on November 26, 2019, couldn't possibly compete for talented players with giants like Kentucky and Michigan. The present gap between Power Five Conference schools and everybody else would almost certainly widen.

Dealing with these questions will add much complexity to a system that already nitpicks what players and their parents eat for lunch on a recruiting trip. Unfortunately, most advocates of paying the players dismiss them as trivial. In advocating a totally free-market approach, Patrick Hruby calls other issues "bullshit."[10]

As Christian Schneider, a columnist for the *Milwaukee Journal Sentinel*, writes, "The idea that injecting more money into college athletics would reduce corruption is preposterous. Once the money spigot is open, it will only provide more opportunities for universities, agents and boosters to gain an advantage. Even if athletes were paid, schools would still compete against each other for recruits—which means the temptation would always be there for a university to offer high school athletes even more."[11]

It's likely that one market restraint—the NBA's so-called one and done rule barring players under 18 from turning pro—will end in 2021 or 2022. That would permit players with superstar potential to turn pro without going to college at all. Less talented players could go straight from high school to the G League, the NBA's developmental circuit. This change will bring into much sharper focus the fact that the universe of so-called exploited players is quite small. The number is confined almost entirely to the big revenue sports of basketball and football. Several hundred college players are chosen in the NFL draft and a mere 60 in the NBA draft. Does it make sense to upend the entire system to accommodate the few hundred who can turn pro? It's hard to argue that players who can't go pro are being exploited: their athletic scholarships provide a pathway to economic independence and a richer life.

If pay for play does come to fruition, universities will be forced to admit, once and for all, that being in the entertainment business is a top priority. Given such an admission, how could they possibly keep the tax exemption that generates such huge cash flow to their athletic operations? What gets lost repeatedly in this ongoing debate is the intangible value of a full athletic scholarship to a good school. But try making this argument to an advocate of paying the players. You'll get the stunned look of someone who thinks you're a loon. Try quoting Charles Barkley, one of the all-time basketball greats, who says of paying the players: "That's crazy." The response is likely to be, "Barkley's got his, but what does he know?"

Yet the value of a full, four-year scholarship at Duke comes to more than $250,000. Moreover, its value in terms of enrichment of life cannot be calculated. Just one dimension of that benefit—the opportunity to bond for life with classmates, who will come to your wedding, recommend your son or daughter to a good school and even help them find the job of their dreams—does not have a price tag. Neither can the pleasure of reading and appreciating a good book, or being able to assess a company's product and services accurately. These issues aren't trivial; they speak directly to the overarching issue of integrity, which universities lose when they fail to put academics first. Most big-time sports programs already have.

A few months after John LeBar's Mom was diagnosed with Alzheimer's, she began getting out of bed and wandering at night, which is common with that affliction. His Dad devised an ingenious solution to keep her from harming herself: He tied one end of a nylon stocking to her ankle and the other to his. We need solutions that are just as practical to help outstanding athletes, and the fans who adore them, understand and embrace why their universities must always be deeply grounded in integrity—that they, too, are responsible for achieving that aim.

Putting academics first is one of the greatest cultural issues of our times. College athletes are treated like rock stars with celebrity derived from near constant exposure on television. Youthful emulators—especially in economically disadvantaged communities—often believe that following in their footsteps is the only path to success. The Victorian Era philosopher, Thomas Carlyle, wrote, "The great law of culture is: Let each become all that he was created capable of being." Herein contemporary American Culture faces one of its greatest challenges: the full development of human resources that are stunted by understandable yet impractical dreams.

The true avatars of excellence in American culture aren't quarterbacks who can throw the ball 50 yards with pinpoint precision; instead, they are young men and women who prepare for 50-year careers in law, medicine, architecture, business and other realms. Many will be scholar-athletes, who practice hard by day and study hard at night—achievers who learn how to manage time, how to be part of a team and even how to learn from losing. They will learn as well how to maintain composure when tensions are high, to get up after getting knocked down and to realize that losing is not the end of the world. Armed with this knowledge, they will go on to build bridges, roads and hospitals, find cures to dreaded diseases, write books that change minds and benefit their communities and the world in ways far too numerous to count.

We can never forget that universities that do their job help maximize the potential of human capital, the most precious resource any society has. We need to encourage universities and the students they teach not to pursue the false gods of commercialization; to trust time-tested values instead—especially the ideal of the scholar-athlete. In a world that becomes more complex daily, putting academics first has never been more important. Each generation must face what President Franklin Roosevelt called, at the height of the Great Depression, a rendezvous with destiny. The times are much changed for the generation coming of age today, but basic values have not changed; they will always endure.

Notable Scholar-Athletes
A Representational but Not Definitive Listing

Name	School	Dates	Record
Arthur Ashe	UCLA	1943–93	From a poor family but taught to read at age four by his mother. First black player named to the U.S. Davis Cup; member of winning Davis Cup teams 1968–71. Only black to win singles titles at U.S. Open, Austrian Open and Wimbledon. Wrote three volume *A Hard Road A Hard Road to Glory: A History of the African American Athletes.* Active in the U.S. Civil Rights movement. Died at 49 of complications following a heart attack.
Hobey Baker	Princeton	1892–1918	Majored in history, politics and economics at Princeton and finished with above average grades. Considered first American star in ice hockey by the Hockey Hall of Fame. Also starred in football at Princeton. Only player in both the hockey and college football halls of fame. Awarded the Croix de Guerre by France in World War I. Killed in a test flight at the end of the war with orders to return home in his pocket.
Bill Bradley	Princeton	1943–	Named NCAA Basketball Player of the Year in 1965 for his play at Princeton. Spent a decade in the NBA, playing on two title teams. A Rhodes Scholar, he served three terms in the U.S. Senate. Ran unsuccessfully for President in 2000.
George H.W. Bush	Yale	1924–2018	Earned his degree at Yale, entering an accelerated program that enabled him to finish in two and one-half years. Held numerous leadership positions in high school and college. Played first base at Yale in the 1940's and competed in the first two college World Series. An avid tennis player, he skydived on his 85th birthday. Served as U.S. President 1989–93.

Name	School	Dates	Record
George W. Bush	Yale	1946–	Though he called himself an averaged student, he earned an undergraduate degree from Yale and a MBA from Harvard. Ran a marathon at age 43 and sub-seven-minute mile years later. After 9/11, threw a perfect strike while wearing a bullet proof vest to open game three of the World Series at Yankee Stadium. Served as U.S. President 2001–09.
Walter Camp	Yale	1859–1925	After graduating from Yale in 1880, he studied at Yale Medical School for three years but dropped out due to illness. Led Yale as a player and coach to football dominance in the last quarter of the nineteenth century. Known as the Father of American football, Camp introduced many innovative rules to the game, including the line of scrimmage and the system of downs. A skilled and popular writer, he selected the most prominent All-American football teams for many years.
Jimmy Carter	U.S. Naval Academy	1924–	Played on the Plains High School basketball team. Served on active duty after graduating at Annapolis and beginning in 1952 joined the fledging nuclear submarine program under legendary Admiral Hyman Rickover. Served as U.S. President 1977–81.
Pete Dawkins	West Point	1938–	An All-American at West Point and winner of the Heisman Trophy in 1958. A Rhodes Scholar, who served with valor in Viet Nam. He ended a distinguished military career as a brigadier general.
Dwight Eisenhower	West Point	1890–1969	Starting halfback and linebacker on 1912 West Point football team. An average student, he excelled in English. As an army second lieutenant, he served as aide to Generals John Pershing and Douglas McArthur. In WW, served as Supreme Commander of Allied Forces in Western Europe. Led successful D-Day invasion of Normandy in 1944. Served as President of Columbia University after the war and as U.S. President 1953–61.
Jay Fielder	Dartmouth	1971–	Received a Scholar-Athlete Award from the National Football Foundation and Hall of Fame. Set school records for touchdown passes and quarterbacked several NFL teams. Named in 2002 to Jewish National Museum Sports Hall of Fame.
Gerald W. Ford	Michigan Yale Law School	1913–2006	Star center and linebacker on 1932 and 1933 national championship teams at Michigan. Coached at Yale while attending Law school. He later coached at Yale and attended Yale Law School. After a distinguished naval career in the Pacific In World War II, elected to the U.S. House of Representatives, where he served for 25 years and eventually became Minority Leader. When Richard Nixon resigned in 1974, Ford became President. Widely known for his fairness, the pardon he gave Nixon in 1974 probably led to his defeat in the 1976 election.

Name	School	Dates	Record
Ulysses S. Grant	West Point	1822–1885	An expert horseman, who set a high jump record at West Point that stood for 25 years. As a general in the Civil War, he led Union forces at the pivotal battle of Vicksburg and to ultimate victory at Appomattox. Served as U.S. President 1869–77. An avid reader at West Point, he wrote a best-selling autobiography late in life.
Mia Hamm	University of North Carolina	1972–	An above average student at the University of North Carolina, she is considered the greatest American female soccer player of all time. Led the UNC Tar Heels to four consecutive NCAA national championships from 1989–93. A two-time Olympic gold medalist, she played on two FIFA Women's World Cup championship teams.
Lyndon B. Johnson	Texas State University	1908–73	Played baseball and became an active debater in high school. Sharpened his debating skills in college. Elected in 1937 to U.S. House of Representatives and to the U.S. Senate in 1948 by only 48 votes in a total of nearly a million. In 1948 he was elected as Senate Minority Leader and became president after President John F. Kennedy's assassination in 1963. After being elected president in his own right in 1964, he secured enactment of historic civil rights legislation. Faced with growing unpopularity during the Viet Nam war he decided not to run for reelection in 1968.
Dick Kazmaier	Princeton	1930–2013	All American football player and Heisman Trophy winner, he was named Ivy League Player of the Decade in 1960. Played football, basketball, baseball and ran track and field in each year of college. Turned down offer to play football for the Chicago Bears to go to Harvard Business School.
John F. Kennedy	Harvard	1917–63	Cum laude graduate of Harvard who also attended Harvard Business School. A letter-winning swimmer at Harvard, he was a good golfer and sailor. Commanded a PT boat in the Pacific in World War II. Elected to U.S. House in 1946, the U.S. Senate in 1952 and as U.S. President in 1960. Faced the Soviets down in the Cuban Missile Crisis. Authorized a program in 1961 to land a man on the moon. Assassinated in Dallas on November 22, 1963.
Jack Kemp	Occidental College	1935–2009	Led Buffalo Bills as quarterback to three NFL Eastern Division titles between 1964 and 1968. Served nine terms as Western New York representative in Congress 1971–89. A strong advocate of civil rights, he was widely admired for his advocacy of supply side economics. Served as Secretary of Housing under President George H.W. Bush and was the Republican candidate for vice president in 1996.

Name	School	Dates	Record
Billie Jean King	Cal State LA	1943–	Although she did not graduate from college, she demonstrated her intelligence and leadership in many gender equity causes and as an author. A much-admired crusader for social justice, she won of 39 women's Grand Slam tennis titles and is considered one of the greatest to ever play the game. Inducted into International Tennis Hall of Fame. Awarded Presidential Medal of Freedom in 2009.
Jackie Joyner-Kersee	UCLA	1962–	Starred in track and field and basketball at UCLA. Won three gold, one silver and three bronze medals in heptathlon and long jump at four different Olympics. Voted by *Sports Illustrated for Women* as Greatest Female Athlete of All-Time. As founder of Jackie Joyner-Kersee Foundation, became a philanthropist in children's education, racial equality and women's rights.
Nancy Hogshead-Makar	Duke University	1962–	First woman to be awarded a swimming scholarship at Duke. Went undefeated as a collegian and became four-time ACC Champion and a two-time All American in swimming. Won three golds and one silver medal at the 1984 Olympics in Los Angeles. An excellent student, she earned a law degree from Georgetown University and later taught in law school. The founder of Champion Women, she is a leading national authority on Title IX and gender equity.
Lee McClung	Yale	1870–1914	Graduated in 1891 after a stellar career on football teams that recorded 54 wins against only two losses. As a halfback, McClung is credited with creating the cutback play. He may have been the best-known football player in the country in 1890–91. After college, he worked his way up in the railroad industry and became a senior executive with Southern Railway. He returned to Yale as its Treasurer in 1904 and was appointed U.S. Treasurer in 1909 by President Taft.
Tom McMillan	Maryland	1952–	Starred at the University of Maryland and played 11 years in the NBA. A Rhodes Scholar, he served in Congress from 1987 to 1993. He is the author of *Out of Bounds* which examines ethics in sports. Also served on the Knight Commission to reform college sports.
Ralph Metcalfe	Marquette	1910–78	Silver medal winner in 100-meter dash at the 1932 and 1936 Olympics. Won bronze medals in the 200-meter dash at the same games. Earned a master's degree at Southern Cal and later taught at Xavier University. Served in the U.S. House of Representatives representing the for the 1st District of Illinois from 1971–78.

Name	School	Dates	Record
Jack Mildren	Oklahoma	1949–2008	An Academic All-American, he achieved fame as "Godfather of the Wishbone" from his days (1969–71) as quarterback for the University of Oklahoma. Position demanded quickness, strength and intelligence. Played three seasons as a defensive back for the Baltimore Colts and New England Patriots. Served as Lt. Governor of Oklahoma from 1991–95.
Richard M. Nixon	Whitter	1913–1994	Excellent student, champion debater and member of the basketball team in High School. Played football at Whittier College. Earned law degree from Duke University and later practiced law. Served as U.S. Vice President 1953–61 and as President 1969–74. Brought Viet Nam War to an end and opened the door to a U.S.-China relationship. Forced to resign the presidency in the face of almost certain impeachment in 1974.
Aaron Molyneaux Hewitt	Harvard	1820–71	First African American at Harvard University, he was the first superintendent of physical education in American higher education. As Director and Curator of Harvard Gymnasium, he introduced many innovations in gymnastics, boxing and use of the dumb bells.
Barack Obama	Columbia	1961–	Played basketball on high school varsity. A skillful golfer. Became first black president of the Harvard Law Review and later taught at Chicago Law School. Signed many landmark bills into law, including the Affordable Care Act. Served as U.S. President 2009–17. Awarded Nobel Prize for Peace in 2009. In 2018, a Gallup poll found him to be the most admired man in American for the 11th consecutive year.
Tom Osborne	Hastings College	1937–	Earned both a master's and a doctorate in educational psychology at the University of Nebraska. Played quarterback and wide receiver at Hastings College. Coached football at Nebraska 1973–97, winning three national championships. Served as Nebraska Athletic Director. Inducted into College Football Hall of Fame in 1999. Served three terms in the U.S. House of Representatives from Nebraska's 3rd congressional district (2001–07).
Alan Page	Notre Dame	1945–	Led Notre Dame to a national championship in 1966 and was named an All-American. First defensive player to win NFL's Most Valuable Player Award. Earned law degree at University of Minnesota and later served as an associate justice on Minnesota Supreme Court. Awarded the Presidential Medal of Freedom in 2018.
Amy Perko	Wake Forest	1965–	Has served as Chief Executive of the Knight Commission on Intercollegiate Athletics since 2005. Named to Wake Forest University Sports Hall of Fame, she was a three-time Academic All-American in basketball.

Name	School	Dates	Record
Fritz Pollard	Brown	1894–1986	Played halfback on a Brown University team that went to the Rose Bowl in 1916. A chemistry major, he was named an All-American. Broke the color line in pro football in the early 1920s when he led the Akron Pros to league championship of what later became the NFL. Served as head coach of Akron Pros in 1921, the first black to hold that position. Named to two football halls of fame posthumously. In 1981, Brown University conferred an honorary Doctor of Laws on Pollard.
Ronald Reagan	Eureka College	1911–2004	Although an average student, he excelled in campus politics, sports and theater. Became a play-by-play announcer of Chicago Cubs baseball on WHO Des Moines, in the early 1930s. Took a screen test in 1937 that led to a seven-year contract with Warner Bros. Starred in 1940 in the widely praised film, *Knute Rockne, All-American* about a legendary Notre Dame football coach. Elected President of the Screen Actors Guild in 1947. Served as California governor, 1967–75. Elected U.S. President in 1980 and reelected in 1984. An advocate of supply side economics, the economy was revived during his administration. An avid horseback rider, he returned to California, where he lived in the Bel Air section of Los Angeles and on his Santa Barbara ranch.
Craig Robinson	Princeton	1962–	The brother of former first lady, Michelle Obama, he starred in basketball at Princeton and later earned a MBA in finance from the University of Chicago. He served as head basketball coach at Brown University and Oregon State University. Became an ESPN basketball analyst in 2014.
Paul Robeson	Rutgers	1898–1976	A two-time All-American and class valedictorian at Rutgers, who later earned a law degree from Columbia University. His powerful bass voice made him an international singing sensation in the 1920s. Perhaps best known for his role in the Broadway musical, "Show Boat." A strong social conscience led to his identification with leftwing causes. And his pro-Soviet leanings made him a target of McCarthy era investigations, causing his income and status to sink significantly.
Myron Rolle	Florida State	1986–	Bahamian American who starred in football at Florida State and was named as a third team All-American. Turned down the chance to play professional when awarded in 2009 a Rhodes Scholarship to study at Oxford University. Earned a degree in medical anthropology there. Graduated from FSU medical school in 2017. Began a residency in 2017 in neurology at Massachusetts General Hospital and Harvard University.

Name	School	Dates	Record
Teddy Roosevelt	Harvard	1858–1919	A sickly child plagued by asthma, he discovered the benefits of physical exertion early in life and became an advocate of manly sports and outdoor adventures. In 1898, exhibited great personal bravery in leading the Rough Riders in their famed charge up Kettle Hill in the Spanish-American War. Elected governor of New York in 1898 and began to shape principles that would shape his presidency. Elected U.S. Vice President in 1898 and became president in 1901 when then-President William McKinley was assassinated in Buffalo, NY. Serving in that office until 1909, he was a widely praised "trust buster" who broke up large oil, railroad and other businesses. He personally mediated an end to the Russo-Japanese War in 1905 and was awarded the Nobel Peace Prize for his role in achieving a settlement of that conflict.
Frank Ryan	Rice	1936–	Played quarterback for Rice University and later for the Los Angeles Rams, Cleveland Browns and Washington Redskins. Earned a PhD in mathematics while still playing football. Became athletic director and lecturer in mathematics at Yale University in 1977 and Yale's Associate Vice President for Institutional Planning in 1987. Assisted U.S. House of Representatives in installing its first electronic voting system.
Jim Ryan	Kansas	1947–	The last American to hold the world record for the mile run. Participated in the '64, '68 and '72 Summer Olympics. Played instrumental role in devising a program to help children with hearing loss. Elected in 1996 to U.S. House of Representatives for 2nd District of Kansas. Served there until 2007. In 2006, the *National Journal* rated Ryan the most conservative member of Congress.
Amos Alonzo Stagg	Yale University	1862–1965	Played football at Yale and was named in 1899 to the first college football All-America team. Inducted into the College Football Hall of Fame as a player and coach in 1951. Earned fame as football coach at the University of Chicago, where he introduced many innovations, including the center snap and the onside kick. Coached two national championship teams at Chicago and compiled a career coaching record of 314 wins, 199 losses and 25 ties. Earning a divinity degree at Yale, he forged a bond between sports and religion in his life.
Pat Summitt	Tennessee-Martin	1952–2016	As women's basketball coach the University of Tennessee, her teams won 1,098 games and eight national championships—the most by any women's coach. She played on a silver medal-winning team in the 1976 and returned to the Olympics in 1984 as head U.S. women's coach. A good student in college, The *Sporting News* placed her at number 11 among the 50 greatest coach of all time. She was the only woman on the list. She authored or co-authored three books, she was awarded the Presidential Medal of Freedom in 2012.

Name	School	Dates	Record
Duke Slater	Iowa	1898–1966	Among the greatest black football players in the 1920s, he starred at Iowa and played professional football for ten years—first for the Milwaukee Badgers, then for the Rock Island Independents and last for the Chicago Cardinals of the NFL. He was elected to the inaugural College Football Hall of Fame in 1951. When he retired as a professional in 1931, he'd been named all-pro seven times. Slater earned a law degree at Iowa in 1928 and practiced law in the last few years of his pro career. After he left the sport, he became a prominent judge in Chicago—the first of his race to serve in several judicial positions.
Morris Udall	Arizona	1922–98	Lost his right eye in an accident at age six and wore a glass eye the rest of his life. A star in basketball at the University of Arizona, he served as president of the student government. Played pro basketball one year for the Denver Nuggets. Earned a law degree from the University of Arizona in 1949. Served in the U.S. House of Representatives from 1961 to 1991. Succeeded his brother, Stewart, who was named Interior Secretary by President Kennedy. In 1976, he was a leading candidate for the Democratic nomination for president.
Byron White	Colorado	1917–2002	Finished as valedictorian of his high school class and at the University of Colorado. Finished at the top of his law school class at Yale. A three-sport star at Colorado, he led the Buffaloes to an undefeated regular season in 1937. Named an All American that year, he was runner-up for the Heisman Trophy. A star in the NFL, he led the league in rushing in 1938 as a 21-year-old-rookie at Pittsburg. Accepted a Rhodes Scholar in 1939 to study at Oxford University. Attended law school on returning to the U.S. and served in the South Pacific in World War II. Appointed in 1962 by President Kennedy as an associate justice of the U.S. Supreme Court, where he served until 1993. Wrote a landmark dissent in 1984 in NCAA v Oklahoma Board of Regents that declared that the NCAA's television plan for member schools violated the Sherman Antitrust Act. His predictions that college games would become highly commercialized have come true.
John Wideman	Pennsylvania	1941–	An All-Ivy League forward in basketball and the second African-American to be named a Rhodes Scholar in 1962. The only winner of two Pen-Faulkner Awards, he has been widely praised for his novels and teaching.

Name	School	Dates	Record
Woodrow Wilson	Johns Hopkins	1856–1924	Elected secretary of the Princeton Football Association and president of the school's baseball association. Graduated from Princeton in 1879 and earned a PhD in history from Johns Hopkins University in 1886. He became a skilled speaker and prolific author as a member of the Princeton faculty. In 1902 he became the school's president. His reform efforts there earned him national notoriety. He became Governor of New Jersey in 1910 and was elected U.S. President in 1912. He won reelection four years later on a pledge to keep the U.S. out of World War I. Even so, Congress approved Wilson's request for a declaration of war in April 1917. At war's end, Wilson enunciated a 14-point plan for peace that included formation of a League of Nations which was ultimately rejected by the I.S. Senate.
Barry Wood	Harvard	1910–1971	Harvard quarterback named an All-American in 1931. One of the best quarterbacks of his time, he was elected to the College Football Hall of Fame in 1981. Wood earned 10 varsity letters, three each in football, hockey and baseball. Served as president of the student council, elected to Phi Beta Kappa and graduated summa cum laude. He became a leading academic in the fields of medicine and microbiology. At 32, he was named head of the Department of Medicine at Washington University in St. Louis.
Dwayne Woodruff	Louisville	1957–	Earned a law degree from Duquesne University in 1988 while still playing professional football. Elected in 2005 as judge of the Court of Common Pleas in Susquehanna County, Pennsylvania. An all-time great player for the Pittsburg Steelers He has been elected to several halls of fame.

U.S. Presidents Who Were Scholar-Athletes

George H. W. Bush   First baseman for Yale University in the 1940s, playing in the first two College World Series. Played tennis; also skydived on his 85th birthday.

George W. Bush   Ran a marathon at age 43 and sub-seven-minute miles years later. Soon after 9/11, he threw a perfect strike while wearing a bullet-proof vest to open game three of the World Series at Yankee Stadium.

Jimmy Carter   Played on the Plains High School basketball team.

Bill Clinton   Played rugby as a Rhodes Scholar at Oxford; became a good golfer as an adult.

Gerald R. Ford   All-American at the University of Michigan, who played on two national championship teams. He was the team's Most Valuable Player in 1934. He swam, ran and played tennis in his youth and played golf as an adult.

Dwight D. Eisenhower   A West Point linebacker, Ike battled Jim Thorpe in the 1912 Army-Carlisle game, trying to knock the college great out of the game to help the Cadets win.

Ulysses S. Grant   An expert horseman, he and his horse set a high-jump record at West Point that stood for 25 years.

Lyndon B. Johnson   Played baseball in high school.

John F. Kennedy   A letter-winning swimmer at Harvard and a good golfer.

Abraham Lincoln   An outstanding wrestler, he was defeated only once in approximately 300 matches. A member of the National Wrestling Hall of Fame.

Richard M. Nixon   Played football at Whittier College. Had bowling installed at the White House. Once gave Redskins Coach George Allen a play.

Barack Obama   Played basketball on his high school varsity. An avid and skillful golfer.

Ronald Reagan   Reportedly saved 77 people during seven years as a lifeguard. Also an avid horseback rider. Though an average student, he more than made up for that through debating and other extra-curricula activities.

Teddy Roosevelt   A skillful boxer at Harvard and a participant in rowing. He was a lifelong outdoorsman and advocate of "the strenuous life."

Woodrow Wilson   Played center field at Davidson, but didn't make the team at Harvard. He was an avid golfer as an adult.

BIBLIOGRAPHY

Blackwell, James. *On Brave Old Army Team: The Cheating Scandal That Rocked the Nation: West Point, 1951*. Novato, CA: Presidio Press, 1996.

Bowen, William C., and Levin, Sarah A. *Reclaiming the Game, College Sports and Educational Values*. Princeton, NJ: Princeton University Press, 2005.

Byers, Walter with Hammer, Charles. *Unsportsmanlike Conduct, Exploiting College Athletes*. Ann Arbor: The University of Michigan Press, 1998.

Clotfelter, Charles T. *Big-Time Sports in American Universities*. New York: Cambridge University Press, 2011.

Crawford, Matthew B. *Shop Class as Soulcraft: An Inquiry into the Value of Work*. New York: Penguin Books, 2009.

Duberman, Martin. *Paul Robeson: A Biography*. New York: The New Press, 1989.

Finley, M.I. and Picket, H.W. *The Olympic Games: The First Thousand Years*. Massachusetts: Courier Corporation, 2012.

Fort, Rodney and Winfree, Jason. *15 Sports Myths and Why They're Wrong*. Stanford, CA: Stanford Economics and Finance, an Imprint of Stanford University Press, 2013.

Gildea, Dennis, *Hoops Crazy: The Lives of Clair Bee and Chip Hilton*. Fayetteville, AR, Universityof Arkansas Press, 2013.

Gurney, Gerald, Lopiano, Donna A., and Zimbalist, Andrew. *Unwinding Madness: What Went Wrong with College Sports and How to Fix it*. Washington, DC: Brookings Institution Press, 2017.

Hoberman, John. *Darwin's Athletes: How Sport Has Damaged Black America and Preserved the Myth of Race*. New York: Houghton Mifflin Company, 1997.

Kyle, Donald D., and Wiley, John. *Sport and Spectacle in the Ancient World*. New Jersey: John Wiley and Sons, 2014.

Llewellyn, Matthew P., and Gleaves, John. *The Rise and Fall of Olympic Amateurism*. Champaign: University of Illinois Press, 2016.

McIntire, Mike. *Champions Way: Football, Florida and the Lost Soul of College Sports*. New York: W. W. Norton & Company, 2017.

Nocera, Joe. *Indentured: The Inside Story of the Rebellion Against the NCAA*. New York: Portfolio/Penguin, 2016.

Oriard, Michael. *King Football: Sport and Spectacle in the Golden Age of Radio and Newsreels, Movies and Magazines, the Weekly and the Daily Press*. Chapel Hill: University of North Carolina Press, 2001.

Oriard, Michael. *Reading Football: How the Popular Press Created an American Spectacle*. Chapel Hill: University of North Carolina Press, 1993.

Postman, Neil. *Amusing Ourselves to Death: Public Discourse in the Age of Show Business*. New York: Penguin Books, 1985.

Radar, Benjamin G. *American Sports, from the Age of Folk Games to the Age of Televised Sports*. Lincoln, NE: Pearson Prentice Hall, University of Nebraska, 1990.

Reed, Ken. *How We Can Save Sports, A Game Plan*. Maryland: Rowman and Littlefield Publishing Group, Inc., 2015.

Robeson, Paul *Here I Stand. Boston: Beacon Press, 1958.*

Sack, Allen L., and Staurowsky, Ellen J. *College Athletes for Hire: The Evolution and Legacy of the NCAA's Amateur Myth*. Connecticut: Praeger Publishers, 1998.

Shulman, James L., and Bowen, William G. *The Game of Life: College Sports and Educational Values*. Princeton, NJ: Princeton University Press, 2001.

Smith, Ronald A. *Sports and Freedom: The Rise of Big Time College Athletics*. New York: Oxford University Press, 1990.

Sparrow, Jeff. *No Way But This: In Search of Paul Robeson*. Melbourne: Scribe Publications, 2018.

Sperber, Murray. *Beer and Circus: How Big Time College Sports is Crippling Undergraduate Education*. New York: Holt Paperbacks, Henry Holt and Company, 2000.

Sperber, Murray. *Onward to Victory: The Crises that Shaped College Sports*. New York: Henry Holt and Company, 1998.

Sperber, Murray. *Shake Down the Thunder: The Creation of Notre Dame Football*. Bloomington: Indiana University Press, 2002.

Summitt, Pat with Sally Jenkins. *Sum It Up*. New York: Three Rivers Press, 2013.

Syed, Matthew. *Bounce: The Myth of Talent and the Power of Practice*. London: Fourth Estate (Harper Collins), 2010.

Thelin, John, and Wiseman, Lawrence. *The Old College Try: Balancing Athletics and Academics in Higher Education*. Ashe-Eric Higher Educ Reports, 1989.

Wagg, Stephen, ed. *Myths and Milestones in the History of Sport*. UK: Palgrave McMillan, 2011.

Watterson, John Sayle. *College Football: History, Spectacle, Controversy.* Baltimore and London: The Johns Hopkins University Press, 2000.

Wiggins, David K. *Out of the Shadows: A Biographical History of African-American Athletes.* Fayetteville: University of Arkansas Press, 2006.

NOTES

Introduction ¤ Declining American Values

1. Ronald A. Smith, *Sports and Freedom: The Rise of Big-Time Athletics* (New York: Oxford University Press, 1988), p. 96.
2. Daniel A. Clark, *Creating the College Man: American Mass Magazines and Middle-Class Manhood, 1890–1915* (Madison: University of Wisconsin Press, 2010), p. 89.
3. Google Ngrams charting the frequency of search terms (see Google Ngram viewer).
4. Clark, *Creating the College Man*, p. 35.
5. *NCAA v. Board of Regents of the University of Oklahoma*, dissent of Justices White and Rehnquist, Part II, June 27, 1984.
6. Paula Lavigne, "Rich Get Richer in College Sports as Poorer Schools Struggle to Keep Up," espn.com, September 6, 2016.
7. "College Sports Tainted by Bounties, Carnegie Fund Finds in Wide Study," *New York Times,* October 24, 1929.
8. Ira Berkow, "Sport of the Times: The Grapes of Wrath at Oklahoma," *New York Times,* February 18, 1989.

One ¤ A Brief History of College Sports

1. Robert J. Higgs, "Yale and the Heroic Ideal, Gotterdammerung and Palingenesis, 1865–1914," in *Manliness and Morality: Middle-Class Masculinity in Britain and America, 1800–1940*, ed. J. A. Mangan and James Walvin (New York: St. Martin's Press, 1987), p. 160.
2. The Connecticut Society of the Sons of the American Revolution, *Nathan Hale and the House of Goose Bumps,* www.conecticut.org/nathan_hale_and_the-house_of_g/.
3. Higgs, "Yale and the Heroic Ideal," p. 160.

4. Daniel A. Clark, *Creating the College Man: American Mass Magazines and Middle-Class Manhood, 1890–1915* (Madison: University of Wisconsin Press, 2010), p. 116.

5. *Ibid.*, p. 81.

6. Benjamin G. Radar, *American Sports: From the Age of Folk Games to the Age of Televised Sports* (Upper Saddle River, NJ: Pearson/Prentice Hall, 2009), p. 92.

7. Ronald A. Smith, *Sports and Freedom: The Rise of Big-Time Athletics* (New York: Oxford University Press, 1988), p. 89.

8. *Ibid.*, p. 27.

9. *Ibid.*, p. 29.

10. *Ibid.*, p. 38–42.

11. Luann Bishop, "Historic Tidbits About the Game," Yale News, March 3, 2016.

12. *Baily's Magazine of Sports and Pastimes,* Volume 57.

13. Steven W. Pope, "Negotiating the 'Folk Highway' of the Nation: Sport, Public Culture and American Identity, 1870–1940," *Journal of Sports History* 27, no. 2: p. 328.

14. Richard P. Borkowski, *The Life and Contributions of Walter Camp to American Football,* thesis, Temple University.

15. John S. Watterson, "The Gridiron Crisis of 1905: Was it a Crisis?" *Journal of Sports History* 27, no. 3: p. 294.

16. Smith, *Sports and Freedom,* p. 93.

17. Christopher Klein, "How Teddy Roosevelt Saved Football," www.history.com, September 6, 2012.

18. Radar, *American Sports,* p. 94.

19. Klein, "How Teddy Roosevelt Saved Football."

20. S. E. Morison, Harvard historian. *Three Centuries of Harvard, 1636–1936.* Cambridge: *The Belknap Press of Harvard University,* p. 24.

21. Radar, *American Sports,* p. 94.

22. James Mennell, "The Service Football Program of World War I," *Journal of Sports History* 16, no. 3: p. 248.

23. Mark Inabinett, *Grantland Rice and His Heroes* (Knoxville: University of Tennessee Press, 2009), p. 87.

24. Gerald Gurney, Donna Lopiano, and Andrew Zimbalist, *Unwinding Madness: What Went Wrong with College Sports and How to Fix It* (Washington: Brookings Institution Press, 2017), p. 12.

25. Charles Clotfelter, "Big-Time College Athletics 80 Years Later," *Duke Today,* October 27, 2009.

26. Gurney, Lopiano, and Zimbalist, *Unwinding Madness,* p. 12.

27. Radar, *American Sports,* p. 107.

28. Murray Sperber, *Onward to Victory: The Crises That Shaped College Sports* (New York: Henry Holt and Company, 1998), p. 369, 372.

29. *Ibid.*, p. 286.

30. *Ibid.*, p. 376.

31. *Ibid.*, p. 376.

Two ¤ Towering Achievers

1. Steven W. Pope, "Negotiating the 'Folk Highway' of the Nation: Sport, Public Culture and American Identity, 1870–1940," *Journal of Sports History* 27, no. 2.

2. *Ibid.*, p. 328.

3. *Ibid.*, p. 327.

4. "Sherman's Field Order No. 15," in *New Georgia Encyclopedia,* edited by Chris Dobbs, June 8, 2017.

5. Jared A. Ball, *I Mix What I Like! A Mixed Tape Manifesto* (Oakland: AK Press, 2011), p. 156.

6. Evan J. Albright, "Blazing the Trail," *Amherst Magazine*, Winter 2007.

7. *Ibid.*

8. *Ibid.*

9. *Ibid.*

10. Wiggins, David K, editor of *Out of the Shadows: A Biographical History of African American Athletes;* chapter by Gregory Bond, "The Strange Career of William Henry Lewis," (Fayetteville: University of Arkansas Press, 2006), p. 42–43.

11. *Ibid.*

12. *Ibid.*

13. *Ibid.*, p. 45.

14. *Ibid.*, p. 46–47.

15. *Ibid.*, p. 50. (Note: This is a secondary source. Bond cites the original as Emmet Jay Scott and Lyman Beecher Stowe, *Booker T. Washington, Builder of a Civilization* (Garden City, NY: Doubleday and Company, 1916).

16. *Ibid.*, p. 52.

17. *Ibid.*, p. 52–53.

18. *Ibid.*, p. 54

19. Dennis J. Hutchinson, *The Man Who Once Was Whizzer White: A Portrait of Justice Byron R. White* (New York: The Free Press), p. 1.

20. *Ibid.*, p. 43–45.

21. Andrew G. Schultz and David M. Ebel, "Tribute to Supreme Court Justice Byron R. White," 51 *University of Kansas Law Review*, 213 (2002) p. 215.

22. Hutchinson, *The Man Who Once Was Whizzer White*, p. 20–22.
23. *Ibid.*, p. 47–48.
24. *Ibid.*, p. 60.
25. *Ibid.*, p. 89–94.
26. *Ibid.*, p. 134–135.
27. *Ibid.*, p. 141–143.
28. *Ibid.*, p. 157.
29. *Ibid.*, p. 157.
30. *Ibid.*, p. 173–176.
31. *Ibid.*, p. 175–178.
32. *Ibid.*, p. 191–192.
33. Joan Biskupic, "Ex-Supreme Court Justice Byron White Dies," *USA Today*, April 15, 2002.
34. Sally Jenkins, "NCAA Lost Its Teeth in Court in 1984, and No One's Been in Charge Since," *Washington Post*, September 23, 2011; also, *NCAA v. Board of Regents, University of Oklahoma*, dissent by Justices Byron White and William Rehnquist, Part I, June 6, 1984, Part II.

Three ¤ The Rise of Iconic Women

1. Women's Sports Foundation website, https://www.womenssportsfoundation.org/, September 2, 2016.
2. *Ibid.*
3. Joanne Lannin, *Billie Jean King: Tennis Trailblazer* (Minneapolis: Lerner Publications Company, 1999), p. 72.
4. Barbara Wells Sarudy, 19th Century American Women, http://womeninushistory.tripod.com/, February 14, 2014.
5. Pat Summitt with Sally Jenkins, *Sum It Up: 1,098 Victories, A Couple of Irrelevant Losses, and a Life in Perspective* (New York: Three Rivers Press, 2013), p. 79.
6. Kyle Boone, "UNC women's basketball coach resigns. . .", CBS Sports, www.cbsnews.com, April 19, 2019.
7. Spenser Davis, "Duke's Mike Krzyzewski Praises Vols Legend Pat Summitt After Breaking All-Time Wins Record," *Atlanta Journal-Constitution*, March, 17, 2019.
8. Interview with Allen Paul, January 19, 2018.
9. Marcus Noland and Tyler Moran, "Study: Firms with More Women in the C-Suite are more Profitable, *Harvard Business Review*, October 9, 2014.
10. Interview with Allen Paul, February 2, 2018.

Four ¤ The Mirror of Public Ideals

1. Michael Oriard, *Reading Football: How the Popular Press Created an American Spectacle* (Chapel Hill: University of North Carolina Press, 1993), p. 191.

2. Daniel J. Clark, *Creating the College Man: American Mass Magazines and Middle-Class Manhood, 1890–1915* (Madison: University of Wisconsin Press, 2010), p. 86.

3. *Ibid.*, p. 86.

4. Oriard, *Reading Football*, p. 61.

5. *Ibid.*, p. 59.

6. *Ibid.*, p. 61.

7. John Sayle Watterson, Biographical Essay in Appendix, *College Football: History, Spectacle, Controversy* (Baltimore and London: The Johns Hopkins University Press, 2000).

8. *Ibid.*, p. 69.

9. *Ibid.*, Appendix.

10. *Ibid.*, p. 78–79.

11. *Ibid.*, p. 21.

12. *Ibid.*, p. 21–22.

13. *Ibid.*, p. 76.

14. *Ibid.*, p. 127–129.

15. Frank Boyle, "Frank Merriwell's Triumph: How Yale's Great Athlete Captured America's Fancy, or, Purified the Penny Dreadfuls and Became Immortal," *Vault/Sports Illustrated*, December 24, 1962.

16. *Ibid.*

17. Alexander Nazaryan, "Stover at Yale Turns 100: But Don't Worry, His Ivy League is Still Alive and Well," *New York Daily News*, October 10, 2012.

18. Thomas M. Frank, "Sporting Legend Returns," *New York Daily News*, August 4, 2002.

19. Michael Oriard, *King Football: Sport and Spectacle in the Golden Age of Radio and Newsreels, Movies and Magazines, the Weekly and the Daily Press* (Chapel Hill: University of North Carolina Press, 2001), p. 103, 214.

20. *Ibid.*, p. 103–105.

21. *Bulletin 23 of the Carnegie Foundation for the Advancement of Higher Education*, New York, 1929.

22. *Ibid.*

23. Oriard, *King Football*, p. 106.

24. Gerald Gurney, Donna A. Lopiano, and Andrew Zimbalist, *Unwinding Madness: What Went Wrong with College Sports and How to Fix It* (Washington, DC: The Brookings Institution, 2017), p. 12.

25. "McMillian's Brilliant Sprint Gives Centre Victory over Harvard," *St. Louis Post Dispatch,* October 30, 1921.

26. "Chicago Legend Passes On. Berwanger Dies at 88," *University of Chicago Chronicle,* July 11, 2002.

27. "The Top 11 Scenes in Football Movie History," www.espn.com, April 4, 2008.

28. Murray Sperber, *Shake Down the Thunder: The Creation of Notre Dame Football* (Bloomington and Indianapolis: Indiana University Press, 1993), p. 465. Murray Sperber provides rich accounts of the Rockne Era at Notre Dame and the making of Warner Brothers' 1940 film *Knute Rockne: All American* in his books *Onward to Victory* and *Shake Down the Thunder.* He was granted full access to the Rockne files at Notre Dame and was the first researcher to examine them. The quotation cited can be found on page 11 of *Onward to Victory.*

29. *Ibid.,* p. 12.

30. *Ibid.,* p. 10.

31. *Ibid.,* p. 474.

32. *Ibid.,* Oriard, p. 316.

Five ¤ Shattered Ideals

1. The account that follows is based largely on detailed descriptions in Charley Rosen's *Scandals of '51: How the Gamblers Almost Killed College Basketball* (New York: Seven Stories Press, 1999).

2. Frank Litsky, "Junius Kellogg Is Dead at 71; Refused Bribe in '50s Scandal," *New York Times,* September 18, 1988.

3. *Ibid.*

4. Rosen, *Scandals of '51,* p. 2.

5. Litsky, "Junius Kellogg is Dead at 71."

6. Rosen, *Scandals of '51,* p. 3.

7. *Ibid.,* p. 3.

8. *Ibid.,* p. 4.

9. *Ibid.,* p. 5.

10. Murray Sperber, "Scandal/Scoundrel Game," in *Onward to Victory: The Creation of Modern College Sports* (New York: Henry Holt, 1998), p. 302.

11. Rosen, *Scandals of '51,* p. 6.

12. Joe Goldstein, "Explosion: 1951 Scandals Threaten College Hoops," ESPN Classics (www.espn.com), November 19, 2003.

13. Rosen, *Scandals of '51,* p. 7.

14. Litsky, "Junius Kellogg is Dead at 71."

15. Sperber, "Scandal/Scoundrel Game," p. 307.

16. *Ibid.*, p. 306.

17. *Ibid.*, p. 306.

18. William F. Reed, "Hidden World," *Sports Illustrated,* November 6, 2017, p. 71.

19. *Ibid.*, p. 72.

20. *Ibid.*, p. 73.

21. *Ibid.*, p. 73.

22. *Ibid.*, p. 73.

23. *Ibid.*, p. 72.

24. Wright Thompson, "For the 1951 Point Shavers, a Life Lived in Infamy," www.espn.com, August 9, 2007.

25. Sperber, "Scandal/Scoundrel Game," p. 307.

26. *Ibid.*, p. 332.

27. *Ibid.*, p. 308.

28. *Ibid.*, p. 334–345.

29. Richard H. Parke, "West Point Ousts 90 Cadets for Cheating in Classroom; Football Players Involved," *New York Times,* August 4, 1951.

30. "The Big Money," *Time Magazine,* February 26, 1951.

31. Frank Deford, "Code Breakers: Fifty Years Ago, Red Blaik's Powerhouse at Army," *Sports Illustrated,* November 13, 2000. In *Brave Old Army Team: The Cheating Scandal That Rocked the Nation: West Point, 1951*, author James Blackwell describes the colloquial "poop" as information being fed by tutors in the academy's cheating scandal. His book provides a comprehensive look at how the scandal developed, expanded and, ultimately, was detected.

32. Deford, "Code Breakers."

33. Sperber, "Scandal/Scoundrel Game," p. 354–355.

34. Martin Duberman, *Paul Robeson: A Biography* (New York: The New Press, 1989), p. 19. NOTE: In the rich literature on the life and impact of Paul Robeson, Duberman's biography stands out for its meticulous research and often stirring prose. The author has relied in this brief account primarily on Duberman's work. Robeson's own account, *Here I Stand,* written in 1953, is noteworthy for the insights it provides into why Robeson became so enamored with the Soviet Union and the passion he developed for colonial peoples. *No Way But This: In Search of Paul Robeson* by Jeff Sparrow, an Australian, is a useful, on-site investigation of Robeson's worldwide travels and how he is remembered in various locales.

35. *Ibid.*, p. 18.

36. Duberman, *Paul Robeson*, p. 284–285.

37. *Ibid.*, p. 286.
38. Anthony Tommasini, "Classical View; Of Basses, Baritones and Hedges," *New York Times,* April 19, 1998.
39. *Ibid.*, p. 286.
40. *Ibid.*, p. 118.
41. *Ibid.*, p. 119.
42. *Ibid.*, p. 185.
43. *Ibid.*, p. 189–190.
44. *Ibid.*, p. 317.
45. *Ibid.*, p. 320.
46. *Ibid.*, p. 342.
47. *Ibid.*, p. 497–499.
48. *Ibid.*, p. 516–517.
49. *Ibid.*, p. 538.
50. *Ibid.*, p. 539, 549.
51. *Ibid.*, p. 549–550.

Six ¤ Moral Collapse

1. Kristen Sheely interview with Allen Paul, February 12, 2018.
2. Ken Sheely interview with Allen Paul, February 24, 2018.
3. Kristen Sheely interview with Allen Paul, February 12, 2018.
4. Ken Sheely interview with Allen Paul, February 24, 2018.
5. Third Amended Complaint, *Kristen L. Sheely, et al., plaintiffs v. NCAA, et al., defendants*, Montgomery County, Maryland, Circuit Court, December 3, 2014.
6. Ken Sheely interview with Allen Paul, May 21, 2018.
7. Third Amended Complaint.
8. *Ibid.*
9. *Ibid.*
10. *Ibid.*
11. *Ibid.*
12. *Ibid.*
13. Anna McFarland interview with Allen Paul, May 20, 2018.
14. *Ibid.*
15. Ken Sheely interview with Allen Paul, February 24, 2018.
16. *Ibid.*
17. *Ibid.*
18. Kristen Sheely interview with Allen Paul, February 12, 2018.

19. *Ibid.*
20. Ken Sheely interview with Allen Paul, February 24, 2018.
21. Text of Ken Sheely remarks at Derek Sheely Memorial Service, December 1, 2011, p. 11.
22. Matt Crossman, "Sharing Derek Sheely," SB Nation, https://www.sbnation.com/longform/2013/12/17/5217634/sharing-derek-sheely-a-helmet-to-helmet- hit-took-the-life-of-a-22, December 1, 2013.
23. Text of Ken Sheely remarks at Derek Sheely Memorial Service, p. 3.
24. Email from Brandon Henderson to info@thedereksheelyfoundation, March 22, 2012.
25. Kristen Sheely interview with Allen Paul, February 12, 2018.
26. Paul Anderson interview with Allen Paul, March 16, 2018.
27. *Ibid.*
28. Associated Press, "Lawyers Announce $1.2M Settlement of Lawsuit Filed by Derek Sheely's Parents," espn.com, August 8, 2016.
29. Michael Dresser, "NCAA, State Reach Settlement in Case of Frostburg Football Player Who Died After Head Injury," *Baltimore Sun,* July 27, 2016.
30. Jon Solomon, "Life After Football Death," CBSSports.com, August 26, 2015.
31. Email from Ken Sheely to Allen Paul, May 18, 2018.

Seven ¤ Molding High Achievers

1. Matthew Sayed, *Bounce: The Myth of Talent and the Power of Practice* (London: Fourth Estate (HarperCollins Publishers, 2010), p. 12.
2. *Ibid.*, p. 12.
3. *Ibid.*, 15.
4. *Ibid.*, p. 3–6.

Eight ¤ The Passionate Professional

Transcribed interviews with David and Roberta Robinson between October 2016 and February 2017.

Nine ¤ The Gold Standard of Courage

1. Transcribed interviews with Nancy Hogshead-Makar between October 2017 and February 2019.
2. "Tell Me When It's Over," interview with Rob Trucks, *Deadspin* (an ESPN website), July 31, 2012.

3. *Ibid.*

4. *Ibid.*

5. Transcribed interviews with Nancy Hogshead-Makar between October 2017 and February 2019.

6. *Ibid.*

7. Transcribed interviews with Nancy Hogshead-Makar between October 2017 and February 2019.

8. Joe Schwartz, "Bill Friday surveys the state of college sports (full interview)," *Indy Weekly* (Durham, NC), August 31, 2011.

Ten ¤ Miracles in Guatemala

Transcribed interviews with Chip Davis, his family, Rev. Linda McCarty and Joe and Vera Wiatt between January 2017 and February 2018.

Eleven ¤ The Spartan Way

Transcribed interviews with Will, Amy and Betty White, Skip Finkbonner, Austin Gower, Ken Henson and Jim Latham between January 2016 and August 2018.

Twelve ¤ The Public Intellectual

1. Caille Millner, "Fashion Victims?" *Harvard Magazine,* May 1, 2000.

2. *Ibid.*

3. John Seabrook, "Nobrow Culture," *The New Yorker,* September 20, 1999.

4. Interview with John Stauffer, September 11, 2018.

5. Syllabus, "American Protest Literature," prepared/taught by John Stauffer, spring semester, 2002.

6. Interview with John Stauffer, September 11, 2018.

7. *Ibid.*

8. John Stauffer, *The Black Hearts of Men: Radical Abolitionists and the Transformation of Race* (Cambridge, MA: Harvard University Press, 2001).

9. Books of limited edition photography feature handmade books by artisans, often with platinum prints. From 50 to 70 copies generally are sold to libraries and large private collections.

10. Interview with Zoe Trodd, January 19, 2016.

11. Interview with Manisha Sinha, December 20, 2016.

12. Neil Postman, *Amusing Ourselves to Death: Public Discourse in the Age of Show Business* (New York: Penguin Books, 1985), p. xix.

Thirteen ¤ A Life in Full

Transcribed interviews with Mark Meyers between October 2016 and April 2018.

Fourteen ¤ The Ripple Effect

1. The account of the earthquake's impact was drawn largely from the *Encyclopedia Britannica.*
2. This chapter is based on transcribed interviews with Paul Auerbach between August and October 2018.

Fifteen ¤ A Road Trip Down South

1. Contests, players and results in the first six paragraphs of Chapter Fifteen are documented in annual report brochures in Duke athletic archives.

Sixteen ¤ Nineteen in a Row

1. Much of the material for this chapter are drawn from UNC Tennis archives, http://www.netitor.com/photos/schools/unc/sport/m-tennis/auto_pdf/unc-mtenhistory.pdf, p. 8.
2. Interviews with Mike McMahon on October 11 and 12, 2018.
3. *Ibid.*
4. Ibid., UNC Tennis archives.
5. *Ibid.*, p. 9.
6. *Ibid.*, p. 10.
7. *Ibid.*, p. 10.
8. Kip Coons, "Duke Ends Clemson Win Streak," *Durham Herald-Sun,* April 5, 1982.
9. Neil Amdur, "Dickson Moving Up and Fast," *New York Times,* May 1, 1983.
10. Frank Dascenzo, "'Grudge Win' Duke's Biggest Ever," *Durham Herald-Sun,* April 5, 1982.
11. *Ibid.*
12. Kip Coons, "Duke Ends Clemson Win Streak," *Durham Herald-Sun,* April 5, 1982.

13. Ron Morris, "Arlosoroff Beats Odds, Duke's Foes," *Durham Herald-Sun,* April 16, 1982.
14. J.A. Allen, "Golden Era of the '80s: Tennis Soars in Popularity," *Bleacher Report* (on-line), October 15, 2009.
15. John Koblin, "Tennis Television Ratings Tumble," *Observer* (on-line), September 4, 2010. The Neilson rating (the percentage of televisions around the Country Tuned In For Tennis) was 9.9.

Seventeen   ¤   Unexpected Endings

1. Memorandum from Chuck Kriese to R.W. Robinson, Associate Director of Athletics, Clemson University, April 26, 1982.
2. U.S. Court of Appeals for the Fourth Circuit ruling on October 25, 1984, p. 3.
3. "Reinstatement of Chaim Arlosoroff's Eligibility," Memorandum from Duke University to NCAA Council, undated.
4. *Ibid.*
5. Letter from Tom Butters, Duke Director of Athletics, August 2, 1982.
6. *Ibid.*
7. "Reinstatement of Chaim Arlosoroff's Eligibility," p. 3.
8. U.S. Court of Appeals ruling, p. 1.
9. *Ibid.*, p. 4–6.
10. Jason Michael Pemstein, "Constitutional Law: Is the NCAA Eligible for a New Interpretation of State Action?" Digital Commons at Loyola Marymount University and Loyola Law School, March 1, 1987, p. 337.
11. *Arlosoroff v. NCAA*, No. 83-1702, U.S. Court of Appeals, January 28, 1985.
12. Dan Treadway, "Why Does the NCAA Exist?" *The Huffington Post,* December 6, 2017.
13. Letter from Harold L. Landesberg to Charles Kriese, October 13, 1982.
14. "Severe Sanctions Levied on Clemson," *New York Times,* November 23, 1982.
15. Interview with Chaim Arlosoroff, August 28, 2017.
16. Interview with Shaul Arlosoroff, September 22, 2017. Note: For the most complete account of his father's life, see *Arlosoroff* by Shlomo Avineri (New York: Grove Weidenfeld Publishers, 1990).

Eighteen   ¤   Unbreakable Bonds

1. "The Bassett Affair," *Duke Magazine,* November 30, 2002.
2. "The Bassett Affair of 1903," Duke University Libraries, University Archives, https://library.duke.edu/rubenstein/uarchives/history/articles/bassett-affair.

3. *Ibid.*

4. Bre Bradham, "'The Luckiest Man on the Planet': President Vincent Price Discusses His First Year in Office," *Duke Chronical,* July 27, 2018.

5. Margaret Harris, "Bonk in His Element," *Duke Magazine,* August 1, 2001.

6. *Ibid.*

7. *Ibid.*

8. Amy McDonald, "How not to PIE a Duke Professor," Just for Fun Duke Archives, March 14, 2015.

9. Harris, "Bonk in His Element."

10. Johnny Moore, "The One & Only Dr. Bonk," *Go Duke The Magazine,* March 13, 2013.

11. *Ibid.,* Bre Bradham.

12. Interview with Laura Kohler, conducted by Allen Paul on January 4, 2018.

13. *Ibid.*

14. Rachael B. Doyle, "Meet the Black Architect who Designed Duke University 37 Years before He Could Have Attended It," www.cub.com, December 6, 2017.

15. Interview with Ted Van Dyk, conducted by Allen Paul on December 21, 2018.

Nineteen ¤ Club Sports Point the way

1. Interview with David Bradley by Allen Paul, February 5, 2019.

2. Interview with David Swanko by Allen Paul, February 10, 2019.

3. Interview with Brent Selman by Allen Paul, January 27, 2019.

4. Interview with Mike Forbes by Allen Paul, May 23, 2018.

5. Interview with Mike Forbes by Allen Paul, January 22, 2019.

6. Interview with Adrian Rivas by Allen Paul, January 30, 2019.

7. Interview with Sarah Putney by Allen Paul, January 24, 2019.

8. "Duke Ice Hockey 2003–04 ACCHL Champs; Final Record 17–3–1," *Duke Chronical,* March 17, 2004.

Twenty ¤ Barriers to Reform

1. Paula Lavigne, "Rich Get Richer in College Sports as Poorer Schools Struggle to Keep Up," ESPN/ABC, https://abcnews.go.com/Sports/rich-richer-college-sports-poorer-schools-struggle/story?id=41857422, September 4, 2016.

2. Charles T. Clotfelter, *Big-Time Sports in American Universities* (Cambridge, UK: Cambridge University Press, 2011).

3. Will Hobson and Steven Rich, "College Athletic Departments Are Taking in More Money Than Ever—and Spending It Just as Fast," *Washington Post,* November 25, 2005.

4. *Ibid.*

5. *Ibid.*

6. *Ibid.*

7. Clotfelter, *Big-Time Sports in American Universities*, p. 126–129.

8. Chris Smith, "The Money on The Line In The College Football National Championship Game," *Forbes,* January 9, 2017.

9. *Ibid.*

10. Clotfelter, *Big-Time Sports in American Universities*, p. 144.

11. *Ibid.*, p. 207–211.

12. Walter Byers, *Unsportsmanlike Conduct* (Ann Arbor: University of Michigan Press), 1995, p. 69.

13. *Ibid.*, p. 69.

14. David Brooks, "The Amateur Ideal," *New York Times,* September 22, 2011.

15. Katherine Ellen Foley and Ephrat Livni, "A New Brain Injury Lawsuit Could Be the Undoing of College Football as We Know It," https://qz.com/1302232/the-fate-of-ncaa-football-is-tied-up-in-a-new-brain-injury-lawsuit/, June 11, 2018.

16. Patrick Hruby, "The NCAA Is Running Out of Excuses on Brain Injuries," *Deadspin* News and Blog Website, May 24, 2018.

17. Michael Dresser, "NCAA, State Reach Settlement in Case of Frostburg Football Player Who Died After Head Injury," *Baltimore Sun,* July 27, 2016.

18. Jon Soloman, "Schools Can Give Out 4-Year Scholarships, But Many Don't," CBSSports.com, September 16, 2014.

19. Orin Starn, "College Athletes' Devil's Bargain: Play or Learn," Raleigh *News and Observer,* December 2, 2017.

20. Gilbert Gaul, *Billion Dollar Ball: A Journey Through the Big-Money of College Football* (New York: Viking, 2015), p. 105–106.

21. Ronald A. Smith, *Pay for Play: A History of Big-Time Athletic Reform* (Champaign: University of Illinois Press, 2010), p. 63.

22. Tom Green, "Renovations at Jordan-Hare Stadium on Schedule To Be Finished for Auburn's Home Opener," www.al.com, July 26, 2018.

23. Michael Casagrande, "Details on Bryant-Denny Stadium Renovation Price Tag, Funding Sources," www.al.com, September 20, 2018.

24. Joel McCreary, "Keeping up with the Clemsons: ACC Schools Under Construction," *Associated Press*, October 3, 2018.

25. *Ibid.*

26. Lavigne, "Rich Get Richer in College Sports as Poorer Schools Struggle to Keep Up."

27. *Ibid.*

28. Andrew Zimbalist, "Antitrust Exemption May Aid College Sports' Untenable Situation," *Sports Business Journal,* www.sportsbusinessdaily.com, November 28, 2016.

29. Byers, *Unsportsmanlike Conduct,* p. 224.

30. *Ibid.,* p. 222–223.

31. Lavigne, "Rich Get Richer in College Sports as Poorer Schools Struggle to Keep Up."

32. *Ibid.*

33. Brad Wolverton, Ben Hallman, Shane Shifflet, and Sandyha Kambhampati, "The $10-Billion Sports Tab: How Colleges Are Funding the Athletic Arms Race," *Chronicle of Higher Education,* November 15, 2015.

34. Dennis Dodd, "College Football Heads in Wrong Direction with Largest Drop in 34 Years," www.cbssports.com, February 13, 2018.

35. Jacob Bogage, "Youth Sports Study: Declining Participation, Rising Costs and Unqualified Coaches," *Washington Post,* September 6, 2017.

36. "Knight Commission Sees Integrity of College Sports At Risk," public news release, October 30, 2017.

37. Arne Duncan and Carol Cartwright, "The NCAA Is Too Far Gone for Incremental Reform," *Chronical of Higher Education,* June 7, 2018.

38. Morgan Moriarty, "Big Ten's Jim Delaney Got $20 million, But There's No Money to Pay the Players," www.sbnation.com, July 24, 2017.

39. Jonathan Alexander, "Fedora Says Football Under An 'Attack' That Could Hurt Country," *News and Observer,* July 19, 2018.

40. Gaul, *Billion Dollar Ball,* p. 20.

41. Hobson and Rich, "College Athletic Departments Are Taking in More Money Than Ever—and Spending It Just as Fast."

42. Associated Press, "Walter Byers, First Executive Director of NCAA, Dies at 93," www.espn.com, May 31, 2015.

Twenty-One ¤ The Folly of Pay for Play

1. John Hoberman, *Darwin's Athletes: How Sport Has Damaged Black America and Preserved the Myth of Race* (New York: Houghton Mifflin Company, 1997), p. xxxiii.

2. *Ibid.*, p. 4.

3. Alana Semuels, "The White Flight from Football," *The Atlantic*, February 1, 2019.

4. "Estimated Probability of Competing in Professional Athletics," NCAA Research, http://www.ncaa.org/about/resources/research/estimated-probability-competing-professional-athletics, April 3, 2019.

5. Leslie Bloom, "How Long Is the Average Career of an NFL Player?" *Houston Chronical,* March 5, 2019.

6. Sam Becker, "Think Athletes Are Overpaid? These Numbers Might Change Your Mind," https://www.cheatsheet.com/money-career/professional-sports-stars-salaries.html/, March 12, 2018.

7. Ryan Swanson, "Want to Clean Up College Athletics? Pay the Players," *Washington Post,* October 2, 2017.

8. John Thelin, "Here's Why We Shouldn't Pay College Athletes," http://money.com/money/4241077/why-we-shouldnt-pay-college-athletes/, March 1, 2016.

9. John Thelin, "Paying College Athletes: How Will Colleges Afford the Price?" *Inside Higher Ed,* February 12, 2018.

Twenty-Two ¤ The Road to Reform

1. A quote often attributed to Louis Armstrong and to his jazz contemporary, Fats Waller. A second version of the quotation, more commonly attributed to Waller, is: "If you gotta ask, don't mess with it."

2. "American College Athletics," Report of the Carnegie Foundation, Chapter 1, October 24, 1929.

3. Gerald Gurney, Donna Lopiano, and Andrew Zimbalist, *Unwinding Madness: What Went Wrong with College Sports and How to Fix It* (Washington: Brookings Institution Press, 2017), p. 12.

4. "Carnegie Report Called Fruitless," *New York Times*, January 14, 1929.

5. "Why Mercer Is Playing Alabama and Auburn This Season," www.al.com, November 17, 2017.

6. www.ncaa.org.

7. Murray Sperber, *Beer and Circus: How Big-Time College Sports Is Crippling Undergraduate Education* (New York: Henry A. Holt and Company, 2000), p. 34.

8. Sally Jenkins, "It's Not That the NCAA Doesn't Know What It's Doing; It's That the NCAA Doesn't Know What It's Supposed To Be Doing," *Washington Post,* November 10, 2014.

9. "Congressionally Chartered Organizations: Key Principles for Leveraging Non-Federal Resources," Government Printing Office, June 13, 2013.

10. "Congressionally Chartered Nonprofit Organizations ("Title 36 Corporations"): What They Are and How Congress Treats Them," EveryCRSeport. com, June 17, 2011.

11. United States Olympic Committee, teamusa.org/about-the-usoc/leadership. com, January 2019.

12. NCAA.org/governance/committees/ncaa-board-governors.

13. John Marshall, "Travel an Extra Grind for Division I's Smallest Schools," *Associated Press*, January 14, 2018.

14. Gilbert Gaul, *Billion Dollar Ball: A Journey Through the Big-Money of College Football* (New York: Viking, 2015), p. 104.

15. Sally Jenkins, "It's Not That the NCAA Doesn't Know What It's Doing; It's That the NCAA Doesn't Know What It's Supposed To Be Doing."

16. Jayma Meyer and Andrew Zimbalist, "Reforming College Sports: The Case for a Limited and Conditional Antitrust Exemption," *The Antitrust Bulletin* 62 (2017), p. 32.

17. *Ibid.*, p. 36.

18. *Ibid.*, p. 49.

19. *Ibid.*, p. 54.

20. *Ibid.*, p. 55–57.

21. *Ibid.*, p. 53.

22. *Ibid.*, p. 57–58.

23. Sperber, *Beer and Circus*, p. 270.

24. Cody Cottier, "Athletics Account for Half Decrease in Reserves—Sports Disproportionate Draw on Savings Raises Questions About WSU Priorities," *Daily Evergreen,* April 3, 2018.

Twenty-Three ¤ Renewing Our Integrity

1. Percy Bysshe Shelly, *Ozymandias,* a poem first published by *The Examiner* (London), January 11, 1818.

2. Benjamin Franklin, "List of Scoundrels," *Founders Online,* National Archives, January 4, 1782.

3. Matt Brown, "The Reversed College Football Result," www.sportsonearth. com/article/156300200/miami-duke-fifthdown-1940-cornell-dartmouth, November 2, 2015.

4. Sally Jenkins, "Zion Williamson Injury Makes Clear: The NCAA Has Turned Education Into a Risk," *Washington Post,* February 21, 2019.

5. Brian Murphy, "Ex-Duke Star's Mom Likens College Basketball System to Slavery, Prison," *News and Observer,* May 8, 2018.

6. "Freshman Wendell Carter Jr. Becomes 7th Selection in 2018 NBA Draft, Selected by Chicago Bulls," *Duke Chronical,* June 21, 2018.

7. Taylor Branch, "The Shame of College Sports," *The Atlantic,* October 2011.

8. Patrick Hruby, "This is How to Pay College Athletes," *Deadspin,* March 6, 2018.

9. Sally Jenkins, "Zion Williamson Injury Makes Clear."

10. Ibid, Hruby, "This is How to Pay College Athletes."

11. Christian Schneider, "Paying College Athletes After NCAA Scandal at Louisville? We Already Pay College Athletes," *Milwaukee Journal Sentinel,* March 6, 2018.

Index

About the Authors

DR. JOHN LEBAR

Dr. John LeBar earned his doctorate in education at Duke University where he coached varsity tennis and fencing. He later served as Director of Undergraduate Studies. His '82 team won Duke's first Atlantic Coast Conference Tennis Championship. He was an avid athlete growing up and swam on a Kansas State Championship Team. He co-wrote *Learning Tennis Together* (published by Leisure Press) with a coaching colleague. Every player he coached was a scholar-athlete, most went to graduate or professional school and nearly all have led high-impact lives.

ALLEN PAUL

Allen Paul's bestselling book, *Katyń: Stalin's Massacre and the Triumph of Truth,* has been called the definitive work on a crime that remains one of the most troubling in Russo-Polish relations. A bestseller in four countries, it remains in print nearly thirty years after Scribner's first published it. Allen earned a graduate degree in international politics from the School of Advanced International Studies at Johns Hopkins University. After college, he worked for the Associated Press and later as a speechwriter in Washington, DC.

Further information about *Marching Toward Madness* can be found at www.marchingtowardmadness.net